WUHAN, 1938

A

Philip E. Lilienthal (signature)

■   ■   ■

B O O K

The Philip E. Lilienthal imprint
honors special books
in commemoration of a man whose work
at University of California Press from 1954 to 1979
was marked by dedication to young authors
and to high standards in the field of Asian Studies.
Friends, family, authors, and foundations have together
endowed the Lilienthal Fund, which enables UC Press
to publish under this imprint selected books
in a way that reflects the taste and judgment
of a great and beloved editor.

WUHAN, 1938

WAR, REFUGEES, AND THE MAKING OF MODERN CHINA

STEPHEN R. MacKINNON

INCLUDES PHOTOGRAPHS BY ROBERT CAPA

UNIVERSITY OF CALIFORNIA PRESS
BERKELEY LOS ANGELES LONDON

University of California Press, one of the most distinguished university presses in the United States, enriches lives around the world by advancing scholarship in the humanities, social sciences, and natural sciences. Its activities are supported by the UC Press Foundation and by philanthropic contributions from individ-uals and institutions. For more information, visit www.ucpress.edu.

The author gratefully acknowledges permission to reprint the following copy-righted material: from W. H. Auden and Christopher Isherwood, *Journey to a War*, London: Faber & Faber, © 1939, 1973; from Joseph W. Esherick, ed., *Re-making the Chinese City: Modernity and National Identity, 1900–1950*, Hono-lulu: University of Hawaii Press, ©2000; from Han Suyin, *Destination Chung-king: An Autobiography*, London: Jonathan Cape, Ltd., ©1943; from James C. Hsiung and Steven I. Levine, eds., *China's Bitter Victory: The War with Japan, 1937–1945*, Armonk, NY: M. E. Sharpe, ©1992; from Hsu Kai-yu, ed. and trans., *Twentieth Century Chinese Poetry: An Anthology*, New York: Doubleday and Company, Inc. (Random House), © 1968; from Agnes Smedley, *Battle Hymn of China*, New York: Alfred Knopf, Inc. (Random House), ©1943, 1970; from Jonathan D. Spence, *God's Chinese Son: The Taiping Heavenly Kingdom of Hong Xiuquan*, New York: W. W. Norton, ©1996.

University of California Press
Berkeley and Los Angeles, California

University of California Press, Ltd.
London, England

Library of Congress Cataloging-in-Publication Data

MacKinnon, Stephen R.
 Wuhan, 1938 : war, refugees, and the making of modern China /
Stephen R. MacKinnon ; includes photographs by Robert Capa.
  p. cm.
 Includes bibliographical references and index.
 ISBN: 978-0-520-25445-9 (cloth : alk. paper)
  1. Sino-Japanese War, 1937–1945—China—Wuhan Shi. 2. Wuhan Shi
(China)—History—20th century.
 I. Capa, Robert, 1913–1954. II. Title. III. Title: War, refugees, and the
 making of modern China.
 DS777.5316.W8M33   2008
 951.04'2—dc22   2008002078

Manufactured in the United States of America

17 16 15 14 13 12 11 10 09 08
10 9 8 7 6 5 4 3 2 1

A PROMISE KEPT

TO JANICE RACHIE MacKINNON (1943-1999)

CONTENTS

ILLUSTRATIONS

TABLES

ACKNOWLEDGMENTS

THE GENESIS OF THIS BOOK WAS in the early 1990s when a small group
of historians—Arthur Waldron, Edward McCord, Diana Lary, Chang-
tai Hong, Chang Jui-de, Hans J. van de Ven, and Johanna Waley-Cohen—
met in a workshop to discuss the importance of war to an understanding of modern Chinese history. The group followed up by organizing
several research conferences on the issue, which resulted in special issues
of journals and conference volumes. I benefited enormously from regular dialogue with this core group of interested historians.

Drawn at first by the romantic atmosphere of the Wuhan moment, I
was then struck by the magnitude and consequences of China's wartime
refugee crisis. I wondered why the role of the tricity—Wuchang, Hankou, Hanyang—as de facto capital in 1938 had been left out of standard
narratives of modern Chinese history. Research in earnest on this question began in 1992 with an extended sabbatical at Huazhong University
in Wuhan. I subsequently published an article and two book chapters on
the Wuhan refugee experience of 1938 (see bibliography). These endeavors
led, by 1999, to the decision to write a book.

I want to thank the Committee on Scholarly Communication with the
People's Republic of China and the Pacific Cultural Foundation for support of the project. In turn, many individual scholars helped along the
way. Special gratitude goes to Diana Lary, whose breadth of knowledge
and encouragement helped me complete the project. Likewise, Arthur Waldron and Edward McCord read the manuscript in its entirety and pro-

vided useful suggestions. Earlier, in Wuhan in the 1990s, local scholars Mao Lei, Pi Mingxiu, and Liu Wangling guided me through libraries and archives, and in Beijing, the staff of the library at the Modern History Institute of the Chinese Academy of Social Sciences was always courteous and helpful in providing access to the institute's extraordinary Republican period collection. Of the scholars at the institute, I particularly appreciated the advice of Yang Tianshi and Gu Weiming.

More recently, the editorial advice, encouragement, and companionship of Anne Feldhaus have been invaluable. At a critical stage, the final distillation of the manuscript benefited immeasurably from the editorial talents of Gene Tanke. I am grateful also for the patience and diligence of Reed Malcom, Kalicia Pivirotto, and Rachel Berchten of the staff of the University of California Press and copyeditor Adrienne Harris in seeing the manuscript through to publication. Becky Eden provided professional help with the maps. Robert Capa's biographer, Richard Whelan, deserves a special thanks for help acquiring reproduction rights to the legendary photographer's remarkable Wuhan photographs. Capa and his photos personify the Wuhan-Madrid connection of 1938.

Finally, the dedication of this book is bittersweet—to my wife of thirty-two years, Janice Rachie MacKinnon, who died in 1999 while helping with the first draft of the manuscript. Her steadfast support and love made it all possible.

Area
Shown
in
Detail

N

Great Wall
Yellow River
Beijing
Tianjin

Jinan

YELLOW
SEA

Lanzhou

Zhengzhou
Xi'an
Longhai
Railroad
Beijing-Guangzhou
Railroad

Xuzhou

Huai
Nanjing
Shanghai

Dabei
Mountains

SICHUAN PROVINCE
Chengdu

Wuhan

Yichang

Boyang
Lake

EAST CHINA
SEA

Chongqing
Yangzi River

Changsha

Hengyang

Guilin

Xi Jiang

Kunming

Nanning
GUANGXI
PROVINCE

Guangzhou

YUNNAN
PROVINCE

SOUTH CHINA
SEA

0   100 200 300 mi

MAP 1. CHINA IN THE 1930S, COPYRIGHT 2007 STEPHEN R. MACKINNON.

PROLOGUE

ONE DRAMATIC STORY from the early days of the Anti-Japanese War (1937–45) remains largely untold: the saga of the refugees who clogged the rivers and roads of central China in flight from the ravages of the advancing Imperial Army. This forced migration of nearly a hundred million people not only changed Chinese politics; it altered the social, cultural, and economic landscape of modern China. The implications first became clear at Wuhan during the spring of 1938, just after the massacre of civilians by Japanese troops at Nanjing. A potpourri of refugees from all over coastal China, who seemed at first to have only poverty and fear in common, converged on the tricity complex of Wuchang, Hanyang, and Hankou, which straddles the Yangzi River at midcourse, and found ways to work together.

During the next ten months, from January to October 1938, Wuhan was the staging ground and logistics base for two million Chinese troops defending the central Yangzi region against Japanese attacks, by land and air, from the north and east. To the Chinese commanders and the populace of Wuhan, and to foreign observers, a Japanese victory did not seem inevitable. The tricity was not directly under siege until bombing became heavy toward the end of August; and earlier, during the spring, Chinese victories had been impressive.

In the end, Wuhan fell, at enormous human cost to both sides. The number of widows and orphans rose dramatically. In less than a year, the Chinese forces, with practically no medical attention available to their wounded, lost up to a million men, wounded or dead—more than their combined losses during the next seven years of war. And the fall of Wuhan uprooted millions of civilians, adding more refugees to the streams of humanity that once again pushed southwest down roads and river ways into Sichuan, Guangxi, and Yunnan provinces, where they remained for the duration of the war.

Still, most Chinese historians agree that the sacrifice in personnel, equipment, and refugee misery at Wuhan was worthwhile. During the siege of the city, the Japanese suffered their greatest losses of the war, and these setbacks had a sobering effect: by the end of 1938, they chose not to pursue the Nationalist government into Sichuan and turned their attention to expanding their grip on the north (and fighting Soviet Russia for control of Mongolia in 1939). In effect, the siege of Wuhan during the summer of 1938, and the battle of Xuzhou that preceded it, prolonged the war in China until the U.S. entry in 1942—no mean achievement.

Thus the story of Wuhan in 1938 has two dimensions—the military and the social—that are of crucial importance to the history of modern China. Because we still lack a comprehensive military history of the Anti-Japanese War, I have sought here to reconstruct the hard facts of the military defense of Wuhan and the central Yangzi before discussing social and cultural matters in depth. At the same time, I have tried to show the intimate relationship between the military and social contexts. Indeed, this interrelationship is the key to understanding why Wuhan did not suffer the panic and chaos that engulfed Nanjing and Jinan when these cities were under siege by the Japanese in late 1937. Without a thorough study of the military context, an appreciation of the transformation of refugee society and culture that took place at Wuhan in 1938 is impossible.

Modern wars have usually produced a restriction of civil liberties and a tightening of political controls, but at Wuhan in 1938, the opposite occurred. In a highly charged atmosphere of carnage, heroism, and desperate hope, the metropolis blossomed as the de facto wartime capital. Forging unity by tolerating political diversity became more important than preserving authoritarian party politics. The freewheeling treaty-port energy of refugees from Shanghai and Tianjin was brought to Wuhan and reshaped to serve the war effort, especially in the cultural field. The Guomindang and Chinese Communists engaged in open political competition, while joined nominally in a United Front government that tolerated renegade ex-Communists like Chen Duxiu and Zhang Guotao as well as various third-party organizations and publications critical of both sides. To a degree unmatched in any Chinese capital before or since, Wuhan enjoyed parliamentary-style debate and political experimentation, the flowering of a free press, and the unleashing and redirection of enormous creative energies in cultural spheres. Internationally, the heroism at Wuhan was seen as an idealistic last stand against ruthless invaders and their loathsome fascist ideologies. It attracted prominent chroniclers of the Spanish Civil War fresh from Madrid—among them the filmmaker Joris Ivens and photographer Robert Capa—as well as the celebrity writers W. H. Auden and Christopher Isherwood, who toured the battlefields and wrote an epic, book-length tribute in prose and verse.*

The Wuhan period suggests that the Anti-Japanese War brought changes to Chinese society, culture, and politics analogous to those that occurred after World War I in Europe. The sense of loss and cultural transformation was sweeping. The more elitist prewar culture of cosmopolitan Shanghai and bohemian Beijing never returned. The death of more than twenty million people, the majority of them civilians, and the profound physical and psychological scars of this war are still painfully remembered today. Moreover, because the Anti-Japanese War was followed immediately by a devastating civil war, by 1949 more than half the surviving Chinese population had been orphaned or widowed or had their lives broken in other ways by the brutalities of war.

In retrospect, however, we can recognize areas in which war had transformative effects on the surviving Chinese population, notably in promoting greater equality for women and turning attention to public health, education, and economic reconstruction in the rural hinterland. The refugee relief and public health efforts that began during the war became the building blocks for a national public health system in both the People's Republic of China (PRC) and Taiwan. More immediately, war propaganda began to knit together culture and society into a unified whole. Refugee intellectuals from academia and the literary salons of Beijing and Shanghai embraced mass culture and politics, and never more fervently than during the defense of Wuhan, which the Western and Chinese press often characterized as China's "Madrid."

The first chapter of this book describes the physical setting of prewar Wuhan and its political role in the history of the Chinese Republic. Chapters 2 and 3 discuss in detail the military context of the spring and sum-

---

* Auden and Isherwood, *Journey to a War*. The year 1938, of course, was also the time that Germany occupied Austria and Hitler met with Chamberlain and others at Munich. Japan's relations with the Axis powers, Germany and Italy, became warmer.

mer of 1938 and then offer a narrative history of the long and bloody battle for Xuzhou and the siege of Wuhan. These chapters show how military events produced shared governance of Wuhan, with key commanders in the field sharing power with Generalissimo Chiang Kaishek. Chapter 4 addresses my central theme, the human story behind the military history: how the refugee population of Wuhan, in coping with the traumas of war, forced positive social changes and actions by the state.

Chapter 5 describes how the needs of refugee society and the harsh realities of the military situation produced dramatic shifts in cultural activity at Wuhan under the leadership of transplanted intellectuals from coastal cities. This focus leads naturally to chapter 6, which looks at the mobilization of students and youth—a key concern for political leaders and intellectuals alike. More than anyone, student refugees embodied the Wuhan spirit, volunteering as welfare workers and rallying almost daily on the streets of Hankou and the campuses of Wuchang. The last chapter is a narrative treatment of the international dimension of the Wuhan crisis, showing that global reaction to events at Wuhan changed dramatically over ten months, leading by October to a "Madrid effect" and a Chinese propaganda victory.

The book thus moves back and forth chronologically through the months in 1938 when Wuhan was China's de facto wartime capital. A guide to key events and places during the defense of Wuhan appears in an appendix. Moreover, two dozen black-and-white photos taken at the time, chiefly by the renowned photojournalist Robert Capa, enhance the text. The intended result is a kaleidoscopic, interwoven series of narrative chapters that juxtapose portrayals of the sweeping changes in the social and cultural life of Wuhan's refugee population with accounts of the extraordinary military and political developments that took place in the city's defense.

The final chapter notes the fleeting nature of the Wuhan moment in history and addresses its importance, explaining how the wartime refugee experience reshaped the society, culture, and politics of modern China and why "the Wuhan spirit" is still celebrated today both on the mainland and in Taiwan.

ONE

WUHAN BEFORE THE WAR

LINKED ONLY BY FERRY CROSSINGS over hundreds of yards of treacherous river, each of Wuhan's three cities—Wuchang, Hanyang, and Hankou—had a distinct identity and history. The relationship between the communities was often tense, aggravated perhaps by the infamously bad weather—hot and steamy in the summer, cold and clammy in the winter. Yet the metropolis we now call Wuhan dominated the economic and political life of the central Yangzi River region for well over a millennium.

Twentieth-century Wuhan's economic center was the bustling port of Hankou, whose pursuit of Western-style commercial and cultural modernity rose to a new level after it became a railroad terminus early in the century. Across the Yangzi River, Wuchang, while clinging to the urban morphology of the traditional administrative capital, led the search for political identity: in 1911–12, 1927, and 1938 it thrust Wuhan onto the center stage of national politics. The tension between the crass commercial modernity of Hankou and the fervent political posturing of Wuchang gave twentieth-century Wuhan a split personality that is still evident today in differences in local dialect, culture, and architecture. Caught in the middle was a smaller, working-class third city, the down-to-earth industrial center of Hanyang.

Thus, taken as a whole, the urban sprawl of Wuhan during the Republican period was amorphous, unplanned, and difficult to define. Spatially and administratively, it had no center: no unified police force, school system, waterworks, fire department, or city administration. The major force that connected these communities also pushed them apart on occasion: the unpredictability of the two fast-moving, giant river systems (Yangzi and Han) and their wildly fluctuating water levels. The cities were frequently cut off from one another by periodic flooding or political upheaval. Even under the best of conditions, the distance to be covered against the swirling pull of the current made ferry crossings seem hazardous to the newcomer. Not until 1957, with the construction of bridges linking the three cities of Hankou, Hanyang, and Wuchang, did Wuhan become the more integrated municipality it is today.

Another distinguishing feature of Wuhan's modern history was the recurrent physical destruction and rebuilding that its inhabitants came to expect. The trading center of Hankou, in particular, was repeatedly laid waste by war after the middle of the nineteenth century. It was razed and seized three times by Taiping rebels in the 1850s, burned to the ground by Qing troops in 1911, badly damaged by war and revolution in 1926–27, and pummeled by Japanese bombing raids in 1938 and U.S. B-29 raids in 1944. Wuchang was spared until the 1920s and 1930s, when the city's new commercial and industrial districts were badly damaged: first by rioting warlord troops in 1921, then by fighting in 1926–27, and finally by wartime bombing raids. Hanyang suffered a similar fate. Yet out of the ashes of war, the Wuhan cities quickly rebuilt and reemerged more confident, prosperous, and optimistic about becoming the most progressive of China's interior cities.

THE INVENTION OF MODERN WUHAN

Modern Wuhan's identity grew out of a deeply rooted but divided history that began with the political centrality of Wuchang. Since at least the Han dynasty, Wuchang had been strategically important because of its location at the Yangzi's juncture with the Han River. Wuchang was the capital of Hubei Province, one of China's richest and most populous provinces, and since the Ming period, its scholar-officials had overseen the entire Huguang region (Hubei and Hunan). The Huguang governor-general was arguably the third most important provincial official in the Qing empire (the first being the Zhihli governor-general, who oversaw the region around Beijing). Political importance made Wuchang an intellectual and educational center as well, the place where student candidates prepared for and took the civil service examinations. Laid out as an administrative city on the southern bank of the Yangzi, its towering walls projected political power and protected the city from flooding. By

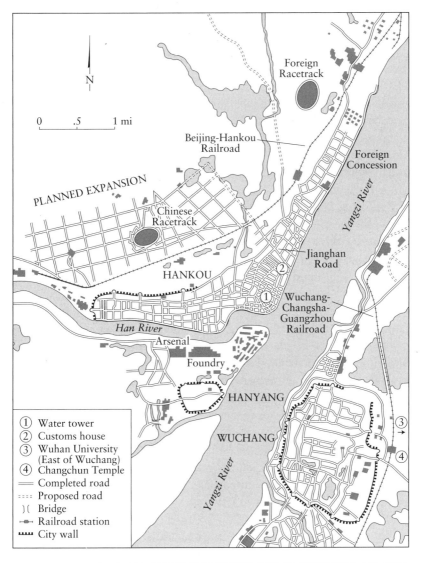

MAP 2. WUHAN, CA. 1927. BASED ON MAPS IN SU YUNFENG (1981), PI MINGXIU (1993), AND *SHINA SHOBETSU ZENSHI* (1917–20). REPRODUCED FROM MACKINNON, "WUHAN'S SEARCH FOR IDENTITY" (2000), WITH PERMISSION OF THE UNIVERSITY OF HAWAII PRESS.

function and design, it fit the traditional Chinese urban model in which the role of commerce was secondary.

Across from Wuchang, at the northwest juncture of the Han and Yangzi rivers, lay Hanyang. Although also walled and almost as old as Wuchang, Hanyang remained a much smaller, sleepy county seat throughout the nineteenth century. During the Qing period, Hanyang's new sister, Hankou, to the northeast across the Han, was the primary focus of growth, transforming itself from a fishing village into the commercial hub of central China. When Hankou was razed by Taiping troops in the 1850s, it had a population larger than Wuchang's: half a million residents sprawled along the banks of the Han and Yangzi. In 1862, though nearly deserted and in ruins, Hankou was declared a treaty port, and it soon became a hub of the lucrative international tea trade. Backed by rich tea merchants, the port quickly recovered as the primary exchange center for domestic and foreign trade in the central Yangzi region. Hankou was large and unruly again by the end of the century, and its social and economic life was almost purely commercial. Not directly governed from Wuchang, it stood on the periphery of the administrative orbit of neighboring Hanyang, the county seat across the Han River with a population of only twenty thousand inhabitants. By the 1890s the tricity region's population was over a million, with the majority split between Hankou and Wuchang.

Thus, in Chinese urban history, Hankou's blatant commercial culture was unorthodox, which makes it of interest to modern scholars in search of a budding civil society or sprouts of capitalism.[1] Needless to say, Hankou and Wuchang did not always get along. Twice, in 1855 and 1911, Wuchang's officials refused to commit troops to Hankou's defense, and the city was burned to the ground as a result. But like their European counterparts in London, Amsterdam, and Paris, Hankou's burghers turned the devastation of their city into an opportunity for growth and renewal.

The clash of cultures between Hankou and Wuchang and the story of how necessity brought the two cities together at the turn of the century can best be told through the careers of two leading citizens: Wuchang's late Qing scholar-reformer Zhang Zhidong and Hankou's entrepreneur and real estate developer Liu Xinsheng. Their different visions ran parallel and then merged around railway-construction projects during the first decade of the twentieth century.

The scholar-official Zhang Zhidong was appointed Huguang governor-general in 1893. From his palatial *yamen* at Wuchang, he wielded direct political authority over three provinces and had influence throughout central China as the highest-ranking official in the region (including Shanghai). By the time of his appointment, Zhang Zhidong's Self-Strengthening reform agenda was a well-known national model.[2] His career had followed the classic bureaucratic pattern, beginning with winning the top *jinshi* degree and drafting a series of important memorials to the emperor (for action by the Empress Dowager Cixi) on the need for unprecedented economic, educational, and military institutional reform. From Wuchang he was able to put into practice much of what he preached. His first action in 1893 was to establish the Wuchang Textile Bureau. A series of reform measures followed, including the creation of a large state-sponsored steel and munitions complex at Hanyang and the establishment of new schools at Wuchang that taught Western scientific subjects. The state encouraged and financed study abroad under certain circumstances (largely for military training). The government hired German advisers to train and help equip a modern Self-Strengthening Army and run the munitions factory at Hanyang. It encouraged joint stock-trading companies and initiated explorations into the financing and construction of railroads.[3]

Also in the 1890s, Wuchang and Hankou began to forge a symbiotic relationship in pursuit of economic growth. Domestic and foreign trade at Hankou jumped up because of the rapid expansion of steamship traffic up the Yangzi. The foreign-concession area that had been designated in the 1860s suddenly filled out, with newly established German, Russian, French, and Japanese zones bustling with activity after 1895 (chiefly because the Treaty of Shimonoseki granted foreigners the right to open factories in treaty ports). Customs receipts indicate a tripling of foreign trade between 1890 and 1910, to 135 million taels a year.[4] The strategic importance of Hankou in domestic commodity trade increased in 1905 with the completion of one of Zhang Zhidong's pet projects, the Beijing-Hankou railway, China's first north-south line. At the same time, the existing heavy-industry complex at Hanyang prospered. And across the river in Zhang Zhidong's bailiwick at Wuchang, light industry (textile factories in particular) appeared after the inauguration of that city's first commercial zone. Thus Zhang Zhidong's bureaucratic stewardship of reforms in Wuchang encouraged the rise of an environment genial to foreign trade at Hankou, which then created opportunities for aggressive Chinese entrepreneurs. One of the most successful was Liu Xinsheng, who within two decades rose from rags to riches as comprador, merchant baron, and finally real estate developer.

Liu Xinsheng's career began simply and unpleasantly in the hide markets of Hankou. In addition to possessing sound entrepreneurial instincts, he had good timing or excellent luck. For reasons that remain obscure, in the 1880s, just when foreign trade began to expand rapidly in the treaty-port zones of Hankou, young Liu left the hide trade, converted to Christianity, learned French, and became a comprador for a leading French trading company. He quickly made a fortune in commissions by arranging deals for the French. By the turn of the century he was a local tycoon, branching out into real estate and forming partnerships with scions of Hankou's old trading elite: families who had enjoyed national renown since the eighteenth century for their civic virtue, as founders of charitable social welfare societies, or *cishan hui.*

The most important of Liu's allies was Cai Fuqing, the patriarch of the highly respected Cai clan, whose commercial interests in Hankou dated back to the sixteenth century. Together with other leading tea, silk, tung oil, and hide merchants, in the early 1900s Liu and Cai drew up plans for expanding infrastructure and constructing new buildings, banking centers, and hospitals in the Hankou metropolitan area. Two large structures had particular symbolic value. The first was the Chinese-managed Huasheng racetrack in Hankou, built to rival the British track in the foreign-concession area. The second, completed in 1909, was a six-story Western-style water tower near the Bund. These structures competed for attention with the heavily colonnaded Western and Japanese banks as well as with the large Victorian-looking customs house in the foreign-concession area to the north of the Chinese city. Finally, in concert with Zhang Zhidong, Liu and Cai, with several gentry-merchant friends, began to plan a southern extension of the Beijing-Hankou railway, to run from Wuchang to Canton.[5]

Thus by 1911 Hankou had risen from the ashes of the Taiping debacle to become a major domestic trade center and treaty port. Then, on October 10, 1911, fighting broke out in the tricity area between Qing-dynasty units and mutineers as self-proclaimed republican rebel forces. Although the mutiny began with the capture of Wuchang, the city and its scholar-bureaucrats managed to remain safe and unscathed behind its high walls by siding with the "revolution." The destructive violence occurred elsewhere. Before a cease-fire was negotiated, Hanyang became a war zone, and in late October Hankou was burned to the ground by Qing troops advancing down the railway from the north. Hankou reportedly burned for four days and four nights. The only large structures left standing in the smoldering ruins outside the foreign-concession areas were the racetrack and the water tower. Yet within a few months, in a very public endorsement of the new Republic of China, the chamber of commerce and merchant associations of Hankou, led by the Cai clan and Liu Xinsheng, inaugurated a campaign to raise money for an ambitious reconstruction plan.

Their efforts paid off almost immediately, and between 1912 and 1927 Wuhan experienced a golden age of growth and prosperity. Fed by an international environment that benefited Chinese business interests during World War I, foreign trade accelerated well into the 1920s, and the domestic commercial economy of Wuhan recovered and reached new heights. The introduction of sophisticated large-scale processing and manufacturing facilities for overseas markets was on the rise. The enterprises at Hanyang that Zhang Zhidong had started—the Hanyeping Iron and Steel Works, the brick factory, and the wire and nail factory—as well as the ceramic-tile works at Wuchang, moved from official supervision *(guandu shangban)* to merchant control. Steam-powered manufacturing processes (in cotton-textile mills, wheat-flour mills, rice mills, cigarette factories, tea-processing plants, oil presses, and cotton-packing plants) became widespread after 1911. One measure of Wuhan's competitiveness was its success in driving foreign yarn and cloth products out of the middle Yangzi market. In 1915 Wuhan had more than 300 privately owned cotton-weaving mills in Wuhan that collectively employed nearly twelve thousand workers.[6] Scholars note that by the late 1920s 13,017 manufacturing and commercial establishments were operating in the Wuhan area, of which 236 reportedly were mechanized. This number included 6 cotton mills (5 Chinese owned, 1 Japanese owned), which together employed more than twenty thousand workers.[7] In heavy industry, by 1922 the new Yangzi Ironworks at Hanyang was the largest operation of its kind in central China outside of Shanghai. Finally, Hankou had become a major financial center, with a stock market and banking sector important enough by the 1920s to influence Shanghai and Tianjin. In 1924 a feature article in the important Shanghai journal *Dongfang zazhi* (Eastern Miscellany) described Wuhan as a successful example of how a strong merchant-driven effort could quickly modernize economic and civic life.[8]

Not surprisingly, such rapid growth concentrated money and power in the hands of a small group of Hankou businessmen, led by Liu Xinsheng, the richest and most powerful of the city's merchant barons. As a real estate mogul, Liu now played an even greater role in directing the physical growth of Hankou's Chinese city. Under his auspices, Hankou acquired a new look, with a string of buildings going up in the heart of the old commercial district. Streets were rerouted, thoroughfares widened, and plans laid out for a grid-patterned district west of the railway line. East of the railway line, around Jianghan Road on the border of the foreign-concession area, the New Market complex was erected and became the heart of the Chinese city. Indeed, most of the major buildings of republican Hankou, Wuchang, and Hanyang were built between 1912 and 1927. Often designed by foreign architects from Shanghai, they produced a decidedly Western look, particularly in downtown Hankou.

Wuchang across the river saw less dramatic change until 1918, when the completion of the Wuchang-Changsha railway line forced the dismantling of the eastern wall and a reshaping of the downtown area as well as expansion of the business district to the east of the old wall. The necessary demolition was aided by the fighting in the city, which was brief but very destructive, after the mutiny of warlord Wang Zhanyuan's troops in June 1921. This event marked the first time Wuchang experienced serious war damage; but paradoxically it provided the opportunity to reshape the city around the new railway terminus. Thus, by the early 1920s, the north-south railway connections on either side of the river were forcing economic integration. On the surface at least, Wuhan as a whole seemed to be acquiring a modern industrial façade comparable to that of Tianjin and even Shanghai.[9] The foreign press noticed and began to call Wuhan "the Chicago of China."[10]

Also during the 1920s the civic and cultural life of Wuhan reached a kind of apex, which was most evident with the blossoming of a popular local press. Even before the 1911 revolution, Wuhan's press had been pioneering and controversial. Fiery anti-Qing-dynasty publications like the *Jianghan ribao* put out by students living in Japan were influential. The number of publications exploded during the 1911–12 revolution, and a second burst followed in 1927.[11] Thus, throughout the Republican period, Wuhan was on a par with Tianjin, and behind only Shanghai and Beijing, in the quality and quantity of its newspapers and periodicals.

The political upheaval that produced the explosion of new publications in 1927 also brought Wuhan's "golden age" to a sudden end. In October 1926, after the Guomindang's Northern Expedition reached the Yangzi valley, the new Republican government chose Wuhan as its provisional capital. Within a few months, the first integrated municipal government for Wuhan as a whole had taken shape, with a full panoply of municipal departments. The new regime, initially dominated by Wang Jingwei and others on the Guomindang left, took a strong anti-imperialist stand under the charismatic foreign minister Eugene Chen and built popular support around Wuhan's well-organized labor and student movements. One of the few Wuhan natives in the government at a high level was Dong Biwu, who received a ministerial appointment. Dong was a middle-school teacher who turned political activist in the 1911 revolution and then after 1919 participated in the May Fourth Movement, an iconoclastic intellectual and cultural revolution that shook China's major metropolitan areas. Dong was present at the first meeting of the Chinese Communist Party in Shanghai in 1921, and founded the Hubei branch in 1923. In 1924 he was invited to Canton to join the reorganized United Front Guomindang party, led at the time by Sun Yatsen and later by Chiang Kaishek. Dong remained the Guomindang's favorite Communist into the 1940s. Affable and always smiling, he was a popular local figure with strong Republican credentials and connections within the Nationalist Party stretching back to the 1911 revolution.[12]

The 1927 Wuhan revolutionary government's most notable success was the recovery of Chinese sovereignty over the British Concession zone in Hankou.[13] Nevertheless, it received only weak support from the Hankou merchants, who especially resented the new municipal government centered in Wuchang and its interference in Hankou affairs. More important, in the late spring of 1927, Chiang Kaishek and then Wang Jingwei moved decisively to the right, first by seizing power and purging Communists in Shanghai and Canton and then in the fall by sending troops to attack the government at Wuhan itself.[14] The fighting seriously damaged parts of Wuchang, Hankou, and Hanyang. By the end of 1927 the Wuhan government had collapsed and the tricity had fallen under the heavy-handed control of Guangxi warlords. The resulting state repression of the local press, as well as of student and labor communities, was severe. The new municipal government that had coordinated administration of the three cities was dismantled (to the relief of the Hankou tycoon Liu Xinsheng and others). Wuhan's most visible Communist, Dong Biwu, had to flee for his life, first into exile in Japan and then to Moscow.

From late 1929 to December 1937 Wuhan was under the tight control of the CC (or Chen brothers) Clique of Chiang Kaishek's Nanjing government. To a degree, the heavy-handed tactics of the CC Clique in competing with the Political Study Clique for dominance of local government had a negative effect on the city's domestic economy, but more fundamental challenges came from external economic developments. By 1932 a combination of factors—including two years of devastating floods, environmental degradation, poor provincial leadership, the global economic crisis, and protectionist trade policies—produced a deep depression in the countryside around Wuhan.[15]

Ironically, the floods of 1931 and 1935 that devastated the surrounding countryside and impoverished the populace benefited the Hankou merchants and the city's economy. During high-water periods, foreign freighters of eight to ten thousand tons found they could berth at Hankou, thus circumventing transshipment of their cargoes at Shanghai. The result was an upsurge in foreign trade and expansion of the foreign community to four thousand souls, about half of whom were Japanese commodity traders. And with foreign businessmen came more Western missionaries with philanthropic projects. The leader in organizing welfare programs, hospitals, and new schools was the Episcopalian bishop Logan Roots. By 1938 the YMCA and YWCA were well entrenched as social-service providers in Hankou and to lesser degree, in Wuchang and Hanyang. The enlarged foreign presence created a more cosmopolitan atmosphere around the Bund, but Wuhan was hardly turning into Tianjin or Shanghai. The foreign community remained small and brazenly fun loving. As an old Shanghai "China hand," *New York Times* correspondent Hallet Abend, quipped, "Hankow had the worst foreign hotels of any city of its size in the Far East, but boasted the largest and one of the finest country and race clubs in all of China."[16]

Overall, the urban economy of the tricity complex stagnated in the 1930s, but it did not crash because the tricity had a strategic position as the international commodity trade and industrial processing center for the entire middle Yangzi region. The rich merchants who had to evacuate their mansions and paddle up and down Jianghan Avenue during the 1931 and 1935 floods continued to prosper and live comfortably. Still, the metropolitan area was swollen with refugees. Hundreds of thousands of desperately poor peasants flooded into Wuhan, living in shantytowns along its outskirts. The total urban population soon exceeded two million (with two-thirds afloat in Hankou). In a pattern similar to that in Shanghai and other large cities, social control under such circumstances largely fell into the hands of a gangster king with triad origins. In the tricity complex, the person filling this role was Yang Qingshan, who cut lucrative deals with Nationalist officials in Wuchang, notably Hubei Province chief General He Chengjun, a Wuhan native and operative for the conservative CC Clique.[17]

Yang Qingshan operated a large network of thugs who ran rackets and intelligence operations out of hundreds of Wuhan teahouses. Although illiterate and a product of the local secret-society underworld, Yang was well connected and widely feared. In 1934 when Yang's mother died, General He Chengjun attended the funeral in person, and Chiang Kaishek sent condolences.[18] In the mid-1930s, when the simple technique for controlling demonstrations—preventing students from using public and private ferries to cross the Yangzi from Wuchang to Hankou—was not effective, Yang led a series of violent crackdowns on anti-Japanese demonstrations in both cities. Then in the spring of 1936 he engineered a shocking assassination—in broad daylight on the streets of Wuchang—of the highest local official belonging to the Political Study Clique, Yang Yongtai.[19] And finally, Yang Qingshan's violent tactics intimidated and drastically shrank the size of Wuhan's historically lively and mostly noncommunist press. In one study published in 1943, the author, himself a journalist, charted the age at death of twenty-six Wuhan colleagues he had known personally: three had died in their fifties, seven in their forties, and the rest in their thirties and twenties—usually violently.[20]

In dealing with unruly students, however, the heavy hand of Yang Qingshan was a last resort. Wuchang had been a proud center of educational reform since the time of Zhang Zhidong. In the 1920s its three universities had thrived because of strong support from local elites and a feeder system of over thirty middle schools. Students had provided shock troops to the revolution of 1927. And later, in Wuhan as elsewhere after the Japanese occupation of Manchuria in 1931 and the attack on Shanghai in 1932, containing students' protests against corruption and unrest about the Chiang government's reluctance to go to war was a big problem. The government's answer was bold and reform minded: restructure the atmosphere on campus—literally—by rebuilding university life from the ground up. In 1930 the Nanjing government closed two of the three Wuchang universities (the third, a missionary-run university, was permitted to continue under new leadership) and began building in their place a new flagship institution under strong central government control.

The establishment of Wuhan University was an impressive achievement and is important to our story because its campus became the wartime seat of government in 1938. Carefully planned at the national level by a blue-ribbon commission and constructed by a team of Chinese architects led by the American F. H. Kales, the resulting complex combined Chinese and Western architectural and landscaping styles. Completed in 1932, the university's gardenlike campus layout and imposing "Chinese renaissance" structures sat on a hilly suburban site overlooking Wuchang to the west and Donghu Lake to the north.[21] The new university's president, Wuhan native Wang Shijie, had been a leading academic at Beijing

University in the 1920s and had served as Chiang Kaishek's foreign minister in the early 1930s. To fill key posts in the university, as much as possible Wang conducted nationwide searches to recruit senior faculty with
wide visibility and pro-Guomindang political credentials. Thus the university's creation had a clear political purpose: as a flagship institution
under firm central-government leadership, it was to set a national example of how to control and rechannel student activism.[22]

How effective this strategy was is open to question. Wuchang remained
the seat of government while being home to a large and combustible
student-intellectual community that existed quite apart from the commercial life in Hankou or the workers' quarters in Hanyang. In 1935
major student demonstrations against the government broke out at both
universities and moved to the streets of Hankou in sympathy with the
December 9 protests against Japanese aggression that were then taking
place in Beijing, Shanghai, Xi'an and elsewhere. New rounds of student
arrests and assassinations of dissident intellectuals followed.[23]

By December 7, 1936—at the time of the kidnapping of Chiang Kaishek during the Xi'an incident—Wuhan was in a strange kind of limbo.
Firmly under the thumb of Nanjing, its political and cultural life was
suffocating and heavily censored. The exception was student activism,
which continued on Wuchang campuses. The government permitted
demonstrations in favor of movement toward a United Front and war
with the Japanese after Chiang Kaishek's release from Xi'an and return
to Nanjing on December 25. The domestic commercial economy was in
the doldrums because of depressed conditions in the surrounding countryside. The streets of Hankou were flooded with impoverished peasants looking for work, while tycoons like Liu Xinsheng, who continued
to profit handsomely from international trade at the port of Hankou,
rode around in motorcars.

Thus, on July 7, 1937, when war broke out at Marco Polo Bridge and
the Japanese occupied Beijing by the end of the month, Wuhan seemed
on the surface largely unprepared for the possibility that it might be thrust
into the center of the conflict. Certainly the Japanese attack on Shanghai in August and its fall by November came much more quickly than
expected. But at least as early as 1933 (as I discuss in the next chapter),
the Nanjing government had begun to plan for the defense of the Yangzi
valley, with Wuhan as the strategic, pivotal point of defense. In other
words, as war clouds gathered over China after the fall of Manchuria in
1931 and the attack on Shanghai in 1932, the defense of Wuhan became

the centerpiece of an emerging strategy: to fight a prolonged war of attrition *(chijiu zhan)* against the Japanese.

September 1937 brought several overt signs that major changes were coming. High Guomindang apparatchiks, notably Vice President Wang Jingwei and Minister of Education Chen Lifu (a CC Clique leader), appeared in Wuhan on inspection visits. Military defense engineers and work teams arrived to initiate planning for the building of massive fortifications downriver at Madang and Tianjiazhen, with construction starting in December. And finally, from their capital at Yan'an, the Communist leaders sent Dong Biwu back to Wuhan, where he established a headquarters for the party in a dilapidated old building in the French Concession zone of Hankou.[24]

The event that government leaders and the local population were not prepared for was the sudden influx of a million refugees after the capture and terrible massacre of civilians at Nanjing in December 1937. The Wuhan regional metropolis was already hard pressed to absorb the hundreds of thousands of peasant families whose livelihood had been swept away by the great floods of 1931 and 1935. Wuhan and its refugee population were living under the threat of a terrible siege. From the north and east, Japanese armored units were storming south down the north-south railway system, intent on joining the inland forces that were beginning to work their way west up the Yangzi from Nanjing. The factor that saved Wuhan for ten months was the serious resistance the Japanese encountered from reorganized units of the Chinese army, which numbered more than one million soldiers. So to comprehend the predicament of the refugees and the new sense of community that they built, we must first understand the changing military circumstances surrounding them, especially how key military figures on the Chinese side assumed political leadership roles that made possible the remarkable "Wuhan spring" of 1938.

TWO

DEFENDING CENTRAL CHINA, 1938:
MILITARY LEADERSHIP AND STRATEGY

AT 7:00 A.M. ON THE DAMP, cold morning of January 24, 1938, a single shot rang out in the third-story sanctuary of Forever Spring (Changchun guan) temple, a quiet Taoist retreat nestled inconspicuously on the southern side of Shuangfeng hill, near the railway station just outside the eastern gate of Wuchang. General Hu Zongnan had put a bullet through the head of a kneeling middle-aged figure, General Han Fuju, whose army had just surrendered control of Shandong, north China's most populous province. To this day, General Han remains the highest-ranking officer in the modern history of the Chinese military to be executed for malfeasance and cowardly performance as a commander.

Since at least 1930 General Han Fuju had exercised independent military and political control over Shandong as its governor. With the outbreak of the Sino-Japanese War in the summer of 1937, although the general was nominally beholden to Chiang Kaishek as head of the Nationalist government's Military Affairs Council *(junshi weiyuanhui)*, he continued to govern and organize the defense of this strategically important province and its capital of Jinan without much consultation. After his attempts to negotiate a separate deal broke down, the Japanese launched an offensive, bombing Jinan and moving ground troops rapidly south from positions in the Beijing, Baoding, and Tianjin area. Chiang Kaishek ordered General Han and his Third Group Army to resist to the last man. Accustomed as he was to following Chiang's orders only when it suited him, General Han vacillated. Finally, rather than risk the destruction of a personal army of eighty thousand men, he decided to retreat, leaving Jinan basically defenseless. The result was little fighting and much panic on the part of the civilian population in and around Jinan throughout December.[1] Simultaneously, the Nationalist government's capital at Nanjing was under siege. To Chiang Kaishek and his colleagues, the speed with which the Japanese occupied Jinan and the port city of Qingdao on December 27 and 28 suggested that the Japanese northern army would soon be free to race south down the Jin-Pu (Tianjin-Pukou) railway at nearly full strength. By the end of January it would be in position to join forces with the large army under General Matsui Iwane, which had just captured Nanjing. The losses of Jinan and Nanjing brought on pandemonium, as a large number of Chinese troops and civilians fled in all directions, especially to the south and west toward Wuhan.[2]

As for General Han's fate, the specifics are as follows. On January 5, 1938, the general left his army in the field in southern Shandong and fled to Henan Province. He brought with him much of the Jinan treasury and personal possessions, including a silver coffin. After a meeting on January 11 near Kaifeng with Chiang Kaishek and his top generals, General Han was arrested and brought to Wuchang. The decision to execute him, which took place at a special military tribunal on January 19, was the collective action of the military leadership under the chairmanship of Chiang Kaishek. Independently powerful regional militarists like Li Zongren, Bai Chongxi, and Feng Yuxiang were now willing to work in concert with Chiang and loyalists like General Chen Cheng and the Whampoa Military Academy graduate Hu Zongnan. There was much collective anger. General Han's refusal to stand and fight was seen as having contributed directly to the failure to organize an adequate defense of the capital, Nanjing, and thus to its humiliating loss, which came at a terrible price in civilian casualties. During the tribunal, General Han remained silent, apparently in a state of utter disbelief. Finally, at the end, as he was led off, he allegedly cried out in defiance, "I take responsibility for losing Shandong. But who takes responsibility for losing Nanjing?"[3]

He had a point; the fall of Nanjing was one reason for Chiang Kaishek's loss of direct military authority at Wuhan. But General Han had badly misjudged the changing political climate and the willingness of fellow militarists to fall in behind Chiang Kaishek despite Chiang's erratic recent performance as a battlefield commander. The Japanese Imperial Army, the generals agreed, was implacable, merciless, and perhaps unbeatable. Only by combining did they have a chance for survival; divided, they would certainly fall.

From all sides of the political spectrum, the Wuhan press applauded General Han Fuju's trial and execution and expressed support for Chiang's military leadership. One statement of support came from a new daily, the *Xinhua ribao*, published by the Communist leadership team of Dong Biwu, Zhou Enlai, and Wang Ming, who had just arrived from Yan'an.[4] Of more immediate military significance was the commitment of over half a million troops to the defense of central China from Chiang's former rivals, powerful regional militarists like Li Zongren and Bai Chongxi, whose Guangxi troops were arriving fresh from the south. More understandable perhaps was the commitment of the remaining units of northern regional armies, such as those loyal to the once-powerful Feng Yuxiang. Most of Han Fuju's Shandong army deserted after his execution, either joining the Japanese as puppet troops or turning to banditry or guerrilla warfare.

THE ADOPTION OF A STRATEGY

It has been often said that the Chinese military leadership had no coherent strategy for the Anti-Japanese War.[5] The rapid collapse of resistance forces defending coastal China and then, in December, the fall of the capital, Nanjing, followed quickly by the loss of Jinan and Qingdao, certainly support this view. But in fact, given the advantage of hindsight and newly released documents from both the Japanese and Chinese sides, the reverse now seems true: war planning of a general nature, especially for the defense of the central Yangzi valley, had been going on since at least the early 1930s.[6] By the time of Han Fuju's execution, in late January 1938, the commanders who gathered in Wuchang had embraced the idea of forcing the Japanese into a war of attrition *(chijiu zhan)* that would last for years. The plan was to bog down the Japanese in the vast hinterland of central China, with the first line of battle being at the northern gateway to the Yangzi valley, the railway-junction town of Xuzhou.[7]

Since the 1920s the most vocal advocate of the protracted-war approach had been Jiang Baili, a quixotic figure who resurfaced in 1938 in Wuhan to assume a prominent role as a publicist for the strategy. Jiang's influence was due in part to his guru status as the founder of Baoding Military Academy, which we will explore in greater detail later. But just as important were his many publications on military questions running back before the 1911 Republican revolution. Together with Cai E (the hero of the successful effort in 1915–16 to thwart President Yuan Shikai's monarchical ambitions), Jiang wrote long commentaries on a new edition of *The Art of War (Sunzi bingfa)*, a fifth-century B.C. classic in which the ideas of Sunzi (a person) were likened to those of Clausewitz. Their work became a standard edition and is still in print today.[8] Alarmed by the rise of Chinese militarism or warlordism and the arms proliferation that went with it, Jiang published a major essay in 1922 arguing that disarmament was the only solution for China. He also wrote a series of boldly interpretive essays on history in which he defended the record of the late Qing commanders Zeng Guofan, Hu Linyi, and Zuo Zongtang—praising them especially for disbanding their troops after the defeat of the Taiping rebels.

At the same time, in the early 1920s, Jiang Baili began to anticipate a war with Japan and to suggest in print that a protracted war of attrition was the only appropriate defensive strategy for China.[9] He advocated reorganizing China's defenses around a localized militia system (citing earlier *tuanlian* precedents by Zeng Guofan and Li Hongzhang). His essays from this time on focused on the need for China to build an industrialized and technologically sophisticated base for the coming war with Japan. By the late 1920s he was China's best-known military intellectual; his articles in popular journals and daily newspapers—such as *Shen bao*, *Dagong bao*, and *Guowen zhoubao*—were ultimately collected in a book, *Guofang lun* (On National Defense).[10] In these essays, he argued that because China's coastal cities were indefensible, military leaders should plan an orderly retreat into the interior as soon as possible. Jiang identified the mountainous Nanyue region of southern Hunan and western Hubei provinces as the place to build an economic and military infrastructure that could support a prolonged stand in the coming war. Recalling Napoleon's difficulties in Russia, he called Hunan the potential Ukraine of China.[11]

The essays republished in *Guofang lun* as well as his many translations of Western works on military strategy kept Jiang Baili influential and widely read throughout the 1930s.[12] Although hardly considered a Communist or leftist, Jiang was still often vulnerable because of his lack of political affiliation and perhaps also because of his drinking habit and loose tongue with many friends and students. His wife, to whom he was devoted, was Japanese (as a nurse, she had saved his life from a self-inflicted bullet wound in 1913), and he was criticized for this fact in the mid-1930s. But probably the most important source of his problems was that in the 1920s, for economic and political reasons, he had served as a paid "adviser" to several militarists—notably Tan Yankai, Wu Peifu, and Sun Chuanfang—which put him at odds with the youthful Guo-

mindang as it gathered strength for the Northern Expedition from Canton (led first by Sun Yatsen and then by Chiang Kaishek) in 1925–26.
Jiang's advising activities in 1930 were the last straw. Unable to tolerate
the association of a man of Jiang's prestige with rivals like his ex-Baoding
student Tang Shengzhi, Chiang ordered his arrest.[13]

From 1930 to 1932 Jiang Baili languished in a Shanghai prison—but
comfortably enough, he said later, to read Goethe and Kant while lis-
tening to Beethoven and composing essays entitled "Fascism and Democracy," "War and Life," and "History and Development of European
Thought." He was abruptly released in early 1932 to advise Shanghai's
new commander, Chen Mingshu, a Baoding graduate who was soon to
lead the Nineteenth Route Army in its courageous defense of the city
against Japanese attacks. From 1932 on Jiang was at his most prolific as
a writer, while serving publicly as an occasional military adviser to Chiang Kaishek. Although Chiang himself had attended Baoding in its early
Beiyang Army incarnation, the two men's personal relationship was never
close, and Jiang did not receive a major position until the spring of 1938;
at that time, certain high-level Baoding graduates at Wuhan apparently
engineered his appointment to the rank of lieutenant general. Then in
April, after returning from a fact-finding tour of Germany and Italy, he
was named commandant of China's newly reconstituted elite officer training school, the Army Staff College (Lujun daxue).

THE CONDITION OF CHINESE FORCES AFTER THE FALL OF NANJING

China began the war in 1937 with an estimated regular force of 1.7 million to 2.2 million men. These troops fit into six categories according to
the strength of their political loyalty to their commander in chief, Chiang Kaishek. First were the troops that were under Chiang's direct control. Second came troops who had been loyal to Chiang in the past but
were less under his direct control. Third were provincial troops over whom
Chiang could exercise command in ordinary times, and fourth were a
different set of provincial troops over whom Chiang had little direct influence. The fifth category comprised the Communist forces: the Eighth
Route Army in the caves of the northwest and the New Fourth Army
taking shape in 1938–39 in the hill country of the central Yangzi region
between Wuhan and Nanjing. Sixth and finally were the northeastern or
Manchurian units that had suffered defeat and displacement by the Japanese in 1931. The first two categories—the Chiang loyalists—included
roughly 900,000 men, who were the better armed and trained. The rel-

atively independent provincial armies counted for at least a million men—
poorly armed but more experienced and fiercely loyal to their commanders
in the field. About another 300,000 were split between the Communist
and Manchurian forces.[14]

Most of the troops loyal to Chiang Kaishek had been dispatched to
the central coastal areas and played major roles in the defense of Shanghai and Nanjing, where they suffered tremendous losses. Most devastating in military terms was the loss of 70 percent of the young officer
corps that Chiang had spent precious resources to train in the 1930s.[15]
Although Generals Chen Cheng and Hu Zongnan, both strong Chiang
loyalists, split the overall command, the surviving units—about four hundred thousand men—had retreated in disorganized and often leaderless
fashion up the Yangzi toward Wuhan in the winter of 1937–38.

The independent regional armies of the north, like the units under General Han Fuju in Shandong Province, had taken big hits; many went over
to the Japanese and later served as puppet troops, some turned to banditry, and others continued to resist as informal guerrilla bands. Thus after the first six months of the war, the Chinese troops that remained in
terms of troop strength were the sizable but relatively autonomous armies
located in either the southwest or the northwest, under the command
of such regional militarists as General Li Zongren and Bai Chongxi
(Guangxi), Long Yun (Yunnan), Yang Sen (Sichuan), Zhang Fakui and
Xue Yue (Guangdong), and Yan Xishan (Shanxi-Suiyuan region). The
Communist forces numbered about one hundred thousand and were relatively unscathed in bases to the north and east of Xi'an; but they were
roped off, in essence, by Yan Xishan's regional army and the deployment
of over a dozen divisions under General Hu Zongnan. Thus, despite receiving considerable attention from scholars, the Communist- led units
of the Eighth Route Army took little or no part in the battle for the central Yangzi valley in 1938.[16] Most of the seven hundred thousand or so
men who were the heart of the Chinese defense were from Guangxi,
Sichuan, Guangdong, and elsewhere, in units that had served under the
command of generals like Li and Bai or Chang Fakui and Xue Yue since
the 1920s.[17]

Early in 1938, as retreating troops regrouped around Wuhan and fresh
units came north from Guangxi and east from Sichuan, the generals reorganized the positioning of divisions and command structure for the defense of the central Yangzi by war zone (see map 3). They redefined the
Fifth War Zone as the area north of the Yangzi (Anhui, Hubei, and Henan
provinces) and put it under the command of General Li Zongren. His

army was a mixture of his own Guangxi units and units loyal to General Bai Chongxi with troops that were more loyal to Chiang Kaishek. The latter's leaders were either untested young commanders like Tang Enbo or recently disgraced figures like Jiang Zizhong, a former Feng Yuxiang associate to whom Li Zongren decided to give a second chance (despite his role in the humiliating surrender of Beijing in 1937). Altogether, about fifty divisions (roughly nine thousand men each, or about four hundred fifty thousand) fought on the Chinese side in the Fifth War Zone.[18] Initially their headquarters was at Xuzhou in northern Jiangsu, a strategically important border city at the north-south/east-west juncture of the Longhai and Jin-Pu railway lines.[19]

To the south of the Yangzi and directly under General Chen Cheng was the Ninth War Zone, which encompassed Hunan, Jiangxi, and Hubei provinces, with the tricity of Wuhan as the command center. Chen's army consisted of seventy-eight divisions or seven hundred thousand men, a mixture of units with strong provincial loyalties, like those loyal to the Cantonese general Chang Fakui. They were expected to work closely with units that were more directly tied to Chiang Kaishek and commanded by graduates of the Whampoa Military Academy (where Chiang had been the commandant in the 1920s). Added to the mix were displaced provincial troops of questionable loyalty who had served under regional militarists like Feng Yuxiang and Zhang Xueliang. Also in play was the New Fourth Army, a collection of guerrilla units under General Ye Ting that was in its infancy in 1938.[20]

The Fifth and Ninth War Zone armies, as reassembled in January, represented the approaches the Chinese military leadership took to organizing and positioning troops. As a field organization, the reorganized Chinese forces reflected German models, with large armies grouped together as field armies (as in the Fifth and Ninth War Zones). But at the same time, in the manner of the Soviet Red Army, units were strategically positioned along communications lines. Thus, in the adoption of battle formation, strategists used both front and route armies as well as rear-area service units. The overall result was a lack of coherence in deploying forces to face the Japanese. When commanders drew up more rational and aggressive plans, the armies rarely followed the plans in practice. Moreover, military intelligence about Japanese movements was poor. Prisoners were usually shot on the spot, and interrogation was rare; and with little reconnaissance work, rumors replaced intelligence, sometimes with disastrous results (like the unnecessary preemptive burning of Changsha by Chinese generals in November 1938).[21]

In short, the Chinese overemphasized positional warfare in their strategic deployments, remaining fixed in position except to retreat. The large, layered units were positioned for holding onto communication lines (such as the Beijing-Hankou or Longhai railway lines). Although the Chinese military leadership probably had good transport and logistical reasons for this approach, the net effect was to immobilize or tie down the main fighting forces, which the Japanese could then more easily maneuver around or outflank. The Chinese further limited their mobility by eschewing guerrilla warfare as a normal tactic. And finally, in the name of a protracted-war strategy, Chinese commanders often avoided decisive confrontations with the Japanese, even when they had a tactical advantage, so as to reduce the possibility of meeting irreversible defeat. This approach was understandable considering the devastating losses Chinese troops had absorbed in the defense of Shanghai and Nanjing, as well as the background of many generals, who as provincial militarists had been expert at political and military survival using their soldiers as capital. At critical moments in a battle, the timidity of division commanders outraged Chen Cheng, Li Zongren, Bai Chongxi, and Chiang Kaishek.

By March 1938, at the beginning of the central Yangzi campaign, the Chinese enjoyed a nearly six-to-one numerical advantage over the Japanese: 1.1 million men (or one hundred twenty divisions) against a Japanese force of 200,000 (twenty divisions). But the advantage of numbers dissolved in the face of the massive superiority of Japanese equipment, mobility, and firepower. According to one calculation by an American military observer, the combat effectiveness of a Chinese division (defined as numbers times firepower) ranged from one-third to one-twelfth that of its Japanese counterpart.[22] Not only was Chinese weaponry inferior, but little replenishment of men and arms took place or was even possible. Leaving aside bravery and *esprit*, this gap meant that one hundred Chinese divisions were often no better than twelve Japanese divisions in fighting effectiveness.

Thus, as the battle for Wuhan and the central Yangzi valley unfolded, the Japanese military leaders were supremely confident. In sweeping through Shanghai and then Nanjing, their troops had proven to be much better prepared than the Chinese in training, armaments, and supporting industrial infrastructure (including the routing of supplies south from Manchuria). Moreover, the Japanese leaders—both civilian and military—believed they were on a civilizing mission: to bring modernity—economic, social, and political—and global integration to a nation that was hopelessly mired in the past.[23] Their air superiority gave them a seemingly endless capacity for bombing and strafing before and during an attack, as well as for strategic bombing of Chinese cities behind the lines.[24]

In retrospect, it is apparent that the Japanese leadership had done little strategic planning. Military planners did not foresee a need for long-term maintenance of supply lines. They believed that their blitzkrieg and terror tactics, followed by application of maximum firepower from fast-moving, well-armed, mechanized ground troops, would bring about the quick collapse of Chiang Kaishek's China. They were simply not prepared to fight a war of attrition.[25]

The Chinese for the most part fought with small arms, machine guns, and hand grenades. The effective use of artillery was limited. A Chinese air force existed, but it was defensive and not employable in a tactical sense. Chinese forces fought most effectively at night and in hand-to-hand combat, when their generals could take better advantage of their numerical superiority and organize mass counterattacks.[26]

Finally, the Chinese struggled with the complex and overly politicized command structure that Chiang Kaishek had built up in the 1930s. Orders from Chiang had to pass down through six tiers of commanders before action was possible. Moreover, especially after the debacles at Shanghai and Nanjing, Chiang often tried to micromanage the battlefield by circumventing normal communication channels and sending direct personal orders to commanders in the field—sometimes contradicting directives sent just a few days earlier.[27] Not surprisingly also, in distributing equipment, Chiang favored central army units over which he had direct control and which had loyal commanders like Tang Enbo and Hu Zongnan who belonged to the Whampoa clique. Needless to say, Chiang's favoritism bred discord and insubordination at all levels of the Chinese command hierarchy.[28]

Given these impediments—the confusion of command, lack of firepower, and overemphasis on positional warfare, as well as the demoralizing debacles at Shanghai and Nanjing—how does one explain the Chinese success in 1938, a spirited defense that tied up the militarily superior Japanese Imperial Army in the Central Yangzi valley for ten months? Part of the answer lies in the improved coordination between commanders that followed a revival of the Baoding connection.

THE BAODING CONNECTION

The nature of leadership on the Chinese side underwent a sea change in January 1938, after the execution of General Han Fuju. Chen Cheng was the overall field commander, and despite Chiang Kaishek's attempts to interfere, he ran the defense of the central Yangzi in an informal but disciplined manner. Overcoming old rivalries and conflicting provincial loyalties, Chen and his associate commanders performed as a surprisingly cohesive group. In addition to their shared patriotism, the men had similar educational backgrounds and shared experiences in weathering military crises during the turbulent decade of the 1920s. Most of them, including the senior commander, Chen Cheng, were graduates of the Baoding Military Academy*(Baoding junguan xuexiao)*.

The Baoding Academy was founded one hundred miles south of Beijing in 1912 by Yuan Shikai on the site of a previous Beiyang Army officers' school. From 1912 to 1922 the elite of Republican China's new professional officer corps underwent training at Baoding. The academy's first commandant was the military intellectual Jiang Baili, who established a curriculum that emphasized drills for discipline, technological expertise based on German and Japanese models, classes on strategy and military history, and the promotion of esprit de corps among students and graduates. This curriculum stood in stark contrast to that of Baoding's successor institution, the Whampoa Central Military Academy, which Chiang Kaishek established in Canton in 1924 on a Leninist Bolshevik Red Army model that emphasized political indoctrination.[29] This difference in training produced a split, which became more apparent after the battle of Wuhan, between the younger Whampoa-trained officers and their older Baoding-educated commanders. Not surprisingly, before and after Baoding's closure in 1922, its alumni, who made up the majority of China's generals in the mid-1930s, remained fiercely loyal to their old school and to Jiang Baili personally, whom they honored as an inspirational teacher and the embodiment of the Baoding spirit.

As we shall see, Baoding generals like Chen Cheng, Bai Chongxi, Luo Zhuoying, Tang Shengzhi, Ye Ting, and Xue Yue were the key players in the defense of Wuhan. Li Zongren, the commander of the Fifth War Zone, was a graduate of the Yunnan Military Academy, which was modeled after Baoding, so he shared a similar background and concern for professionalism. The same was true of Zhang Fakui, who attended the academy that Zhang Zhidong established in Wuchang at the turn of the century. Few of these men had studied overseas (except for those of a later generation like Tang Enbo and Sun Liren). Since the 1920s most had struggled against Chiang Kaishek's efforts to marginalize and separate them from their armies. By 1938, however, with the exception of Han Fuju (not a Baoding man), they understood the seriousness of the

Japanese threat and the need to rally around Chiang's leadership and work
with the younger officers who were Whampoa Academy graduates.

In other words, the generals defending Wuhan came together as members of the Baoding generation. Their collective decision to execute Han
Fuju was an epiphany of sorts, giving them a new sense of mission. Over
the next few years the Baoding generals exhibited an esprit de corps and
mutual respect for each other's professionalism that surprised foreign observers. They were committed to working together on the battlefield and
agreed, politely and willingly, to quietly circumvent Chiang Kaishek's directives when necessary.

A related factor was the character of the troops these gentlemen commanded. They were a mixture of conscripts and soldiers of fortune, some
of whom had served for over a decade in units organized by their commanders. As mercenaries or professional soldiers operating essentially in
alien territory (and for troops from Guangxi, Canton, Sichuan, and Shandong, the central Yangzi valley was certainly alien), they were fiercely loyal
to their commanders. But running through all units was a shared sense
of outrage about the Japanese invasion. These soldiers understood the
threat to their home provinces. As a result, desertions were relatively few
and discipline within units was relatively good—in contrast to the forced
conscription and high desertion rate that later characterized many of the
units more directly under the command of Chiang Kaishek loyalists and
Whampoa Military Academy graduates. All of the above was especially
true of the Guangxi divisions under Li Zongren and Bai Chongxi; by the
end of 1938, foreign observers came to regard these troops as among the
best fighting units on the Chinese side.[30]

The improved chemistry of the moment, marked by good communication and the prowess of certain commanders, helps explain the ability
of the Chinese to hold out for ten months and inflict unacceptable losses
on the Japanese side. The division commanders of the Fifth and Ninth
War Zones came together through their will to resist the Japanese, not
through loyalty to Chiang Kaishek. The troops in both war zones were
a mélange of regional forces with different levels of armament and experience. Although poorly armed and trained, most of them remained
intensely loyal and followed orders.

High casualty figures, not high desertion rates, characterized the Chinese side during the battle for control of the central Yangzi valley. Moreover, Chiang Kaishek's loss of crack units and of his best officers earlier
in the war reduced or neutralized the commander in chief's ability to med-
dle or micromanage the battlefield (as he did in Shanghai). At the same

time, the relative political independence of many commanders limited their ability to coordinate operations and to come to each other's aid as the tide of battle turned in a particular place. And so in the end, relentless bombing and the exercise of superior mobility and firepower carried the day. The Japanese took Xuzhou and then Wuhan by the end of 1938.

At times, Chinese and Japanese historians have treated the Xuzhou and Wuhan campaigns as separate events. But to the Chinese and Japanese commanders at the time, the two events were intimately connected. Leaders on both sides saw the campaigns as parts of a pincer move by the Japanese to bring the north China and central China wings of the Imperial Army together south of Xuzhou so that they could deliver a speedy coup de grace to Wuhan by midspring. To block this move, the Chinese high command decided that its armies had to make a major stand at Xuzhou.[31]

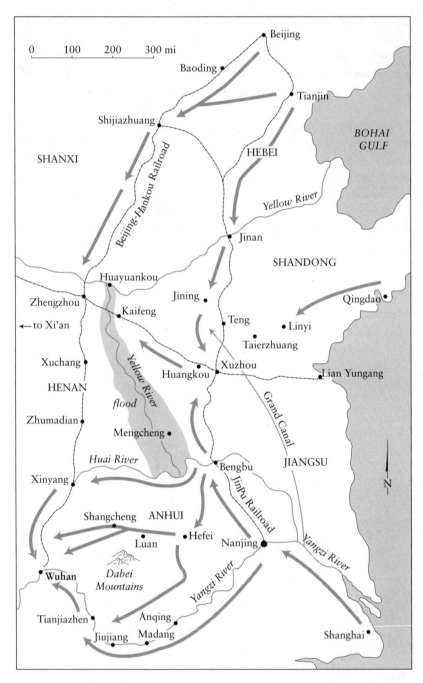

MAP 3. BATTLE FOR XUZHOU AND DEFENSE OF WUHAN, 1938, COPYRIGHT 2007 STEPHEN R.
MACKINNON.

THREE

THE BATTLE FOR XUZHOU
AND THE DEFENSE OF WUHAN

THE BATTLE FOR CONTROL of the central Yangzi region lasted ten months, from January to October 1938. In terms of geography and order of battle, the initiative lay with the Japanese because of their superior firepower and maneuverability on land and in the air. Foreign observers at the time, and many historians agree in retrospect, faulted the Chinese leadership for failing to take the offensive in pursuit of the enemy, especially on those occasions when the Japanese were overextended, tied down, and retreating.[1] Before accepting such views, however, one should consider the difficulties the Chinese forces would have faced in taking the offensive. Their mobility was limited to forced marches or the use of railway lines. Given their lack of heavy firepower, softening up the enemy before an attack was not possible. Much of the time they had little or no artillery, as well as very limited ability to bomb and strafe the enemy from the air.

In January 1938 the Japanese plan was to connect large units from the North China Area Army (under Generals Itagaki Seishiro, Nishio Toshizo, and Isogai Rensuke) with the Eleventh Army (the Central China Expeditionary Force) under General Hata Shunroku, which was headquartered in Nanjing. Units of the North China Area Army began moving south along the JinPu railway from Jinan, and units under General Hata began moving north up the JinPu railway from Nanjing. Once united at Xuzhou, according to the plan, the two armies would launch a coordinated attack in a pincer movement from the north and east on central Yangzi valley strongholds, taking Jiujiang first and then Wuhan. Success by the end of March seemed assured—a success that seemed certain to break the back of United Front resistance under Chiang Kaishek.[2]

At this point, the war council that Chiang convened at the end of January in Wuchang made an important decision: to go all out in committing troops to the defense of Xuzhou, the key strategic city at the junction of the Longhai and JinPu railroads.[3] In retrospect, this decision was perhaps the most important one of the war, because the effectiveness of the Chinese resistance around Xuzhou tied down and embarrassed the Japanese, forcing them to rush reinforcements from Manchuria (under General Doihara Kenji) and Nanjing. Both these deployments seriously delayed previously planned campaigns to the west and north from Taiyuan and up the Yangzi from Nanjing. They also forced the Japanese into a major rethinking of troop deployment and a change in the way that Tokyo directed the war.[4] The prolonged, bloody struggle for Xuzhou forced the Japanese to give high priority to the central Chinese theater.

Recognizing the strategic importance of holding on to Xuzhou, the Chinese military leadership began in January to prepare for its defense. From a core of eighty thousand troops, which Li Zongren commanded at headquarters at Xuzhou, the number swelled to about three hundred thousand, with the import of troops from scattered units positioned along the JinPu or Longhai railway lines. The idea was to catch the much smaller Japanese units as they came by rail and road from the north, south, and east. Once drawn in and overextended, they could be delayed and perhaps even stopped at positions to the north and east of Xuzhou. This tactic was effective. The battle for Xuzhou raged for five months, with both sides taking heavy casualties and claiming victories.

When the Japanese finally took Xuzhou in mid-May, they found an empty city defended by only a few thousand soldiers. But earlier the Japanese had seen costly setbacks. At the end of March, the Japanese had been lured into a major engagement at Taierzhuang about thirteen miles to the northeast of Xuzhou; here, three divisions were beaten back and forced to retreat, with casualties running from fifteen thousand to twenty thousand killed (about the same number died on the Chinese side). Eventually, the Japanese reconquered Taierzhuang, but in this battle and the effort to take Xuzhou, they lost valuable time, and their morale was shaken. On the Chinese side, the reverse was the case. Despite the defeat, Xuzhou was a morale booster. Li Zongren, Bai Chongxi, Zhang Zizhong, Sun Lianzhong, and Tang Enbo became national heroes. As the Chinese troops retreated, they approached the defense of Wuhan with new confidence and determination.[5]

Needless to say, the history of the five-month battle for control of the Xuzhou railway junction is complicated both chronologically and geographically. The Chinese side of the story is especially complex because of the variety of units deployed at any one time or place, with some fighting and some not, under an ever-changing cast of division commanders. As the Japanese closed in on Xuzhou from the north, east, and south, what pattern existed in the thrust and retreat of forces was a zigzagging motion, with action swinging first to the north, then to the east, then to the south, and back and forth again.

In early February Japanese armored units with strong air support attacked Chinese divisions protecting the JinPu railway. The pincer movement first engaged Chinese troops about one hundred miles to the north and south of Xuzhou. As we have seen, the Japanese plan was for units of the North China Area Army to push south toward Xuzhou and for units of the Eleventh Army to push north up the railway line from the Nanjing area, finally to meet triumphantly in Xuzhou. Then, after a short pause to regroup, the large force would proceed west along the Longhai railway line to Zhengzhou. From Zhengzhou, the combined units could proceed south down the PingHan (Beijing-Hankou) railway to lay siege to Wuhan. But by the end of the month a Chinese force of about three hundred thousand had successfully blocked Japanese advances, forcing major battles to the south around Bengbu on the Huai River and to the north at Teng *xian* (county).

The standoff at Teng *xian*, a railway stop about seventy-five miles north of Xuzhou, was particularly important and bloody. The defenders were relatively untested and poorly armed troops from Sichuan. Their commander was Wang Mingzhang, an old comrade and close associate of theater commander Li Zongren. Heroically, the Sichuanese held out until mid-March, when heavy artillery barrages and the growing size of the Japanese force finally overwhelmed them. General Wang lost his life in defense of Teng *xian*.[6] At the same time (mid-February) the Japanese began moving a large force inland from the port of Qingdao, heading across country southwest toward Xuzhou. At Linyi, about thirty miles northeast of Xuzhou, they encountered large deployments of entrenched Chinese forces commanded by Generals Pang Bingxun and Zhang Zizhong. The latter, a former associate of Feng Yuxiang, had suffered the contempt of Chiang Kaishek and the press since he surrendered Beijing without a fight in July 1937. Li Zongren decided to give Zhang a second chance and in January 1938 gave him a command in the Fifth War Zone. Zhang would redeem his reputation in the battle for Linyi.

In March and early April Chinese resistance in the Xuzhou area was at its most effective. Chinese units fought major engagements to the north, south, and east of the city, significantly slowing Japanese advances. Surprised foreign observers even noted that the Japanese might be stopped.[7] Chinese units under Generals Pang and Zhang took a terrific pounding but stopped the Japanese divisions under Itagaki Seishiro in a three-week battle at Linyi. Zhang Zizhong immediately became a national hero and an international celebrity.[8]

In mid-March both forces paused and regrouped for an even greater battle at Taierzhuang—on a railway spur line along the Grand Canal about thirteen miles northeast of Xuzhou. There General Zhang was joined by units commanded by the northerner Sun Lianzhong (also a former associate of Feng Yuxiang) and a young officer, Tang Enbo, whose units included artillery pieces. But General Tang was inexperienced and reluctant to commit his units to the battle. He was a graduate of the elite Japanese military academy, Shikan Gakko, and a protégé of Chiang Kaishek's chief of staff and military alter ego, General He Yingqin. Tang's relations with theater commander Li Zongren were not good. To get General Tang to close in and risk his artillery at Taierzhuang, Li reportedly threatened court-martial and execution.[9]

The small town of Taierzhuang was obliterated in the battle that raged from March 22 to April 7, 1938. Finally, Japanese troops under General Isogai Rensuke ran out of ammunition and had to retire. Much of the combat was at night and hand-to-hand. Both sides lost roughly twenty thousand men before the Japanese withdrew.[10] By mid-April another pause and a stalemate of sorts prevailed, despite the furtive initial attempt by Chinese units under Zhang and Sun, though battered and exhausted, to pursue the Japanese as they retreated north and east into Shandong from the charred remains of Taierzhuang.

By the end of April the tide began to turn in favor of the Japanese as reinforcements of men and supplies arrived. Japanese strength in the Xuzhou neighborhood reached four hundred thousand men as fresh troops and materiel poured in from Tianjin and Nanjing. New Japanese commanders (the infamous Doihara Kenji among them) ordered a series of counterattacks. Their plan was to approach Xuzhou from the southwest, east, and north; surround the city; lay siege; and destroy the large number of Chinese troops deployed in its defense. The Chinese also deployed reinforcements, bringing their total strength in the region to six hundred thousand. At the end of April the fighting on three fronts around Xuzhou was fierce, with much bloodshed on both sides. Slowly, Japanese firepower on the ground and bombing from the air prevailed. On May 9 the Japanese captured Mengcheng, well to the north of the Huai River. From there the southern flank force split into two parts: half went west and then north to cut off the Longhai railway escape route from Xuzhou, and the other divisions moved straight north up the railway line to Su*xian*, just outside Xuzhou. At the same time, to the north, the Japanese units from north China massed at Jining and began moving south beyond Teng *xian*. Along the coast, at Lian Yungang, the Japanese made an amphibious landing to reinforce troops attacking from the east. What remained of Taierzhuang was captured in May—an event of symbolic importance to Tokyo.

On May 17 the noose around Xuzhou tightened appreciably as Japanese artillery hit targets inside the city. By that time, however, an action that was probably the most important and skillful Chinese maneuver of the Xuzhou campaign was already under way: a brilliantly executed strategic retreat to the south and west across the JinPu railway line. On May 15 Li Zongren, in consultation with Chiang Kaishek, had decided to pull back from Xuzhou and attempt an escape; on that day, the evacuation of the civilian and military population of the city began. Li ordered troops to melt into the countryside and then move south and west at night, crossing the JinPu railway and splitting into four groups that would head west. The idea was eventually to regroup in the rugged Dabeishan Mountain region to the south and prepare for the defense of Wuhan. Li's generals left reluctantly, having held out for so long. Tang Enbo reportedly wept.

Marching by night and hiding in the wheat fields by day, in less than a week, forty divisions—between two to three hundred thousand men—quietly slipped out of Japanese reach. At a critical point on May 18, fog and a sandstorm covered the tracks of the retreating troops as they crossed the JinPu railway. On May 21 Li wired Chiang Kaishek that the withdrawal was complete. Two days earlier, on May 19, Japanese units under General Hata Shunroku had marched into the nearly abandoned ruins of Xuzhou, taking prisoner thirty thousand soldiers and civilians.

The events of the next few days were remarkable and remain highly controversial. The Japanese army (North China units) steamed east down the Longhai railway, taking Kaifeng on June 6. The troops were poised to cross the Yellow River and threaten the railway junction with the (north-south) Beijing-Hankou line at Zhengzhou. Chiang Kaishek had flown to Zhengzhou at the end of May and decided to order General Wei Rulin to blow up the dikes of the Yellow River at Huayuankou so that the river would change course and flow south into Anhui Province, joining the Huai and then heading east toward the sea. Chiang hoped to stop the Japanese advance by flooding the invaders' path to the west and south. The dikes were blown up on June 5 and again on June 7, 1938. The devastation and human suffering that resulted were almost incalculable.[11]

The move did force a change in Japanese war plans for the Wuhan campaign. Units of the North China Area Army did not reach Zhengzhou; they had to retrace their steps and head south, down the JinPu railway, to join General Hata's forces near Nanjing. Thus the destruction of the dikes redirected the attack on Wuhan but did not seriously delay it. The attack began in early July as a two-pronged drive upriver from Nanjing.[12]

The blowing of the dikes at Huayuankou brought the five-month Xuzhou campaign to a dramatic and tragic end. For the Chinese side, the outcome was bittersweet. Initially, because of the victories at Linyi and Taierzhuang, the Chinese were jubilant, especially in the refugee-swollen de facto capital of Wuhan.[13] The loss of Xuzhou was a blow, yet the strength of the defense and the escape of Li's troops seemed to demonstrate that the Japanese were becoming bogged down in central China. Chances seemed improved for Wuhan; the tricity might be able to hold out. The Japanese commanders were angry. Having reorganized and reinforced in June, they were determined to end the "China incident" at Wuhan.

Historians, like observers at the time, disagree about who made the key decisions on the Chinese side and who should receive credit for the impressive defense of Xuzhou. Chinese historians on Taiwan in the 1950s, and recently a few on the mainland, favor crediting Chiang Kaishek for sagely micromanaging defensive strategy from Wuchang.[14] Certainly, Chiang bombarded field commanders with private communications and instructions via telephone and telegrams. Diana Lary credits the effectiveness of the Chinese defense to the Guangxi generals Li Zongren and Bai Chongxi, especially Li.[15] Foreign military attachés like Evans Carlson and journalists like Israel Epstein pointed to midlevel commanders Tang Enbo, Zhang Zizhong, and Sun Lianzhong—who persevered despite incompetent meddling by Chiang Kaishek, Li, and Bai—as the true heroes of the campaign.[16]

Some critics have charged that the Chinese generals were insufficiently aggressive in their strategic moves. Advisers like the German von Falkenhausen and the Russian Kalyagin, along with the American military attachés Carlson, Joseph Stilwell, and Frank Dorn, pointed out that the failure to effectively pursue Japanese divisions retreating from Linyi and Taierzhuang gave the Japanese time to regroup and counterattack. In retrospect, this expectation seems unrealistic, given the inadequacy of equipment, the absence of airpower, and the badly battered state of Chinese troops at the time. The Japanese had been stopped but not beaten. The high morale of the Chinese troops alone could not have driven the Japanese into the sea.[17]

One factor that has gone relatively unrecognized is the importance of the skillful retreat by the two to three hundred thousand Chinese troops that General Hata thought he had trapped at Xuzhou in late May 1938. Badly battered, but with about half his troops intact, General Li and the divisions of the Fifth War Zone survived the Xuzhou campaign and were able to regroup in the Dabeishan Mountains. This step was significant because it delayed the attack on Wuhan and forced General Hata to fight his way up the heavily fortified Yangzi River, capturing river communities town by town until he could lay siege to Wuhan.

Still, on the Chinese side, the human cost of the battle for Xuzhou was great, deeply shaking the confidence of the man most in charge, Li Zongren. The hero's welcome he received on his return to Wuhan did not help. Apparently haunted by the ghosts of those lost in the defense of Xuzhou, Li was hospitalized for mysterious reasons—for depression as much as for physical ailments. (The official explanation was that an old bullet wound had flared up.) Bai Chongxi took over the Fifth War Zone duties and command of the four hundred thousand or so troops bivouacked in the Dabeishan area, waiting for the Japanese to attack from the east.[18]

DEFENDING WUHAN

In June 1938 the Japanese amassed four hundred thousand men for the assault on Wuhan. The attack was initially to be a two-pronged pincer offensive under the overall command of General Hata, moving west and south from Xuzhou as well as west up the Yangzi River (see map 3). A column of North China Area Army units was to move southwest overland from Hefei on the JinPu railway. The other thrust, by a larger force of combined Eleventh Army and naval units, was to push a steady assault moving upstream and west from Nanjing along the southern bank of the Yangzi.[19] In neither case was the geography favorable. For the units pushing cross-country in a southwesterly direction, the trek was particularly rough; they faced a patchwork of small mountain ranges and narrow valleys with many river crossings and few passable roads. Summer was also in full force, producing a very hot and malaria-ridden environment.

The Chinese marshaled at least eight hundred thousand men for the defense of Wuhan and the central Yangzi valley. In practice, the grand strategy and deployment of troops was as much the work of the theater commander Chen Cheng and the generals under him as it was the work of Chiang Kaishek. Basically, the approach was to place troops in the most defensible or important places along the path of the advancing Japanese. Fifth War Zone troops under General Bai Chongxi defended the region north of the Yangzi River, and Ninth War Zone troops deployed along the southern bank. In the north, the idea was to tie up the Japanese in the rough terrain south and north of the Dabeishan Mountains and thus prevent them from cutting off the Ping Han railway north of Wuhan. In the south (the Ninth War Zone), the Chinese worked furiously to construct riverine defenses that might block the main assault below Jiujiang and push the Japanese farther south into the Boyang Lake district.[20]

The Chinese side benefited from the hilly, roadless terrain (though it was unfamiliar to many of the troops and commanders), the support of the local populace, and the gift of sufficient time to dig in and erect earthen defenses. The summer of 1938 was hot, steamy, and disease ridden; foot soldiers on both sides were crippled by dysentery and malaria. The Japanese, besides their obvious superiority in firepower and mobility, enjoyed an important natural advantage: during the summer of 1938 the Yangzi was near its high-water mark. Throughout the campaign, this waterway facilitated effective shelling of Chinese defense positions by Japanese gunboats and helped a flotilla of supply ships reach advancing troops.

Japan opened with a resounding victory. On June 15 the first defensive stronghold on the Yangzi at Anqing (over one hundred miles east of Nanjing) fell after only one day of fighting. The two divisions of Sichuan soldiers under General Yang Sen (the militarist who had dominated Chengdu in the 1920s) were outmaneuvered and quickly overwhelmed by an amphibious landing behind their defenses. General Yang fled in disgrace, not to be heard from again.[21] From Anqing, which had an airfield, the Japanese were able to coordinate a combined army-navy assault on Jiujiang, the major riverine port and railway junction that was another one hundred miles upstream. (By rail, Jiujiang was the northern terminus for traffic in different directions to Hangzhou, Nanchang, and Canton.) In hopes of preventing the capture of Jiujiang, Chinese engineers and a thousand coolies had been working at night since May to build impressive defensive installations with artillery emplacements at Madang, which was midway en route to Jiujiang at a place where the banks of the Yangzi formed a natural defensive embankment.[22]

Tragically, the defense of Madang turned into a debacle. On June 24 the Japanese surprised the Chinese by landing upstream from Madang, cutting off major defending units at the county seat of Pengze. The local commanders were off on a training junket at the time, so Pengze fell quickly, almost without a struggle. Suddenly Madang was surrounded, and when the Japanese began to use poison gas, the defenders panicked. The elaborate earthen defenses at Madang fell without ever facing the frontal assault they were built to defend against. The end came as Japanese gunboats crashed through river barriers on June 29. The loss of Madang was a major embarrassment and left the route to Jiujiang almost undefended. Chiang Kaishek court-martialed the officers in charge of Madang and ordered the execution of the divisional commander for Pengze, General Xie Weiying (a Whampoa graduate), who had ignored telephone calls from Bai Chongxi and others warning him to reinforce Madang at the time of the surprise attack.[23]

The Cantonese generals Zhang Fakui and Xue Yue, with a force of over two hundred thousand men, were in charge of the defense of the Jiujiang-Ruichang area. Their mission was to meet the Japanese and push them south into the Boyang Lake district. Both were seasoned commanders, players in the militarist politics of the 1920s who had served under Chiang Kaishek during the Northern Expedition of 1926–27. Xue Yue was a Baoding graduate with closer ties to Chen Cheng than to Chiang Kaishek, and Zhang Fakui (educated at the Wuchang Military Academy) was accustomed to operating independently from bases in Guangzhou. For the defense of Jiujiang, Xue Yue commanded about eighty thousand troops. At first, the Chinese units stood their ground at Hukou, to the north of Boyang Lake, losing the city on July 8 after a brutal five-day battle. The battle for Jiujiang, the major port city in Jiangxi Province, began on July 23. It was over by July 28. Although the evidence is inconclusive, the Japanese may have used poison gas again in their attack. In any case, the defense led by Xue Yue was haphazard and disorganized. Moreover, the call for retreat came early and suddenly, leaving the civilian population at the mercy of the conquerors. Japanese troops were ruthless in their treatment of the remaining civilian and military population, repeating a mini-Nanjing massacre at Jiujiang.[24]

If the goal of the massacre and destruction at Jiujiang was to terrorize the populations and armies upstream into submission, it failed. Chinese resistance at the next major target, the commercial center of Ruichang, ten miles inland from Jiujiang, on the road west toward the Wuhan-Canton railway line, went much better. It lasted for a month and drew the Japanese into a major seesaw battle. General Zhang Fakui's large force made the Japanese pay heavily for every kilometer they advanced. At about the same time, Japanese units thrust south toward Nanchang and quickly bogged down in the Lu Shan Mountains. Overextended and with their supply routes cut off, the Japanese turned back and rejoined the battle around Ruichang.[25]

To the north, in the Fifth War Zone, Chinese resistance was better organized and more effective, slowing down the Japanese advance earlier in the campaign. The commanders were familiar names from the Xuzhou campaign: Sun Lianzhong, Jiang Zizhong, Tang Enbo, and others. South of the Dabeishan mountain range at Taihu (more or less directly north of Madang), the Chinese managed to tie up the Japanese for three weeks, until the invaders took this position on July 25. The Japanese took all of August to push west to Guangji, where they met stiff resistance that lasted until September 9. The battle at Guangji (just north of the Yangzi) was a prelude to a major encounter at Matouzhen on the river, where General Xue Yue and his Cantonese divisions redeemed their reputations. At one point in the battle over a critical position at Shaho, Xue Yue threatened the life of a young division commander (Yu Jishi, a Whampoa graduate) to prevent him from retreating and leaving the remaining units to the mercy of the Japanese.[26]

Thus the Japanese were finding in September that they needed three weeks to advance ten miles up the Yangzi. They needed this time in part because a Chinese force of one hundred thousand led by Xue Yue counterattacked effectively at the end of August at Huangmei, ten miles to the south of the river, and pushed the Japanese back into the mountains. As a result, the Japanese commander, Imamura, had to bring in emergency reinforcements from other positions. His troops remained caught in an ongoing battle, which became especially bloody at a place southeast of Ruichang called Wanjialing; the fighting ended only after the fall of Wuhan itself at the end of October.[27]

The final big battle on the Yangzi occurred at the river fortress of Tianjiazhen, where Chinese engineers, with Russian advisers and thousands of coolies, had been erecting massive battlements since the end of 1937. The resulting struggle was one of the bloodiest of the campaign, raging until September 29, when the Japanese (after using gas) finally captured an uninhabited smoldering ruin. The way was now largely cleared for the final army-navy assault upriver on Wuchang.[28]

At about the same time (August-September), to the north of the Dabeishan mountain range, the Japanese units of the North China Area

Army launched an end-run thrust from Hefei (in Anhui Province) to the west, with an eye to capturing control of and cutting off the Beijing-Hankou railway line at Xinyang. Li Zongren had resumed his command of the Fifth War Zone and seemed to be in charge of the defensive maneuvers to stop this thrust from Anhui. Initially, the Japanese were slowed for weeks as they attempted to cross the Pi River at Luan. Once across the river, however, resistance withered, and they moved rapidly through Shangcheng. They met significant resistance again at Huangchuan, where the hero of Linyi, General Zhang Zizhong, managed to pin them down for over a week.[29]

The Japanese finally reached Xinyang on the Ping Han railway on September 30. The Chinese expected General Hu Zongnan and his divisions to mount a significant defense, in part to cover the retreat of Li Zongren's battered and exhausted Guangxi divisions into the mountains to the west. Instead, Hu Zongnan and his army disappeared to the north, and the Japanese took Xinyang without a fight. Li Zongren, the theater commander, was furious, but Hu Zongnan was the closest of the Whampoa generals to Chiang Kaishek and was too senior for Li to threaten him with disciplinary action.[30]

With control of the Beijing-Hankou railway, the Japanese could now swiftly move troops and equipment directly south to attack the tricity from the north at Hankou, in concert with amphibious landings from General Hata's flotilla to the south, on the edge of Wuchang. With the noose tightening rapidly, Wuhan was about to be encircled.

The orderly evacuation of troops and equipment—as well as of Chiang's military headquarters at Hankou (his headquarters at Wuchang had been destroyed by bombing in August)—began in late September and was well under way by early October. Chiang and Chen Cheng were determined not to repeat the mistakes made at Shanghai and Nanjing and not to risk the sort of narrow escape that Li Zongren had engineered at Xuzhou. Earlier, in July and August, a Herculean effort had begun to remove and transport Wuhan's industrial capacity, especially the city's munitions production, upriver. By the end of October, thousands of tons of equipment were stockpiled on wharves upriver at Yichang, waiting to be shipped up the gorges to Chongqing for the duration of the war.[31]

Under simultaneous attack from the north, east, and south, Wuhan capitulated on October 25. Canton had fallen more quickly four days earlier, made more vulnerable perhaps by the absence of the seasoned Cantonese units that were fighting under generals Zhang Fakui and Xue Yue in the defense of Wuhan.

Finally, the capture of Wuhan seemed to leave Changsha defenseless against an imminent attack from the east, or so Chiang Kaishek concluded.[32] This assessment turned out to be erroneous, largely because of poor intelligence. In panic, and over the strenuous objections of Chen Cheng, Chiang seized on a scorched-earth tactic and gave orders for the city to be torched. And so, on November 12, 1938, Changsha—the capital of Hunan Province, one hundred miles south of Wuhan—was burned to the ground. Once the magnitude of this mistake and the suffering of the civilian population were apparent (the Japanese did not try to take Changsha until a year later), Chiang ordered a military tribunal and the execution of the three top leaders of the police who had set the blaze. Zhang Zhizhong, the general in charge—a trusted associate of Chiang as the governor of Hunan and a Whampoa graduate—escaped explicit blame.[33]

In military terms, the ten-month siege had been extraordinary. The Chinese had begun the year 1938 in a panic over the loss of Shanghai, Nanjing, and Jinan. Ten months later, the mood was different. Although the sacrifice and destruction had been tremendous, the retreat from Wuhan was orderly. The Japanese were clearly bruised and overextended, with little stomach left for pursuing the Chinese army to the west in the near future. The policy of strategic retreat in the context of a war of attrition was vindicated.

The successes of the Chinese army during the battle for Wuhan came at a terrible human cost: over half a million men killed or wounded in the long series of battles up and down the Yangzi valley. Soldiers received little medical attention, disease was rampant, and food was scarce. Most of the troops were hundreds of miles from home. Yet in 1938 few deserted. But the soldiers were not alone in bearing the brunt of war. The sacrifices of the surrounding civilian populations were probably even greater. The destructive power of modern warfare made the battles of 1938 devastating, and so much worse than anything civilians had experienced before. The Japanese use of modern transport, firepower, rapid mobility, and radio communications was new and overwhelming in impact. The Chinese had no comparable technological prowess. Still, their use of film, the popular press, and radio for propaganda purposes helped mobilize the masses, and their employment of telephones, railway lines, machine guns, and grenades allowed them to carry out prolonged, armed resistance.

Finally, the forced migration of huge populations, including elites, was of epic proportions and unprecedented scale. The defense of Wuhan turned most of the population of the central Yangzi valley from Nanjing to Yichang into refugees at one point or another. Both urban and rural communities were decimated by the constant back-and-forth fighting and bombing. Surviving family members could do little more than run. Millions of families were torn apart and displaced by the war; the suffering of women and children was particularly grave and long lasting. Refugees who had fled earlier from the north and the coastal areas met the refugees streaming into Wuhan. The experience of managing this cauldron of refugees, with its unprecedented mixture of social classes and regional backgrounds, would transform the tricity politically, culturally, and socially.

FOUR

WUHAN'S REFUGEE CRISIS

ALTHOUGH THE AMERICAN EYEWITNESSES Anna Lee Jacoby and Theodore White exaggerated the lack of existing records, they were essentially correct in saying that the movement of peoples and the creation of refugee societies all over China's hinterland are among the great untold stories of the Anti-Japanese War. In *Thunder Out of China* (1946), they wrote:

> Through the long months of 1938, as the Chinese armies were pressed slowly back toward the interior, they found their way clogged by moving people. The breathing space of winter had given hundreds of thousands time to make their decision, and China was on the move in one of the greatest mass migrations in human history. It is curious that such a spectacle has not been adequately recorded by a Chinese writer or novelist. Certainly the long files of gaunt people who moved west across the roads and mountains must have presented a sight unmatched since the days of nomad hordes; yet no record tells how many made the trek, where they come from, where they settled anew.[1]

The Anti-Japanese War did not produce a Chinese Tolstoy.[2] Instead, the poets, woodblock carvers, and foreign observers best captured the horror and desperation of the refugee experience. The poet Yuan Shuipai left the following stream-of-consciousness account of being bombed on a train stuffed with refugees.

> Seven days and seven nights eating, sleeping, defecating
> on top of a freight car
> From one hundred to three hundred swept up at the entrance to the tunnel

Big fire, Big fire, Big fire
Bodies, Bodies, Bodies
The suggestive pictures on the walls
Musclemen pushing their way forward
Leg, Leg, Leg
Curve, Curve, Curve
A pair of eyes protruding from the flames
And the flames shooting out from the eyes
City follows city, the rail line
From village to village, narrow trails and cavalries.[3]

GRASPING THE DIMENSIONS OF REFUGEE FLIGHT

The historian has the problem of describing the demography of refugee flight in more analytically satisfying terms. A major issue is the lack of reliable numbers. Estimates of the total refugee population during the war period (1937–45) run from three million to ninety million. The scholar must rely on random contemporary accounts, both foreign and domestic, and on the few official "war damage" reports that the Chinese compiled after the fact. The resulting data are spotty in coverage and regional in focus and therefore lead inevitably to impressionistic conclusions. Systematic annual surveys of refugee movements like those that the United Nations, International Red Cross, and U.S. State Department currently undertake simply do not exist for the period we are exploring.

First, we need a bit of historical perspective on the problem of war refugees in modern Chinese history. In picturing the chaos that engulfed the lower Yangzi after the fall of Shanghai and Nanjing in late 1937, we would do well to remember Jonathan Spence's eloquent translation of contemporary Chinese descriptions of the destruction and social cost wrought by the Taiping wars of the mid-nineteenth century in the same areas:

[There are] the masses of refugees and homeless villagers who wander in the area, displaced again and again by fighting that seems to have no end. These farmers and small-town dwellers of the Yangzi delta have now to contend with at least eight different kinds of troops who march and countermarch around their former homes. . . . For more than a year . . . from Shanghai through Suzhou toward the Yangzi, or even to the walls of Nanjing . . . across a fifty-mile swath of land one might see almost every house destroyed, wantonly burned by one side or the other, stripped of its doors and roof beams. That wood then serves either as fuel for the troops or as makeshift supports for temporary bridges across the myriad canals and creeks.[4]

Although aggregate figures on the number of refugees for the Taiping period are elusive, the documentation is often better than that for the Anti-Japanese War period. Historians agree that the Taiping wars displaced over thirty million people in the provinces of Jiangsu, Zhejiang, Anhui, Jiangxi, and Hubei.[5] Shanghai's foreign-concession authorities reported a huge jump in refugee population, including an influx of Chinese merchant elites. Inland, the picture was less clear. But we know, for example, that the population of Wuxi *xian* (county) dropped 78 percent between 1830 and 1865 (from three hundred thirty thousand to seventy thousand).[6] Once peace was restored, refugee elites returned and rebuilt cities like Wuxi, Suzhou, and Nanjing; as a result, these cities' populations gradually recovered and exceeded prewar levels by the end of the century.

From the Taiping period to the 1930s, China experienced frequent foreign and domestic wars, but these affairs were restricted geographically, so displaced populations were confined to specific regions. During the Taiping, Nian, and Boxer rebellions, as well as in the Opium War and in the clashes between regional militarists in the 1920s, the devastation of one region could be severe while neighboring locales remained tranquil and even prosperous. Thus in 1854–56 and again in 1911, Qing armies burned Hankou to the ground and halved its population without touching Wuchang, its twin city across the river. By the twentieth century, urban populations in particular had learned to view war as a temporary pestilence they had to wait out. At worst, in fear for their lives and with their property destroyed by armies still roaming in the vicinity, families would flee and take refuge in a neighboring province or tranquil zone. Others, usually the poorest, hid in the countryside nearby or somehow managed to survive in the rubble of their neighborhoods. Once war ended and a semblance of civil order was restored, the survivors returned in large numbers to rebuild on the ruins.[7] In post-Taiping Hankou, the results were spectacular: after the city was razed in 1856, Hankou's population jumped from less than half a million to more than a million in thirty years.[8]

The Anti-Japanese War (1937–45) obviously differed from these previous conflicts. The especially terrifying element for the civilian population was the speed and geographical reach of the combined air and land operations of the Japanese. Coastal China from Manchuria to Canton came under nearly simultaneous attack, and within a year the Japanese took control of twenty-one provinces, with the express purpose of terrorizing the civilian population into submission. More than any other factor, the brutality of the Japanese attack and occupation of cities in the first six months of the war produced the greatest forced migration in Chinese history. With massacres occurring at a rapid pace, beginning in north China and culminating at Nanjing in December 1937, refugee flight grew exponentially. The carnage was so pervasive that much went unrecorded. In recent works, Tim Brook and Fred Wakeman have described in detail the utter devastation and panicked populations that the Japanese armored units left in their wake as they moved up the lower Yangzi corridor from Shanghai to Nanjing.[9]

Relying heavily on missionary accounts, Diana Lary has told the story of the terrible violence and destructiveness of Japanese troops during the battles for Xuzhou during the spring of 1938.[10] Later that year the suffering grew when Chinese commanders ordered the blowing up of the Yellow River dikes in June and the burning of Changsha in November. These catastrophes forced whole communities to pull up stakes and flee well in advance of the Japanese arrival. China's urban population was undergoing forced redistribution. A major shift inland of China's cultural and professional elites occurred; and after the war many refugees never recrossed the country to return home. Decades were to pass before the economies of major battlefront cities like Taiyuan, Jinan, Jiujiang, Changsha, Wuhan, and Nanjing returned to prewar levels.

Anecdotal evidence is abundant, but the statistical evidence of refugee flight on a massive scale is skimpy and conflicting. Lloyd Eastman relied on a single secondary source in adopting a low figure of 3 million to 4 million refugees for the entire war period.[11] More recently, using archival figures from a 1946 Guomindang survey, Ch'i Hsi-sheng estimated that 95 million people were on the move.[12] At the beginning of the war, in 1937 and 1938, conservative Guomindang estimates indicated that at least 60 million people were in flight. The highest percentages of refugees came from the inland provinces of Henan, Shanxi, Hunan, and Hubei. Coastal trade centers like Shanghai and Fuzhou/Xiamen remained more economically viable under the Japanese and lost relatively little population. Table 1 shows the percentage of population fleeing from various provinces and cities.

Refugee flight came in waves. The first was during July and August of 1937, from the north toward the south, forced by the occupation of the Beijing and Tianjin area and the brutality of the Japanese at Tongzhou, Baoding, and elsewhere. With the Beijing-Hankou railroad blocked at Baoding and Shijiazhuang, masses of civilians fled by boat to Cheefoo (Yantai) or Qingdao and then by train into Shandong. Lao She recorded the chaos caused by the influx of refugees at Jinan in a memorable eyewitness account for the newspaper *Dagong bao*, December 4 and 5, 1937.

TABLE 1 WARTIME REFUGEES
AND HOMELESS PEOPLE, 1937-45

Province or City	Number of Refugees	Percentage of Population
Jiangsu	12,502,633	34.83
Nanjing	335,634	32.90
Shanghai	531,431	13.80
Zhejiang	5,185,210	23.90
Anhui	2,688,242	12.23
Jiangxi	1,360,045	9.55
Hubei	7,690,000	30.13
Wuhan	534,040	43.56
Hunan	13,073,209	42.73
Fujian	1,065,469	9.25
Guangdong	4,280,266	13.76
Guangxi	2,562,400	20.37
Hebei	6,774,000	23.99
Beijing	400,000	15.45
Tianjin	200,000	10.00
Shandong	11,760,644	30.71
Henan	14,533,200	43.49
Shanxi	4,753,842	41.06
Manchuria	4,297,100	12.12
Suiyuan	695,715	38.20
Chahar	225,673	11.08
Total	95,448,753	26.17

SOURCE: *Nanmin ji liuli renmin zongshu biao*, 1946, official archival report cited by Ch'i Hsi-sheng in Levine and Hsiung, *China's Bitter Victory*, 180. Reproduced by permission of M. E. Sharpe, Inc.

From August to October of 1937 Jinan's population mushroomed from three hundred thousand to over six hundred thousand. Two months later, in December, General Han Fuju refused to defend the city and withdrew. Shortly thereafter, when the Japanese marched into the city, they found a ghost town with a population of less than one hundred thousand.

The mass exodus from Shandong and Henan lasted three months, with many refugees heading for Shanghai.[13] Others fled west to Taiyuan (Shanxi) and Xi'an (Shaanxi). In this movement, urban dwellers were joined by a large number of peasants. According to Japanese surveys, certain rural areas became significantly depopulated. Some 25 percent of Baoding County's mostly peasant population fled rather than face continued Japanese occupation and the atrocities that went with it.[14]

The second wave occurred later in the fall of 1937, as urbanites on the run from the central coast moved up the Yangzi River to Nanjing.

This process began with the three-month battle for Shanghai and the Japanese carpet bombing of Zhabei. The battle involved almost a million men, of whom the Chinese lost over three hundred thousand. In panic, over six hundred thousand civilians fled the Chinese sections of Shanghai. Half headed West, and the rest (about two hundred fifty thousand, of whom about one hundred thousand were children) pushed into the foreign-run International Settlement areas, where social services broke down and produced this scene:

> Refugees poured into the ten square miles of the French Concession and International Settlement, swelling the population from 1.5 to 4 million within a few weeks and increasing the size of the average household to 31 people. Many left the 175 refugee camps to return to their native villages, but tens of thousands of homeless clogged the streets and hundreds of thousands more slept in office corridors, stockrooms, temples, guild halls, amusement parks, and warehouses. With winter came disease, starvation, and exposure; and by the end of the year 101,000 corpses had been picked up in the streets or ruins.[15]

The panic flight from surrounding cities may have been even more extreme, reminiscent of the depopulation forced by the Taiping wars eighty years earlier. Overnight, the population of Suzhou dropped from two hundred thousand to fifty thousand. At Wuxi the exodus was even worse, dropping from three hundred thousand to ten thousand.[16] Two-thirds of Hangzhou's six hundred thousand residents disappeared. Overall, a 1939 source estimated that over 16 million fled the Nanjing-Hangzhou-Shanghai battle zone during the fall of 1937.[17]

The third big wave started in December and January of 1938, as the result of the massacre of civilians at Nanjing. Ningbo on the coast was bombed and 80 to 90 percent of its population reportedly fled. By early spring 1938, the refugee "hordes" that White and Jacoby describe in *Thunder Out of China* were converging on Wuhan and Canton. Joining them was a final wave from the north. Millions, many of whom were peasants, fled the Huainan region as the enormously destructive battle of Xuzhou raged during the spring of 1938 or were left homeless by the intentional blowing up of the Yellow River dikes.[18] Many headed for Wuhan. The British journalist Freda Utley visited a refugee camp in Wuchang and interviewed a group that had just arrived from Anhui:

> Old men and women and young mothers sat upon straw mats with babies and young children, thin, sad, hopeless in their misery, and many of them sick. I questioned one young woman who lay, very ill, upon a mat with a tiny baby beside her. . . . "Where is your husband?"

> "He has joined the guerrillas in Anhui."
> "Are you all alone, or have you a family here?"
> "Alone, all my family has been killed."
> "How old is your child?"
> "Two weeks old; he was born on the road and I managed to walk on
> and get as far as this."[19]

Staff workers at the camp told Utley that they doubted that the woman
or her child would survive. By late spring 1938 Wuhan's population had
grown from 1 million to 1.5 million, and a year later Chongqing's population would double from four hundred thousand to about eight hundred thousand.[20] And at the same time (1938), to the southeast, peasants fled inland along the Fujian coast or south to Canton. When Canton
fell in October, a million people migrated into Hong Kong and Macao
and were forced out again by the Japanese occupation in 1941.

Thus, despite the inadequacy of aggregate figures, the mass migration
was clearly unprecedented in size and impact. Twenty-one provinces suffered significant refugee flight and the economic and social dislocations
that went with it. China's population was forcibly redistributed and
remixed. The educated classes complained most loudly. Suddenly city
dwellers accustomed to an upper-class life were living in poverty in the
countryside. Gone were the servants, the large family compounds, and
the comforts of Shanghai and Beijing—a state of affairs that shocked May
Fourth movement intellectuals like Wen Yiduo and Yu Dafu. For Chinese peasant families, the traumas were worse and more basic. After har-
rowing experiences on the roofs of trains and cattle cars, they struggled
to survive in the urban refugee camps of central and southwestern China,
where they were thrown together with people who spoke in different di-
alects and differed in class, educational, and regional backgrounds. Thus
the war was a great leveler: it brought more lasting forms of social, cultural, and linguistic integration between the urban and the rural than had
Mao Zedong's forced migration or *xiafang* campaigns of the 1950s and
1960s. In short, refugee flight changed the social and psychological landscape of modern China.

Who were these refugees? What was the sociological makeup of this
desperate, floating population? Although children made up a large number of refugees, the age and gender distribution was wide indeed. A few
prominent intellectuals like Lao She and Xu Beihong left families behind
in occupied cities, but for the most part, whole families were on the move,
minus the elderly. Table 2 provides a sampling of a group of Hunan
refugees who moved west from the Changsha area to Sichuan during the

TABLE 2 AGE AND SEX DISTRIBUTION OF REFUGEES FROM
FIVE HUNAN COUNTIES (SURVEYED IN SICHUAN, 1939)

Age	Male	Female	Total	Percentage
5 and under	638	493	1193	—
15 and under	1868	1469	3337	34.1
16–40	2251	2265	4516	46.1
41–50	590	502	1092	11.1
51–60	277	302	579	5.9
61–80	88	171	259	2.6
Total	5074	4709	9783	

SOURCE: Sun Yankui, *Gunande renliu*, 65–67, citing document from No. 2 archive, Nanjing, 118 *chuanzong*, 16 *anquan*.

fall of 1938; note how few were elderly. Surveys of refugees in Wuhan and later in Chongqing demonstrated again and again the wide representation of peoples from the various regions of China.[21]

The diversity of the refugees' educational and professional backgrounds was striking. Again, the available statistical record is confusing. In a 1938 interview, Xu Shiying, the official in charge of national relief work, told reporters in Wuhan that cultural and educational workers made up 55 percent of the refugee populace; party and government workers, 21 percent; merchants, 10 percent; industrial workers, 6 percent; and peasants, only 2 percent.[22] A later, Chongqing survey of over 1.2 million refugees found 50 percent engaged in small business of one kind or another, with workers and students making up 15 percent of this group and peasants another 23 percent. The problem with these surveys is that they focus mainly on refugees who were living in shelters in the city. In later, more sophisticated surveys that included outlying suburban counties—around Chongqing or Guiyang, for example—the results were probably more accurate and showed a closer balance between peasants, workers, merchants, and students or teachers.[23]

In general, peasants were the most difficult refugee group to track. They were probably the most numerous, but they were also less permanently in flight than other groups. Though a high number of them fled during the initial Japanese advances, their livelihoods tied them to the land. Thus, after 1939, when the fighting became more subdued, an unknown number returned to their homes. In some areas, like Hunan or Yunnan, peasants became refugees again when war returned. Small-business persons and artisans represented a relatively high proportion of the visible refugee community in cities like Wuhan and Chongqing. They were probably the most flexible of the refugees in that their occupations allowed them to set up shop in new surroundings. Clearly, they emerged from the war in the best shape economically—less ravaged by the runaway wartime inflation that was so hard on soldiers, educators, and bureaucrats.

Historically, the number of intellectuals in the refugee population was extraordinarily high, rivaling the numbers during the upheavals of the Ming-Qing transition in the seventeenth century. This group included professors, schoolteachers, students, writers, poets, painters, dramatists, scientists, journalists, editors, and others. Its members were the most articulate and best-organized part of the population—and their fate is the best documented. The majority of intellectual refugees came from Shanghai, Tianjin, and Beijing, and the group included most of the important names in the Chinese literary, art, drama, and university worlds at the time. As a contemporary sociologist said, "[Ninety] percent of the highest level intellectuals migrated west, 50 percent of the mid-level cultural workers, and only 30 percent of the lower-level intellectuals."[24] With them came the national press. Dailies like *Dagong bao, Zhongyang ribao, Shen bao,* and *Saodang bao* moved presses inland and resumed publishing. In time the plight of many refugee intellectuals became desperate, with inflation, increasing censorship, and prolongation of the war creating despair. The attempted suicide in Chongqing in 1941 of the noted Shanghai playwright Hong Shen drew national attention as a cry for help.[25]

Although the war turned Wuhan's economy upside down, it also presented new opportunities for some people. The most fortunate refugees were the ten thousand or so skilled industrial workers who moved from Shanghai at state expense to work in Wuhan's armament industry. The story of the rapid transformation of the Wuhan economy is relatively well known and is often given a triumphal spin in Chinese popular histories of the period.

As we saw in chapter 1, the prewar commercial economy of Wuhan had relied on transshipment of commodities and processed goods in and out of the port of Hankou. The war shut down most of this trade, putting the great commodity merchants and textile magnates of Hankou out of business. And yet within a matter of months of the start of the hostilities the Wuhan economy was operating successfully on a war footing, with an emphasis on industrial production and state control. Clearly, the Wuhan business community contributed to the war effort, by reinventing itself and reinvesting in war-relevant industries, but its efforts were dwarfed by the infusion of investment capital and management experience from state enterprises and coastal entrepreneurs. The addition of machinery, capital, and expertise from Shanghai and elsewhere was the key to quickly transforming the Wuhan economy and providing jobs for refugee workers with the necessary skills and experience.

By the spring of 1938 about one hundred and seventy factories from the Shanghai area had moved to Wuhan and begun operation. Most of these businesses were privately owned and had made the move without much help from the government. Along with the machinery came skilled labor—including large numbers of engineers and technicians. Estimates indicate that over forty thousand skilled workers fled inland during the war, and most of them passed through Wuhan in 1938.[26]

Wartime production in Wuhan peaked just as heavy bombing raids by Japanese planes began in March 1938. By August Wuhan had lost over 12 percent of its industrial capacity to bombing, and clearly the situation was only going to get worse. In addition, the city now faced the threat of a Japanese siege, which might cut off escape to the west. The earlier lack of evacuation preparations during the battle of Shanghai had aided the enemy economically and hurt the Chinese government's ability to arm and feed its troops.

Thus, throughout the summer and fall of 1938, the government made a major effort to prevent Wuhan's industrial base from falling into Japanese hands. Chiang Kaishek appointed geologist Weng Wenhao head of the National Defense Planning Commission, with ministerial rank. His Industrial and Mining Adjustment Administration *(gongguang diaozheng-chu)* began dismantling and removing most of Hanyang's aging state-run steelworks, as well as the nearby arsenal and munitions factories. Throughout the summer Weng oversaw relocation of state and municipal enterprises, including water and energy-generating plants. By autumn the private sector had begun a massive relocation of textile, cigarette, and food-processing businesses to the interior.[27]

All told, more than one hundred eight thousand tons of equipment were transported out of Wuhan. At the state's expense, ten thousand workers were moved as well. In addition to relocating 13 large industrial plants, businesses removed about 250 major light industrial units. By October about 57 percent of the productive capacity of the metropolis had moved farther inland. Thus, by the time the Japanese took Wuhan in late October, over 70 percent of the city's industrial capacity was either destroyed or relocated.[28] Needless to say, this rapid rise and fall in industrial production at Wuhan brought even more chaos into the lives of the refugee population.

The impact of the war on refugees was not just economic and social; it was also profoundly psychological. Old ties of family and geography were torn asunder. Marriages dissolved, prostitution increased, and uncertainty spawned desperate romance. In the process, family members abandoned or seriously neglected children and the elderly in increasing numbers.[29] To quote again the eyewitness Freda Utley:

> Many [families] had been on the march for weeks, some for months. Families which had set out with five or six children had reached Hankou with only one or two. Small girl children were scarce; when the mother and father have no more strength to carry the little children, and when the smaller children are too exhausted to move another step, some have to be left on the road to die. . . . With what agony of mind must some children be abandoned so that the rest can be saved! Who can even imagine the infinite number of small individual tragedies amongst the millions who have been driven from their homes by the Japanese?[30]

But the refugee predicament had a positive side as well. At Wuhan, during the ten months of its heroic defense in 1938, a new sense of community responsibility arose within the bizarre mix of humanity thrown together by the war. People apparently decided that the only hope for survival was to unite in caring for one another while preparing for a last stand against hopeless odds. The result was an unprecedented effort to provide social services for the refugee population of the city, with special attention to women and children.

Although Eastman and others characterize the public and private refugee-relief efforts at Wuhan as woefully inadequate, they equaled the better-known (and better-documented) effort in the foreign-concession areas of Shanghai in 1937–38.[31] First, the services helped a significant number of refugees, perhaps half of those in need. Second, the relief effort connected national integration to social responsibility, reaching beyond family and local ties toward a redefinition of community. And finally, in retrospect, these efforts laid the foundation for the comprehensive social-welfare and health programs later instituted in the PRC and Republic of China (ROC; Taiwan).

In January 1938, shortly after the fall of Nanjing, the newly reconstituted press of Wuhan began to point with alarm at the social crisis gripping the tricity complex of Wuchang, Hankou, and Hanyang. The crisis threatened to undermine the defense of the city and destroy public health. The level of bedlam that had left Jinan bereft and defenseless now threatened Wuhan. Besides, the press argued, society at large had a duty to do something about the plight of refugees, especially the basic needs of children for food and shelter. A flood of articles in the popular press as well as new books and pamphlets focused on the subject.[32] Most widely noted and reprinted were articles by Wuhan's three most prominent women: the first lady, Song Meiling; the journalist Shen Zijiu; and the lawyer-politician Shi Liang.

Shi Liang was the sparkplug behind the Wuhan relief effort. A determined Shanghai career woman, she first became nationally prominent as one of the "seven gentlemen" arrested in November 1936 for organizing the National Salvation movement, which called for war with Japan. She was the person most responsible for establishing women's branches of the National Salvation Association throughout the country, many of which survived well into the 1940s.

Born in 1900 into a scholar-official family in rural Jiangsu Province, Shi Liang was in the first class of women to graduate from Shanghai's top law school. A short, square-jawed woman who projected intelligence, intensity, and toughness, she clawed her way to the top of Shanghai's legal profession by the 1930s. Her career was her life (she did not marry until 1937, and then to an aide), but in private she could be charming and persuasive. She was also politically astute: in the early 1930s she carefully cultivated a close personal relationship with each of the three most powerful women in China, the Song sisters—Ailing, Meiling, and Qingling. In her private law practice, she specialized in civil rights litigation and gained a reputation as a forceful and plainspoken advocate. By 1935 her court appearances, especially in defense of prominent dissidents, became public events, and usually she won. After her arrest in 1936, she received unusually polite treatment in prison, illustrating the respect she commanded as a public figure. One of her closest friends was Zou Taofen, a prominent publisher and liberal, who was also one of the "gentlemen" arrested with her.

The prison experience toughened Shi Liang's resolve as a social activist. After her release in the summer of 1937, she worked full-time in support of the war effort. With the fall of Shanghai in November, she followed two of the Song sisters (Ailing and Qingling) to Hong Kong. Then in February of 1938 she moved to Wuhan with the express purpose of organizing women in the interior for the war effort through the existing National Salvation Association network. But finding herself in the midst of a social crisis of epic proportions, she revised her priorities and became increasingly concerned about the refugee populations then flooding into the city. She mobilized the Song sisters, bringing them together in special appeals for refugee relief. There is little doubt that her careful orchestration of public meetings and press coverage pressured the Guomindang into making refugee relief a high priority. In this effort she had useful allies, like Zou Taofen's Shenghuo publications, which were particularly helpful in carrying her message. Although Communists like Deng Yingchao (a labor organizer and Zhou Enlai's wife) became involved as well, most of the Party's leadership was slow to see the value of refugee relief as a recruitment tool, and it remained peripheral to organizing efforts.[33]

By late spring public opinion in Wuhan, whipped up by Shi Liang and her allies, cried out for government action, although which organizations should take responsibility at the national, provincial, and local levels remained unclear. Much of the initial effort in Wuhan had taken place under private auspices, led by the president of the Hankou Chamber of Commerce, industrialist He Hengfu. Although Chiang Kaishek's central government had established a nominal relief committee in Nanjing during the fall of 1937, the group's work was limited. The government first began to respond in earnest from Wuhan in February 1938, with the announcement of the high-level National Relief Committee (zhenji weiyuanhui), under the Administrative Yuan. In March and April the Guomindang Party held an extraordinary session in Wuchang, and again refugee relief work received high priority in speeches by Chiang Kaishek and others. By the end of April the National Relief Committee was operational and funded under the leadership of a venerable statesman, Xu Shiying, a former ambassador to Japan who had been active in refugee work in Shanghai in the early 1930s.[34] From the end of May into mid-June, the committee investigated what government and private agencies were already doing about providing shelter to refugees. Its report clearly documents Shi Liang's effort to push the state into deeper involvement in relief work.[35]

In the nineteenth century the Qing state had played a role in famine relief, orphanages, and flood-control projects. Relief for the poor, including refugees, as well as attention to public health and local public works, including fire prevention, was provided by local merchant elites acting as philanthropists in the organization of benevolent societies—called cishan tang in Hankou.[36] Although the general expectation was that these relief efforts, which did not include housing, would be temporary, the war changed that assumption.

The National Relief Committee's 1938 report on Wuhan found 111 shelters operating in the tricity area. Of these, 18 were managed by local city-government relief societies *(zhenji hui)* in Wuchang, Hankou, and Hanyang. The report found 13 run by provincial merchant associations *(tongxiang hui)* that had sprung up since 1910; 15, by Christian church organizations; and 4, by the International Red Cross. The traditional benevolent societies for which Hankou was famous, under the leadership of He Hengfu and the chamber of commerce, ran 57 shelters; but these and 4 privately managed shelters served only a few families, or a maximum of thirty people, at each address. Hankou had 88 of the 111 shelters.

The numbers by themselves, however, are deceptive. Although fewer in number than the privately run operations, government-run shelters housed more people: over 20,000 people or about 60 percent of the total, and nearly all were in Wuchang. Traditional self-help merchant-run institutions operated in Hankou and Hanyang. Of this group, the provincial association shelters, of which Jiangsu, Anhui, and Zhejiang were the most important, housed only fellow provincials.[37] The Anhui Benevolent Association, for example, housed 6,933 Anhui-ese by mid-June (a dramatic increase from 675 one month earlier) in nine locations around Wuhan. Church organizations used schools to house about 2,500 refugees, for whom they held special classes. The International Red Cross ran four shelters, three of which were in Hankou, that housed about 700 each, for a total of 2,681.[38]

Varying amounts of food rations usually went with shelter space for refugees, and the shelters attempted to provide medical assistance as well. Much of the staffing was volunteer, recruited from the students and youth who were being organized by groups all over the city. In sum, the report found that by mid-June 1938, shelters were housing 63,876 of the 430,000 people who had descended upon the Wuhan metropolis.[39] Though the effort was not enough, it was significant; the number of refugees served compares well with the numbers helped by foreign merchants and governments in Shanghai's foreign-concession zone in the fall of 1937.[40] The report also showed, for the first time in Chinese history, major participation of state-run agencies in relief work for war refugees.

The National Relief Committee report indicated that the programs were paying special attention to the needs of refugee children, many of whom were orphans. Here again we find the hand of Shi Liang, who was gain-ing a reputation as the heroine of Wuhan. Public concern about the plight of children had first found voice in January 1938, in a public meeting organized by Li Dequan, a social activist and the wife of General Feng Yuxiang. At that meeting, Ms. Li asked Shi Liang to organize a relief campaign for refugee children. The daily presence of child beggars on the streets of Hankou made the need for such work obvious and thus made organizing and fund-raising easier. Shi Liang managed to create a movement to which the Song sisters (Meiling, Qingling, and Ailing) were willing to attach their names. The resulting political coalition was unusual, putting on the same platform women leaders on the left and right—from the communist Deng Yingchao to Song Meiling (Madame Chiang Kaishek). The ecumenical approach worked, attracting volunteers and support across the political spectrum and quickly producing concrete results.

Traditionally, during the Qing dynasty, state-run orphanages served urban communities, so the expectation was that the wartime government would manage child-welfare work. By March the government had created education and nutrition action committees under an umbrella welfare organization, the Wartime Child Welfare Committee, or Zhanshi Ertong Baoyuhui, to care for refugee children. On May 1, in a well-publicized ceremony, the first state-sponsored orphanage opened in the facilities of the former Japanese-managed Tong Ren hospital. Most of the over five hundred orphans housed at the model facility were refugees rescued from the battlefields of Xuzhou.[41]

The wartime achievements of the Baoyuhui were impressive, and the organization became a model for later child-welfare organizations in both the PRC and the ROC on Taiwan. As the organization's executive secretary, Shi Liang was careful to have the organization's steering committee include a coalition of leading Guomindang and Communist women, from Song Meiling to Deng Yingchao. Of the Song sisters, Meiling (Madame Chiang Kaishek) was most active in the organization, giving speeches and visiting orphanages. From Wuhan roots, over forty state-supported childcare centers set up operations in southwestern China during the war. These centers sheltered, educated, and nourished hundreds of thousands of children under the age of twelve.[42] Agnes Smedley described the scene at Wuhan in 1938: "Madame Chiang Kaishek and her women followers were gathering thousands of war orphans from the war zone. One day I went into their headquarters just as another train-load of these ragged, lice-ridden, half-starved children were being brought in. Dozens of women were shaving their heads, bathing and feeding them, and dressing them in fresh blue denim overalls. Long lines of these little tots were then marched through the streets to waiting boats or junks which transported them to the west."[43]

Shi Liang also organized a new national umbrella committee *(funu zhidao weiyuan hui)* dedicated to mobilizing women for the war effort. After a special "summit" on women's issues at Lu Shan in late May 1938, chaired by Madame Sun Yatsen (Song Qingling) and dominated by Communist figures like Deng Yingchao, the committee was formed with much fanfare. However, its goals remained vague and focused on war mobilization, not on traditional issues of women's rights, marriage laws, and voting rights. With relatively few Guomindang women leaders participating, it failed to become broad based and had little direct impact on the lives of women refugees during the early years of the war. Its main activity seemed to be sponsoring well-publicized rallies at which Shi Liang and others gave pep talks to young women students and recruited volunteers for refugee relief work. Clearly, women leaders like Shi Liang were more focused on providing immediate help to refugee families, especially children, and on solving the public health crisis.[44]

The public health effort was an important legacy of the Wuhan period. Malaria epidemics were especially serious among refugees, cutting a devastating swath through both civilian and military populations of Wuhan; women and children were particularly vulnerable to disease, starvation, and exposure. In response, the most extensive pre-1949 effort in crisis management in Chinese public health history was launched from Wuhan in 1938. Led by Harvard-trained Dr. J. Heng Liu (Liu Juiheng), the cream of China's medical establishment from Beijing and Shanghai descended on the tricity to help organize and deliver health care to civilians and soldiers alike.[45]

In 1938 Dr. Liu unified military and civilian health services under one health administration. His right-hand man in Wuhan was a former colleague at the Peking Union Medical College, Dr. Robert K. Lin (Lin Kesheng), an overseas Chinese trained at the University of Edinburgh. Dr. Lin reorganized the Chinese Red Cross at its headquarters in Wuhan and Changsha around a new mission of penetrating the countryside. A remarkably effective and popular organizer, he had fifty-three units staffed with volunteer doctors up and running within months. Each unit had three sections rendering aid to soldiers on the front as well as providing medical services in hospitals along the main lines of communication. The preventive section immunized children, led sanitation campaigns, and staffed camps and local hospitals on an emergency basis. The nursing section was organized similarly; and a third section comprised a team of surgeons who worked in field hospitals.

The shortage of trained medical personnel was a major problem, especially in the army. Estimates indicated that 90 percent of military medical staff had not received professional training. Minister Liu therefore gave high priority to the training of medical personnel and put his best man in charge—again, Dr. Robert K. Lin. In the spring of 1938 Dr. Lin opened an emergency-training center in Changsha that offered a three-month crash course for paramedics. The program attracted a flood of eager applicants. At first located in Changsha and then in Guiyang, Lin's center trained a majority of the medical personnel who operated in rural areas during the war.[46]

The efforts of Drs. Liu and Lin made the most noticeable difference in Wuhan and Chongqing. The men oversaw the establishment of vaccination and public health centers all over Wuhan, and public health and sanitation quickly improved. The government nationalized existing hospitals, established by merchant-funded benevolent societies, and put them on a war footing. Perhaps unavoidably, these successes were limited to cities; in the surrounding countryside, civilians and wounded soldiers received little or no care. Still, Wuhan represented a turning point in the organizational history of Chinese public health.[47]

By the summer of 1938 the central government's National Relief Committee under Xu Shiying had turned its attention to facilitating the evacuation (shusan) of refugees and the provision of services on the road. The Hubei provincial government played a major role in organizing transportation out of Wuhan by railway, boat, or vehicle, or on foot. Between June and November 1938, the central government created eight emergency aid centers along refugee routes (near train stations, major river ports, crossroads, and the like). At the same time, it made provisions to give refugees shelter at designated locations. Nine provinces soon had 26 such central locations with 132 branches, and 166 "guest houses" for refugees were operating by the end of the year. In one way or another, this effort reportedly helped 3.5 million refugees during the fall of 1938.[48]

In short, perhaps because Shanghai, Beijing, and Canton were relatively unscathed by the war, historians have insufficiently appreciated the level of disruption elsewhere and its effects on Chinese society as a whole.[49] The flight to the interior of at least 100 million people was forced by a level of violence that brutalized civilian life and left deep psychological scars. At the same time, signs of renewal were evident during the defense of Wuhan in 1938: a more integrated collective consciousness energized society in new ways. The result was an unprecedented level of community volunteerism and state intervention in relief and health work.

As we shall see, the desperately optimistic atmosphere that prevailed for ten months of 1938 at Wuhan stemmed in large part from the efforts of many of China's best and brightest: intellectual refugees from Beijing, Tianjin, and Shanghai. More than the political and military leadership of Wuhan, a quixotic collection of intellectuals rallied the people of the tricity in defense of their newly adopted home.

FIVE

CULTURE AND THE PRESS

IN 1938 NEARLY ALL of China's important intellectuals descended on Wuhan. In a movement that was independent of any one party or state-controlled entity, writers, dramatists, artists, and philosophers, as well as editors and journalists, began organizing cultural propaganda that would whip up maximum support for the defense of Wuhan among the urban and rural populations of the central Yangzi.

Since the 1980s scholars like Li Zehou, Feng Chongyi, Edward Gunn, and Vera Schwarcz have argued that the Anti-Japanese War was a cultural disaster, bringing a sudden end to the liberalizing renaissance inaugurated by the May Fourth Movement of 1919.[1] The strength of this argument depends largely on one's definition of "culture." Clearly the May Fourth Movement in 1919 targeted intellectual elites and attacked traditional modes of expression in art and literature; its emphasis was on individual expression, science, and democracy. But by 1938 the intellectual environment had changed. Many Chinese now believed that to fight a war of attrition effectively, the entire country had to be energized and politically organized. In this sense, leaders in the media and the arts saw themselves as reinventing Chinese culture on a scale that surpassed even that of the May Fourth Movement. As John Fitzgerald and others have pointed out, since the mid-1920s the definition of *wenhua,* or culture, had been expanding to include the popular culture of the ordinary citizen. Of course, this wider view had its dissenters. One was Liang Qichao before his death in 1929; another was "the last Confucian," the reformer Liang Shuming. Both men worried about the debasement and internationalization of traditional culture. But by the time of Lu Xun's death in 1936 and the emergence of the League of Left Wing Writers in Shanghai, the commitment to reshaping the arts to maximize their appeal to the masses had swept through the Chinese intellectual community. In the heady atmosphere at Wuhan, the momentum of this earlier movement turned the tricity into a laboratory for experiments in cultural change. Many cultural leaders believed that propaganda was as important as weapons in fighting the war. Thus, in the production of a new mass-directed culture, Chinese intellectuals, especially the young students who flooded into Wuhan as refugees, considered themselves to be in the vanguard. A consensus formed that China's chances for survival would improve if the cultural apparatus were reorganized and put on a wartime propaganda footing.[2]

Leading the charge were some of the most famous names on the Chinese cultural scene; novelists like Mao Dun and Lao She; the scholar-politician Guo Moruo; the painter Xu Beihong; the cartoonist Feng Zikai; the poet Aiqing; the strategic thinker Jiang Baili; philosophers Feng Youlan, Ai Siqi, and Zhang Shenfu; and the playwrights Xia Yan, Tian Han, Hong Shen, and Yang Hansheng. For a few, notably Lao She and Guo Moruo, Wuhan in 1938 became a defining moment in their lives. The contradictory undercurrents that separated these two men make their stories compelling and worth telling in detail. But first we need to understand the larger context in which these intellectuals operated.

WUHAN'S FREE PRESS

The explosive growth of the print media in Wuhan was remarkable. Within the first three months of 1938 the number of dailies shot from three to fourteen and the number of weeklies, from twenty to thirty; the number of journals climbed from thirty to over two hundred within ten months. Dozens of new publishing houses set up shop. Every faction and political group seemed to have its own publication. The draconian powers of the secret police under Dai Li, which had operated so effectively in prewar Shanghai, had been neutralized, and in 1938 not a single editor or publisher was arrested or assassinated.[3]

This flowering of free expression was possible because of the basic political restructuring that occurred in Wuhan after the fall of the central government in Nanjing: control over the city (including the media) passed into the hands of a group of senior Baoding generals. In a situation reminiscent of the early 1920s, when the press also experienced greater freedom in many parts of China, rule by military oligarchs opened up opportunities for the press to reorganize, expand, and explore new avenues of expression.[4]

As we saw in chapter 1, Wuhan's press had a long tradition of courageous journalism, having already played a key role in the revolutionary politics of Republican China in 1911 and again in 1927. But the arrival in 1938 of national publications like *Dagong bao, Shen bao,* and the Shenghuo (Life) chain, along with a bevy of talented journalists and editors from coastal treaty ports like Tianjin and Shanghai, stimulated the explosion in productivity and brought calls for greater professionalization.

This sudden burst of activity had several sources. First, repressive censorship, including the threat of arrest and assassination, virtually disappeared when the Baoding generals restrained the heavy hand of Governor He Chengjun (by summer replaced by General Chen Cheng) and his gangster enforcer, Yang Qingshan. In one study of the history of the Wuhan press before 1938, the author charted the age of death of twenty-six fellow journalists or publishers whom he had known personally since the first decade of the twentieth century. Of this group, three died in their fifties; seven, in their forties; and the rest, in their thirties and twenties—usually violently.[5] Given this background, the fact that no editors or publishers were arrested or assassinated in Wuhan in 1938 is all the more remarkable.

Second, the militarists who were running the defense of Wuhan dispensed patronage to a variety of publications, thus widening the playing field for the press. The resulting range of publicly expressed opinion was unprecedented, stretching from publications like *Hongqi* (Red Flag) on the left (backed by the Communist Eighth Route Army) to journals like *Minyi* (People's Opinion) or *Kangzhan xiangdao* (Anti-Japanese War Guide) on the right (supported by protofascist elements in the Guomindang and the Whampoa military clique). In between, of course, were publications that were politically more inclusive and more widely read, including weeklies and monthlies published by the Shenghuo group (discussed later) and *Xuelu* (Bloody Road) edited by Tao Xisheng and others. Two of the five largest daily newspapers, *Wuhan ribao* and *Xinhua ribao,* were operated by the rival Guomindang and Chinese Communist parties, respectively, but they adopted something of a united front in their reporting and editorializing—and rarely attacked each other directly. In the middle politically, and appealing to more elite tastes, was China's paper of record, *Dagong bao,* which moved from Tianjin to

Wuhan in late 1937 under direction of the legendary Zhang Jiluan, who had personal ties with Chiang Kaishek as well as with the liberal wing of the Guomindang and with military figures like Ye Ting and Feng Yuxiang. Shanghai's oldest daily, *Shen bao,* which had fallen on hard times since the assassination of its editor-publisher in 1934, lacked a military sponsor and floundered as a result. Its Wuhan edition had a much smaller circulation and influence than did the other four publications.[6]

The last of the big five, the daily *Saodang bao,* was the most important and widely read newspaper at the time. It had originated in Nanjing under tight oversight by Chiang Kaishek and the Whampoa military clique, but with Chiang losing influence to the new constellation of military figures in charge at Wuhan, direct control of the paper shifted to the Military Council. Throughout 1938 the publication reflected the coalition views of the most powerful military men who controlled Wuhan at the time—theater commander and Hubei governor General Chen Cheng and the Guangxi militarists Bai Chongxi and Li Zongren. The publisher, Huang Shaogu, was an interesting figure, who managed to combine a military career with journalism. A graduate in literature from Beijing University in the early 1920s, Huang cut his teeth as a journalist working on one of Cheng Shewo's popular and profitable dailies (*Shijie wanbao*). In 1926 he had to flee for his life to Xi'an during the warlord Zhang Zongchang's murderous vendetta against Beijing's editors and publishers. He joined the staff of the local warlord Feng Yuxiang, became a general in command of a division, and in 1927–28 was part of the Northern Expeditionary force that liberated Beijing from the Manchurian warlord Zhang Zuolin. Huang then migrated to Nanjing and resumed his career as a journalist, rising quickly to the leadership of *Saodang bao.*[7] He chose as his editor in chief at Wuhan the learned Ding Wenan, who belonged to one of Beijing University's most distinguished scholarly families.[8] Ding Wenan had high standards and paid his staff well. The consensus was that *Saodang bao* carried the best war reporting. The paper's daily accounts of the back-and-forth fighting at Taierzhuang and Xuzhou during the spring of 1938 were the most extensive and eagerly awaited on the streets of Wuhan. They turned young journalists like Liu Zunqi into famous war correspondents.[9]

Competition for readership was fierce, and advertising revenue was scarce. None of the big four were as lucrative as the mass-circulation dailies *Shen bao* and *Li bao* or the big publishing houses like Commercial Press or Shenghuo that had been so important in the prewar treaty-port days. Thus the financial support of well-connected patrons was essential for survival, and publishers vigorously solicited patronage from military figures. But the historically unique feature of the publishing scene at Wuhan was the fact that a variety of backers—pushing different political agendas—stepped forward to help finance publications. As a result, 1938 saw more diversity of public opinion in Wuhan than in any Chinese capital before or since.

Minority political parties, sometimes collectively called the third-party movement, reached the zenith of their visibility at Wuhan because of the expanded freedoms permitted by the Baoding military oligarchs. In July the People's Political Council *(guomin canshenghui)*—an advisory body to the central government with two hundred members, of whom one hundred had no ties to the Guomindang—was convened, providing a public forum on policy for the first time in the history of Nationalist rule. Its creation, which the Nationalist government had announced in March 1938, along with a much freer press, changed the political landscape while Wuhan was the de facto wartime capital. Taking immediate advantage of the situation, four or five important third parties became highly visible at Wuhan during the spring and summer of 1938. None of them had over a thousand members, and none had significant military backing. But in their publications and through participation in the People's Political Council meetings, which were covered closely in the press, minority-party leaders such as Zeng Qi, Zhang Junmai (Carsun Chang), and Luo Longji demanded a voice in government and denounced corruption, dictatorship, and the dogmatisms of both the Communist and Nationalist parties. The best-organized group was the China Youth Party *(Zhongguo qingnian dang)* under Zeng Qi, with publications like *Xinzhongguo ribao* and *Guolun*. The most widely read party organ was *Zaisheng*, edited by Zuo Shunsheng for the National Socialist Party *(guo she dang)* led by Carsun Chang.[10]

Blunt criticism and calls for dialogue and greater democratization, especially by third-party politicians, irritated Nationalist Party ideologues. Some party loyalists like Tao Xisheng soon decamped to Chongqing. Others, like Ye Qing, seemed to enjoy the atmosphere of free debate and entered enthusiastically into the fray, attacking third- party positions and the Communists in widely read publications like *Xuelu*. The Communists were equally irritated, but for different reasons. A chief concern was the ability of a few small Trotskyite Third International publications, namely *Douzhan* [Struggle] and *Douzheng bao*, to gain a platform in Wuhan. Worse still, major Nationalist and third-party weeklies like *Xuelu* and *Zaisheng*, as well as leading dailies like *Saodang bao*, published criticism of the Communists for their attacks on renegade ex-Communist leaders like Chen Duxiu and Zhang Guotao. The publicity that their statements attracted seemed to drive Wang Ming, Zhang Wentian, Bo Gu (Qin Bangxian), and other party leaders in Wuhan into a state of near apoplexy.[11]

Just as influential were the publications for specialized audiences (e.g., youth, women, children, and professionals) published in Wuhan by nationally prominent publishers and editors from Shanghai and Nanjing, who arrived with their own connections and investment capital. Best known today are the Shenghuo publications produced by Zou Taofen, one of the "seven gentlemen" who been arrested in 1936 with Shi Liang for defending human rights and advocating an early declaration of war on the Japanese.

Zou Taofen arrived from Shanghai in December 1937, bringing with him printing equipment and a string of publications for which he recruited editors, many of whom were the biggest names in their fields. Some of his products, like the journal *Kangzhan* (Anti-Japanese War), a literary magazine edited by Mao Dun, were for a general audience. Others, like *Funu shenghuo* (Women's Life), sought to appeal more directly to women.[12] A bimonthly called *Shijie zhishi* (World Knowledge) synthesized international developments, and *Zhanshi riben* (Wartime Japan) focused on Japan. The monthly *July (qiyue)* focused on the arts; *Zhanshi jiaoyu,* on education; and *Shizhou,* on music. Altogether Zou published more than twenty serials, along with a rash of books and pamphlets on a wide variety of subjects. These publications were available at a chain of bookshops (Shenghuo *shudian)* all over the tricity area.

Zuo's Shenghuo publications—which were well edited, attractively packaged, and patriotically left-liberal in tone—seemed more omnipresent in Wuhan than they had been in Shanghai. Running second in popularity were journals and books from publishers who had come from Nanjing, which generally represented the more conservative social views of leaders like the education minister, Chen Lifu. Available alongside the new weeklies like *Xuelu* (mentioned earlier) that had broad appeal was an array of less-important but still-influential older journals like *Zhandou zhoubao, Zhongshan zhoukan, Minyi, Huangpu,* and *Zhongguo kongjun,* in which major Guomindang writers like Ye Qing, Ye Chucang, Zhou Fohai, Tao Xisheng, and Chen Lifu himself appeared regularly.

In the history of modern Chinese journalism, wartime Wuhan is remembered as a crucible in which many major figures in publishing in the PRC and Taiwan forged their careers. In 1992, in Beijing and Taibei, I interviewed two such figures, who were by then very elderly. Although the two men ended up in very different places on the political spectrum, they told similar stories about the difficulties of getting started in Wuhan.

Of the two, Hu Qiuyuan had the more auspicious start. A young, well-connected Wuchang intellectual who had just returned to Wuhan in 1937 from a couple years of study in the United States, he first moved in with relatives and worked as an assistant to the British *Guardian* correspondent Freda Utley. His publishing career began when he won the political and financial backing of General Chen Mingshu, a Baoding graduate who was nationally known for leading the valiant defense of Shanghai against the Japanese (five years earlier, in 1932). In the early spring of 1938, with General Chen's help, Hu took over a bankrupt local paper *(Hubei ribao)*, renamed it the *Times (Shidai ribao),* and gave it a national focus. In line with General Chen's views, he tried to aim his editorials down a middle political path between the positions of the Guomindang and the Chinese Communist Party. His targeted readers were students, and the paper vigorously supported the ideals of democracy and free speech in high-minded essays; it wholeheartedly approved of the People's Political Council when reporting on the group's first meeting in July. Although the paper never had a large circulation, it survived for five months as a daily, until August 1938, and was frequently cited in other publications. At that point, Wang Jingwei, the secretary general of the Guomindang, intervened and shut off access to paper and printing machinery because (according to Hu) Hu had refused to become a mouthpiece for Wang's faction inside the party. More importantly, Hu had lost the support of Chen Mingshu. Thus the paper had to close, but Hu's career as a publisher was launched. His subsequent role as a relatively independent dissenting voice over the next decades within the Guomindang publishing world in Chongqing, Nanjing, and Taibei is well-known.[13]

The second figure, Hu Sheng, arrived in Wuhan as a refugee from Shanghai, where he had been working in left-of-center publications. In Wuhan he accepted the role of publisher-editor of the periodical *Jiu Zhongguo* (Save China), which had begun in Shanghai as part of the National Salvation movement.[14] Hu wanted to reach ordinary, semiliterate citizens with inspiring messages about the war. He had little outside support and few connections, and for financial support he had to rely upon relatives with whom he lived. He ran the magazine on a shoestring, and it survived only because he was able to distribute it through Zou Taofen's Shenghuo *shudian* bookstores. Still Wuhan proved to be the turning point in Hu Sheng's career. At some point during the summer of 1938 he joined the Communist Party. And at the end of the year, after Wuhan fell to the Japanese, he and another young refugee from Shanghai, Qian Junrui, were hired by General Bai Chongxi, the hero of the battle of Taierzhuang, to edit a new newspaper *(Aobei ribao)* that Bai's army was publishing and distributing as it retreated south toward Guangxi.[15]

Another young journalist who proved himself at Wuhan was Liu Zunqi, later the founding editor of *Guangming ribao* in Beijing in the 1950s. Liu was an English major at Yanjing University in Beijing in the late 1920s. In Shanghai in the early 1930s, as an underground Communist, he worked on a number of Western-owned English-language publications, including Harold Isaacs's *China Forum*. At one point, Liu was arrested by the Guomindang, and after his release, he made his way to Yan'an, the Communist guerrilla base. By 1938 he was in Wuhan working as a special war correspondent for the *Wuhan ribao* and the military-controlled *Saodang bao*. His reports from the battlefield on the fighting at Taierzhuang, Xuzhou, Madang, and other places made him a celebrity by the end of 1938.[16]

On the Guomindang side, another figure who came into his own at Wuhan was Dong Xianguang, or Hollington Tong, as he was known to the foreign press. Dong had received a grade-school education in English at Shanghai missionary schools, and before he departed for the United States in 1907 for further study, he tutored Chiang Kai-shek in English for almost a year (both were from the same town near Ningbo). Dong graduated from the School of Journalism of the University of Missouri in 1912, after which he went to Columbia University and worked in New York for a year as an assistant editor of the *Independent* and as a reporter for the *New York Times* and the *World*. He returned to China in 1913 and worked on a variety of English- and Chinese-language papers in Beijing and Shanghai. By the early 1930s he was the editor-publisher of the *China Press*, an English-language daily financed by Kong Xiangxi. In the mid-1930s he joined Chiang Kaishek's government in Nanjing and began working as an official spokesman. In 1938 Chiang appointed Dong vice minister of propaganda *(xuanchuan bu fuzhang)*, a post he would hold for the duration of the war. (He exercised de facto direct authority over the ministry most of the time because of high turnover and incompetence at the ministerial level.) Dong used the post to staff his ministry with budding young professional journalists, whom he recruited on the basis of merit rather than political connections. He gave foreign correspondents, a number of whom he knew personally in Shanghai, the relative freedom to roam outside Wuhan and report from the battlefield.

At the same time, he won Chiang Kaishek's confidence by giving international circulation to compelling stories of the Generalissimo's personal
courage. In short, because of the acumen of Dong and his colleagues, the
Guomindang at Wuhan greatly increased the sophistication of its propaganda apparatus, to which Chiang Kaishek devoted increasing personal
attention.[17]

War correspondents like Fan Changjiang and Liu Zunqi and the editor-publishers Zou Taofen and Zhang Jiluan had become celebrities. Other
journalists, like Dong Xianguang, were in control of ministries. Capi-
talizing on heightened public recognition, journalism as a profession reorganized itself during the war. A new professional association formed
in Wuhan, calling itself the Chinese Young Journalists Society (*Zhongguo qingnian xinwen jizhe xuehui*). Leading reporters like Fan Changjiang,
Ge Baoquan, and Liu Zunqi and editor-publishers like Cheng Shewo (*Li
bao*), Zhang Jiluan (*Dagong bao*), and Zou Taofen (*Shenghuo*) were active participants. The society's journal, *Xinwen jizhe*, attracted readers
outside of journalism circles. Its purpose was to raise standards and encourage debate about the elements of good war reporting. A series of articles in the journal discussed topics such as the importance of making a
distinction between news (*xinwen*) and commentary (*pinglun*).[18] The
number of specialized books on journalism and collections of exemplary
reporting that were published at Wuhan seems to be remarkably high,
considering the production difficulties during wartime. In short, Wuhan
provided a fertile field for free expression in Chinese journalism and a
chance for the national press to expand inland and spread its wings outside the hothouse of treaty-port culture.[19]

BRINGING CULTURE TO THE MASSES: LAO SHE, GUO MORUO, AND WEN YIDUO

The explosion in variety and number of publications at Wuhan represented fundamental changes in Chinese cultural production. The theo-
retical commitment of intellectuals to innovative and high-quality mass
propaganda had been building in Shanghai since the early 1930s. However, in Wuhan the theory was put into concrete practice—in philosophy, literature, painting, theater, the visual arts, music, and other fields.

The creative enthusiasm of the time was contagious, with the actors
believing that the changes taking place were as important as those of the
May Fourth period. Two charismatic leaders, Lao She and Guo Moruo,
led the popularization of culture in the Wuhan experiment, each in his
own way.

LAO SHE   Lao She (1899–1966) grew up fatherless in the poor Manchu neighborhoods of Beijing. He was basically self-educated.[20] He was not a member of the May Fourth elite—the students and professors who took to the streets in 1919 to challenge traditional Chinese culture in the name of science and democracy. In the mid-1920s he went to the United States and England to study; in 1929 he returned to Beijing and then a year later moved to Jinan, where he taught English and began to write fiction. His first works were imitations of Western literature: short stories and one-act plays that appeared in the local press of Beijing. His first best-seller was the serialized novel *Erma* (Ma's Son), a portrait of life in a Beijing Manchu neighborhood. In his stories, he reproduced the vernacular language and feel of street life in the *hutongs* (alleyways) of Beijing. This focus was fresh and original, but it put him outside the mainstream as represented by the critically celebrated novels of Ba Jin, Mao Dun, Ding Ling, and Xu Zhimo, which dwelt on the divided loyalties and dilemmas of upper-class family life in Chinese cities. Put another way, because of his emphasis on the vernacular and local, Lao She's work was considered by many, including the doyen of May Fourth writers, Lu Xun, as good but limited, parochial, and lacking depth. Undeterred, Lao She took pride in his reputation as a master storyteller and in the popularity of his work. His classic, *Rickshaw Boy (Luoto xiangzi)*, ran as a serial in 1936 and became an instant hit.

Another reason Lao She was out of step with the May Fourth generation of writers in Beijing and Shanghai was his aversion to politics. Because of his reluctance to participate in the revolutionary or New Literature debates of the early 1930s, he never completely gained the trust of either of the newly minted Leninist parties that dominated Chinese politics. He was not close to the literary commissars of either the Communist Party (Zhou Yang, Hu Feng, Feng Xuefeng) or the Guomindang (Ye Chucang and Tao Xisheng). Although profoundly disturbed by Japanese advances in the northeast in the early 1930s, he did not join in formal protests, even though, as a famous author, he was under pressure to do so. He remained distantly allied to Lu Xun and the League of Left Wing Writers that was centered in Shanghai. The only political figure with whom he did develop a long-term relationship was the northern-warlord-turned-populist-general Feng Yuxiang. Feng was an early admirer who used Lao She's short stories as texts for teaching literacy to his troops.[21]

On July 7, 1937, Lao She was living in the southwestern suburbs of Beijing, just a few miles away from Marco Polo Bridge, when a clash between Chinese and Japanese troops led to formal declaration of war by the Nanjing government. As the Japanese swiftly occupied Beijing, Lao She left his wife and family to go south to report on the Japanese advance. He was horrified by the scenes he witnessed in the panic-stricken villages and market towns across north China. In a series of articles for *Dagong bao,* he described the widespread devastation and the plight of refugees, especially in Shandong, after General Han Fuju abandoned the provincial capital, Jinan.[22]

Arriving in Wuhan in December 1937, Lao She stayed at first with a friend in a small apartment on the Huazhong University campus in Wuchang. Within weeks he moved across the river to Hankou to help General Feng Yuxiang form a writers colony in a large walled compound suitably named Fuyin Tang (House of Glad Tidings). Joined by fellow writers and his good friends Wu Zuxiang, He Rong, and Lao Xiang (Wang Xiangchen), he found the atmosphere congenial: "[The place] has trees, flowers, grass, and birds, and a huge yard: no problem with exercise, one can even run 100 meters without making a turn. . . . There are many people here, yet everything is in order, so I can read and write at ease. Thanks to the airy room and quiet, peaceful residence, I was able to write a great deal within a few months. I am grateful to my friends and Mr. Feng."[23] With Feng Yuxiang's financial and political support, Lao She, Lao Xiang, and He Rong launched a successful bimonthly called *Kang daodi* (Resist to the End), which offered short stories, songs, cartoons, and plays specifically to inspire the semiliterate working-class population. The editors were committed to developing innovative content in a language and form that ordinary soldiers would understand and that would appeal to the rural as well as the urban masses.

Lao She and his colleagues called their work "new wine in old bottles" *(jiu ping zhuang xin jiu)*—a slogan they derived from the work of the historian Gu Jiegang (1893–1980), who pioneered the Tongsu Duwu (Popular Reading) movement in the 1920s. In addition to running a Popular Reading press, which put out a weekly journal, by the end of the decade Gu had collected more than thirteen thousand folk songs. In the 1930s, motivated by anti-Japanese sentiment, he began publishing drum songs from north China with new anti-Japanese lyrics. The first printing of these songs sold tens of thousands of copies in a few days. By 1936 Gu was running a substantial publishing house in Beijing, putting out eight pamphlets a week and several small newspapers—all in simplified language and using popular folk imagery and phrasing.[24] After the fall of Beijing, the Popular Reading press moved its equipment and staff to Wuhan, for the express purpose of working in concert with Lao She and his colleagues.

Politically, Lao She's activities challenged the hegemony over wartime propaganda exercised by the New Literature writers who were arriving in Wuhan from Shanghai during the spring of 1938.[25] In late March, when the All China Writers Association *(wenxie)* convened for the first time in Wuchang, Lao She urged each of his fellow writers to "forget that you are a man of letters. In other words, forget Shakespeare and Du Fu, and turn yourself into a country storyteller."[26] At the meeting, Lao She urged the association to give top priority to producing popular reading materials, under the slogan Going to the Countryside, Going to the Army *(wenzhang xiaxiang, wenzhang ruwu)*. Henceforth this slogan and Lao She's ideas about popularization became the dominant theme of the association's flagship publication, *Kangzhan wenyi*. By summer its pages reported monthly production of ten pamphlets for soldiers and a variety of magazines and other publications for the popular market, with titles like *Heavy Fire (Danhua)*, *Everyone Reads (Ren ren kan)*, *Wave of War (Zhanchao)*, *Common People (Laobai xing)*, and finally Lao Xiang's "Anti-Japanese Three-Character Classic" ("Kangzhan sanzijing"), which sold fifty thousand copies in its first month of publication.[27]

Lao She appeared to have won the literary battle, but the war was not over yet. By summer, there was significant resistance to his Tongsu Duwu campaign, principally from the members of the League of Left Wing Writers, most of whom had come from Shanghai. As the historian Liang Kan has shown convincingly in a recent essay, the wartime argument about popularization had roots in the early 1930s.[28] Critics of Lao She and his cohorts believed he was attacking the revolutionary New Literature that had originated with the May Fourth Movement and that by the 1930s had the explicit political purpose of raising the "consciousness" of the masses. In other words, slogans like Going to the Countryside, Going to the Army were fine, but the idea of new wine in old bottles was not acceptable. In April a group of left-wing writers met in Wuhan in the Hankou offices of *Qiyue*, one of Zou Taofen's monthlies edited by the Communist writer Hu Feng. They argued that popularization of literature should mean "massification" *(zhonghua)*. The blind imitation of old forms of cultural expression was politically dangerous because it led to "capitulationism"—toleration of the social and political evils within Chinese traditional culture. The influential Communist writer Feng Xuefeng

(1903–76) also made clear that writers needed to pursue socialist agendas when addressing the masses:

> The true, undistorted and specific meanings of the "popularization of
> art" campaign which began seven or eight years ago are clearer now. They
> include the following imperatives: take charge of the masses' cultural and
> artistic life; create mass revolutionary art by training writers from the masses;
> send intellectual writers down to perceive the life of the masses; create new
> art forms and content; first study then compose in popular language; en-
> lighten by introducing revolutionary culture through literacy campaigns
> that raise the masses' educational level; and finally, make revolutionary
> propaganda using simple, popular artistic forms."[29]

Feng and others contended that Lao Xiang's popular "Anti-Japanese
War Three-Character Classic" set a bad precedent: its traditional format
was too confining and "throws us back into the quagmire of classical
Chinese."[30]

Thus the effort to organize writers to address an audience of the less
well educated was conflicted and not altogether successful. Critics on the
left blunted Lao She's efforts. Still, the polarization of views among intellectuals over the "new wine in old bottles" slogan can be overstated.
Some prominent writers, like Mao Dun, sought middle ground and managed to maintain good relations with both sides.[31] In fact, Mao Dun cred-
ited the popularity of his weekly *Kangzhan* to the adoption of a number
of Lao She's "new wine in old bottles" techniques. Nevertheless, with
people taking sides in the debate over *tongsu wenyi*, the work of left-
wing writers reached a limited audience. Although well-organized and
willing to expend much time and energy on their publications, young leftists like Hu Sheng in his publication *Jiu Zhongguo* were not particularly
effective in reaching beyond the better-educated students and professionals. The more meaningful grassroots work at Wuhan was done by
Lao She and his colleagues—not by the leftists.

Lao She seemed to be at the height of his career. In ten months at Wuhan
he produced five plays, two novels, more than a dozen short stories (many
of which appeared on the pages of *Kang daodi*), and a number of critical essays that sought to persuade his peers and his better-educated readers to join the effort of reaching out to the masses. His most important
work during this period was the unfinished novel *Tui* (Shedding), sixteen
chapters of which were serialized in *Kang daodi*.[32] Set in north China
during the immediate aftermath of the Marco Polo Bridge incident, it
traces the fate of five students who fled the Beijing-Tianjin area with millions of others, heading toward Jinan and farther south. On the road,

the students experience a variety of hardships, including betrayal by col-laborators. In the end, the experience fuels their resolve to go to the front and fight. Lao She's play *Defend Wuhan (Baowei da Wuhan)* was a hit and was probably the most widely performed play at the time.[33]

The young writer Han Suyin recorded a performance in mid-October: "The acting fell short of the art we were accustomed to in Peking. The modern costumes, the abrupt, unrhythmic speech, seemed strange to us and a little uncouth. But the audience applauded each patriotic utterance with such zeal that it was difficult to hear anything. Halfway through the play an announcement was made of a fresh victory at the front. The crowd went delirious with joy. Hankou will be saved! Wuhan will be held!"[34]

Lao She's sense of mission in Wuhan had its romantic and quixotic qualities. He was patriotic and committed to reaching ordinary people, and he was relatively unconcerned with being politically correct. In ap-pealing for unity of effort, he was asking his fellow Chinese to put aside class and party distinctions. The new cultural popularization movement aimed to shape messages that would awaken the masses and provide them "spiritual food" *(jingshen liangshi)* for the protracted war ahead. In this view, the key to defeating the Japanese was to offer patriotic ed-ucation using traditional folk forms so as to end the collaboration of the masses.[35] But in his appeals, Lao She essentially addressed the more formally educated, upper-class intellectual refugees who were arriving from Beijing and Shanghai. Sensing their condescension and lukewarm interest in popularization, he repeatedly emphasized that he was simply advocating a revival of the democratic spirit of the May Fourth Move-ment of 1919.*

GUO MORUO   Just as sincere and active as Lao She, but in a different way, was the poet-scholar Guo Moruo. Guo emerged as Wuhan's official im-presario of cultural propaganda. By the summer of 1938, Guo was giv-ing inspiring speeches almost daily at mass rallies in the streets of Wuchang

---

* Years later Lao She would look back on his Wuhan days as his most fulfilling. Nos-talgia was especially strong after 1949, when he saw the artistic promise of unity, democ-racy, and nonpartisanship fade in China. His last great work, the play *Teahouse (Cha guan)*, was performed to sold-out audiences in the 1950s. At almost the same time, the romantic vision of Wuhan came back to haunt him. During the 1957 antirightist campaign, Lao She was attacked as too bourgeois—and saved from banishment only by the intervention of Mao Dun and others. Then, during the height of the Cultural Revolution, charges about Lao She's old Wuhan connections to militarists like Feng Yuxiang and his arguments with the likes of Feng Xuefeng over *tongsu wenyi* resurfaced and led the Red Guards to target him as a counterrevolutionary. Their brutal treatment drove him to suicide in 1966.

and Hankou. At the same time, he did some of his best creative writing: the play *Qu yuan,* which is still performed today, and a book-length autobiographical poetic tribute to the Wuhan spirit, *Hongbo qu.*

Guo Moruo was born into a well-to-do Sichuan gentry family. In the first decade of the twentieth century he studied in Japan, where his erudition and personality attracted the attention of fellow students like the writer Lu Xun and the philosopher Li Dazhao. He did not return to China until 1921, after teaching in universities for nearly two decades and acquiring a Japanese wife, two sons, and a reputation for innovative scholarship and fine poetry. From Japan he participated in the May Fourth Movement of 1919, becoming nationally known as a revisionist scholar who joined Gu Jiegang in bringing scientific methodology to the study of the oracle bones and early Chinese history. With his return to Shanghai in 1921, Guo was determined to live the life of a writer, focusing almost exclusively on writing poetry and plays, but also flirting with left-wing politics. He became a connoisseur of fine calligraphy. Along with Xu Zhimo, Mao Dun, and others, he was a founding member of the fashionable Crescent Moon literary society.

Politicized by the anti-imperialist May Thirtieth Movement of 1925, he was persuaded by Li Dazhao and others to join the fledgling Communist Party. Organized in Beijing and Shanghai by intellectuals like Li, the party helped form a united front with Sun Yatsen's larger Guomindang party in the south. In 1927 Guo made his political debut on the national stage as the minister in charge of culture for the left-wing Guomindang government that had just been founded at Wuhan by the party leader (and rival of Chiang Kaishek) Wang Jingwei. As a government spokesperson for a few months in 1927, Guo was a colorful and articulate presence. His political career was cut short by the violent purge of Communists in Shanghai and elsewhere under Chiang Kaishek's direction during the late spring. With the complete collapse of the Wuhan government by the fall of 1927, Guo feared for his life and fled with his family back to Japan, where he remained until 1937, concentrating on poetry and scholarship and keeping a low profile politically.[36] Guo continued to write prolifically and to practice a fine calligraphic hand.

While Guo was in exile in Japan, Lu Xun wrote a famous essay criticizing his old comrade for becoming a dilettante and spreading himself thinly across too many fields: poetry, archaeology, drama, literary scholarship. In a sense, Guo's strength had become his weakness: he had been too self-confident, too prominent in too many areas, too young. Guo, of course, saw himself differently—as a renaissance man burned by politics after he had first mastered and then challenged traditional learning in several scholarly fields.[37]

Guo was wounded by Lu Xun's attack. Although brilliant and gregarious, he had a mercurial temperament, and his moods often swung between emotional highs and lows. Politics had tarnished his reputation, and he had little further direct contact with the Chinese Communist Party. By 1935 and 1936, as war clouds gathered and students demonstrated in the streets of Beijing and Shanghai, friends were wondering why he stayed in Japan.

The formal outbreak of war in July 1937 triggered an identity crisis for Guo. He needed to prove himself again as a committed patriot and political activist; so, after much soul-searching, he decided to desert his wife, Anna (Sato Tomiko), and their five children and return to Shanghai to join the anti-Japanese National Salvation movement. Then Shanghai fell, and Nanjing came under siege. In November 1937, he moved to Hong Kong, where he stayed for a month working on archaeological issues and planning his next step with old friends like the writer-dramatist Xia Yan.[38]

One day at an art-exhibit opening on Hollywood Road, Guo met two young women who were students and roommates from Shanghai: one a painter, Yu Feng, and the other a dancer, Yu Liqun. He had been a close friend of the dancer's father, a journalist from a prominent Guangxi family. Moreover (although married with five children), he had been involved recently in a love triangle with Yu Liqun's older sister, Yu Lichen, the Tokyo correspondent for *Dagong bao,* who committed suicide that spring (1937) in Shanghai after Guo ended the affair. By his own account, he was still overwhelmed by emotion and guilt (having visited the grave site in Shanghai), when Guo fell in love at first sight with the younger sister Yu Liqun and began madly pursuing her. Although flattered by the famous intellectual's attentions (and presumably unaware of his role in her sister's suicide), Ms. Yu at first did not take Guo seriously; in any case, in late December she and Yu Feng left Hong Kong for Wuhan to join the war effort there. Guo followed in early January 1938 and renewed contact with the Communist leader Zhou Enlai, who had just arrived in Wuhan from Yan'an.[39]

At a meal with Zhou Enlai, Dong Biwu, and Ye Ting—with whom Guo had served in the revolutionary government in Wuhan in 1927— Guo was offered an appointment as head of the cultural propaganda division of the Third Bureau *(di santing).* The offer was the equivalent of receiving a ministry in the new military government forming under General Chen Cheng, and in which Zhou Enlai had the position of political commissar. The United Front agreement between the Communist and Nationalist parties stipulated that a member of each party would serve at every ministerial level in the wartime government. Startled, and perhaps fearing the possible personal and political cost, Guo asked for time to think about his decision. Furthermore, he was obsessed with pursuing Yu Liqun, apparently to the point of exhaustion. He became so ill that friends persuaded him to leave Wuhan and go to Changsha for two weeks of rest and medical care.

On January 29 Yu Liqun arrived in Changsha with a message from Zhou Enlai urging Guo to return to Wuhan immediately because he planned to issue the formal offer for the position as head of the division of cultural propaganda, with subsequent approval by Chiang Kaishek and an announcement by General Chen Cheng on February 1. Zhou's message concluded with an appeal to Guo's ego: he was the only man with the literary experience and talent to find new ways of inspiring the masses to stop the Japanese advance on Wuhan. Yu Liqun added a personal message of her own: she would marry Guo only if he accepted the appointment. Over the previous weeks she had been under heavy pressure from Zhou Enlai and left-wing friends to consent to marry the "old" man (twenty years separated the two); he desperately needed her companionship, and it was her patriotic duty.[40]

Guo Moruo was Zhou's choice because he was acceptable to both the Guomindang and the Chinese Communist parties. Because of his prominence in the 1927 government, his name still had resonance in Wuhan. And despite Lu Xun's criticisms of him as an intellectual dilettante, he had cachet as a famous May Fourth intellectual who had solid contacts and friends on both sides of the Guomindang-CCP divide that ran back to his student days in Japan. Despite his reputation as a philandering scholar and poet, nobody could deny that he was still a major player in Chinese intellectual life. Moreover, his long exile in Japan had exempted him from the heavy factional fighting within both the Guomindang and the CCP in the 1930s. Thus he seemed an acceptable old leftist intellectual—malleable and politically harmless—to both Chiang Kaishek and Zhou Enlai.

Not surprisingly, given the pressure, Guo agreed to take the post and return immediately to Wuhan. Marriage to Yu Junqun followed within weeks (without a formal divorce from Anna).* And once his appointment as head of the propaganda department was made official, Guo threw him-

---

* A politically arranged marriage such as Yu Liqun's—a new twist on the old idea of the family-arranged marriage—was not unusual. Mao Zedong's marriage to Jiang Qing was approved at about the same time by a party vote. Granted, there were extenuating circumstances: Jiang Qing was pregnant. Yu Liqun and Guo would have five children; they named their first child, born in 1939, Guo Hanying (for Wu Han, according to Yu Liqun).

self into the work with gusto, finding redemption in the new job and marriage. He recruited a staff of two thousand artists and writers, who lived and worked together on the sprawling campus of the former Cultural University (closed since 1927) in Wuchang's university district. He organized the community into six sections, appointing as heads respected intellectuals and artists such as the novelist Yu Dafu and the dramatists Hong Shen and Tian Han. The author of a popular current play, Yang Hansheng, was his chief executive assistant. In speeches Guo stressed that the purpose of wartime propaganda was to undermine the enemy by ending collaboration and giving the populace, including the troops, the will to resist during what would inevitably be a long war. The war was to be a fight to the death, and the cultural worker needed to make that truth palatable. Guo spoke almost daily—at rallies, press conferences, and schools, at meetings of chambers of commerce and women's associations, and on the radio. The live radio broadcasts became a favorite medium as the defense of Wuhan approached a state of siege in the fall of 1938.[41]

In retrospect, his work in Wuhan was probably Guo's finest hour. He succeeded in creating a propaganda machine in which Communists and non-Communists worked smoothly together. His ecumenical approach was especially evident in his public appearances. He presided almost daily at functions and rallies throughout the tricity that mixed Communists and third-party figures like Carsun Chang (Junmai) or You Yuren with the likes of Chen Lifu, Kang Ze, Zhou Fohai, Ye Qing, and Tao Xisheng on the Guomindang side. At his sprawling headquarters, he encouraged painters, musicians, and journalists, many of whom had just arrived from Shanghai, to establish new associations and publications that would bring refugee professionals together in the war effort. Finally, he contributed mightily to bringing international acceptance and attention to the righteousness of China's cause, arranging public appearances by dissident Japanese intellectuals like Lu Ditan (husband and wife), who denounced the brutal nature of Japanese aggression. He repeatedly emphasized the connection between Wuhan's situation and Madrid's, comparing the struggle in Europe to the Chinese fight against Fascism.[42]

Thus Guo played the role of impresario for cultural propaganda with flair and inspiration. In trying to mediate the dispute about the best way to put popularization into practice, he seemed to embrace both the opposing approaches, the *tongsu* and *zhonghua* credos put forth by Lao She and Feng Xuefeng. Drawing on his record as a prominent veteran of earlier cultural wars, he insisted that the May Fourth 1919 cultural revolution was now reaching new heights with the wartime thrust of taking culture to the people. Often, his gift for hyperbole got the best of him, as in this statement:

> A revolution in painting must first depart from ancient elegance.
> Folk style values what is true to life and realistic,
> If the image is not realistic, it is then false,
> And the vulgar, when really driven home, is naturally the divine.[43]

Such quotes do not convey Guo's contagious energy and obvious commitment to the cause. Into late October 1938 he was still giving passionate speeches on the streets of Wuhan. He also showed personal courage and was one of the last officials to leave the city as the Japanese stormed its gates.

Between daily appearances on the streets of Wuhan to address mass rallies and meetings, Guo spent time writing in his Wuchang courtyard home, which he had turned into a salon for other writers and artists. He wrote plays and poetry mostly, and by the end of the year became a father again. The marriage to Yu Liqun was an enduring and happy one, and he later said that Wuhan was the happiest period of his life.

In his own work, Guo Moruo had difficulty writing for a popular audience. The plays he wrote in *tongsu* style were much less successful than those of Lao She, Yang Hansheng, or Hong Shen.[44] The style and content of his best work remained elegantly tinged with the classical, in the May Fourth tradition of Lu Xun or Xu Zhimo. At Wuhan he completed perhaps his greatest play, *Qu yuan,* the story of the early Han-dynasty poet who committed suicide rather than betray his emperor (and by implication, China). *Hongbo qu,* his book-length ode to the new marriage and the romantic magic of Wuhan in 1938, was likewise sprinkled with classical allusions and stylistic flourishes.[45] The enduring literary quality of these two works explains why they are among the few writings by Guo Moruo that are still read today.[*]

---

[*] By the end of the war, Guo Moruo made a Faustian bargain with Mao in Yan'an, and his immersion in politics became complete. With the establishment of the People's Republic of China, Guo held various high ministerial-level positions. He became a kind of cultural court jester for the new regime, leading delegations to Moscow and New Delhi while negotiating at home through the complex twists and turns of palace politics in Beijing. Unlike other cultural leaders—Mao Dun, Ba Jin, Zhou Yang, and Ding Ling, for example—Guo held onto a high ministerial-level position during the infamous Cultural Revolution of 1966–76. Politically, however, he was powerless, with tragic consequences for his family. He was unable to save two of his sons—one of whom, Guo Minying, was a talented poet who committed suicide during the Cultural Revolution. Thus, although Guo survived politically into the 1970s, his reputation was badly tarnished by years of sycophancy. When he died in 1980, the state funerals shown on television had a hollow ring. And today Chinese intellectuals mostly remember him with contempt.

WUHAN UNIVERSITY, CA. 1935, WITH CLASSROOM AND ADMINISTRATION BUILDINGS IN THE MONUMENTAL
CHINESE RENAISSANCE STYLE. COURTESY LIBRARY OF CONGRESS.

JIANG BAILI AFTER RELEASE FROM A SHANGHAI PRISON,
1931. FROM *JIANG BAILI XIANSHENG JINIANCE* (1993),
FRONTISPIECE.

PEOPLE RUNNING FOR SHELTER ON THE STREETS OF HANKOU DURING AIR RAID ALARM, MARCH 1938.
PHOTOGRAPH BY ROBERT CAPA, COURTESY MAGNUM PHOTO, COPYRIGHT 2001 CORNELL CAPA.

WOODBLOCK PRINT OF REFUGEES IN FLIGHT, ARTIST LI HUA, FROM *WOODCUTS OF WARTIME CHINA* (1946), 4.

REFUGEES FROM THE YELLOW RIVER FLOOD, NEAR ZHENGZHOU, JUNE 1938. QIN FENG (2005), 115.

WOUNDED SOLDIER AT RECEIVING STATION, NEAR JIUJIANG, JUNE 1938. FROM UTLEY (1939).

YELLOW RIVER FLOOD VICTIMS NEAR HUAYUANKOU, JUNE 1938. FROM QIN FENG (2005), 114.

TRAIN MOBBED BY SOLDIERS AND CIVILIANS FLEEING XUZHOU, MAY 1938. PHOTOGRAPH BY ROBERT CAPA,
COURTESY MAGNUM PHOTO, COPYRIGHT 2001 CORNELL CAPA.

HOMES DESTROYED BY INCENDIARY BOMBS, HANKOU, 1938. FROM UTLEY (1939).

FIRST AID WORKERS ARRIVING ON THE SCENE OF THE BOMBING OF WUCHANG, AUGUST 1938. PHOTOGRAPH BY ROBERT CAPA, COURTESY MAGNUM PHOTO, COPYRIGHT 2001 CORNELL CAPA.

WOMEN LEADERS POSING AFTER THE FOUNDING OF THE WARTIME CHILD WELFARE ASSOCIATION, APRIL 1, 1938. (SHI LIANG IN TOP ROW, SECOND FROM RIGHT; MME. CHIANG KAISHEK [SONG MEILING] IN SECOND ROW, FOURTH FROM LEFT.) COURTESY GU WEIMING.

MME. CHIANG KAISHEK WITH REFUGEE CHILDREN IN WUHAN, 1938. PHOTOGRAPH BY ROBERT CAPA, COURTESY MAGNUM PHOTO, COPYRIGHT 2001 CORNELL CAPA.

LUNCHTIME AT THE ORPHANAGE IN CANTON, JULY 1938. PHOTOGRAPH BY ROBERT CAPA, COURTESY MAGNUM PHOTO, COPYRIGHT 2001 CORNELL CAPA.

MEDICAL COMMISSIONER ROBERT K. LIN (LIN KESHENG). FROM UTLEY (1939).

GUO MORUO SPEAKING TO A LARGE RALLY. FROM GONG JIMIN AND FANG RENNIAN (1982), FRONTISPIECE.

SURPRISE LATE WINTER SNOWSTORM BLANKETING WUHAN, PROVIDING OPPORTUNITY FOR SNOWBALL FIGHTS, MARCH 7, 1938. PHOTOGRAPH BY ROBERT CAPA, COURTESY MAGNUM PHOTO, COPYRIGHT 2001 CORNELL CAPA.

ENTHUSIASTIC FLAG WAVING AT PATRIOTIC RALLY, SUN YATSEN PARK, HANKOU, MARCH 12, 1938.
PHOTOGRAPH BY ROBERT CAPA. COURTESY MAGNUM PHOTO, COPYRIGHT 2001 CORNELL CAPA.

WOMEN STUDENTS UNDERGOING MILITARY TRAINING, WUHAN, SPRING, 1938. PHOTOGRAPH BY ROBERT CAPA, COURTESY MAGNUM PHOTO, COPYRIGHT 2001 CORNELL CAPA.

MARCH IN SUPPORT OF LEAGUE OF NATIONS COVENANT CONDEMNING JAPAN, HANKOU, SPRING 1938. FROM QIN FENG (2005), 23.

WOMAN SPEAKER HARANGUING CROWD ON STREETS OF WUHAN, 1938. FROM QIN FENG (2005), 27.

RECRUITMENT POSTER RIDICULING HITLER AT RALLY IN HANKOU IN AUGUST 1938. FROM QIN FENG (2005), 52.

SWASTIKA ON PASSENGER TRAIN FOR PROTECTION AGAINST JAPANESE BOMBING MISSIONS. DEPARTURE OF GENERAL ALEXANDER VON FALKENHAUSEN AND OTHER GERMAN MILITARY ADVISERS FROM WUCHANG STATION, JULY 5, 1938. PHOTOGRAPH BY ROBERT CAPA, COURTESY MAGNUM PHOTO, COPYRIGHT 2001 CORNELL CAPA.

WESTERN JOURNALISTS AT WUHAN, 1938 (LEFT TO RIGHT): ROBERT CAPA, WALTER BOSSHARD, AND AGNES SMEDLEY. FROM UTLEY (1939).

JAPANESE TROOPS ENTERING FOREIGN CONCESSION AT HANKOU, SALUTING ITALIAN TROOPS STANDING BY, OCTOBER 26, 1938. FROM QIN FENG (2005), 76.

WEN YIDUO AND RESISTANCE TO POPULARIZATION   While Lao She and Guo Moruo were throwing themselves wholeheartedly into the cultural propaganda movement of the early war years, other veterans of the May Fourth era who passed through Wuhan in 1938 were much less enthusiastic about the campaign. The personal and political tensions over such issues are well illustrated in an exchange of letters between the poet and aesthete Wen Yiduo (1898–1946) and his wife, Gao Xiaozhen. Although Wen was sympathetic to the patriotic motivations of major players like his friend Guo Moruo, he thought that the planned level of popularization and politicization of Chinese culture was fundamentally abhorrent.

Wen and Gao were members of leading gentry families from the Wuhan tricity region (Xishui county). After their (arranged) marriage and three years of separation while Wen studied in the United States, Wen returned in 1925. He taught Chinese literature, published translations, and wrote poetry in a variety of north China institutions before settling at Beijing's Qinghua University in 1931. The marriage was a happy one, and by 1937 the couple had five children: three daughters and two sons. Shortly after the Marco Polo Bridge incident on July 7, 1937, Gao departed with her youngest children (the two boys) for the Wuchang family residence, where she waited for Wen to arrive from Beijing. Wen followed at the end of the year with the three girls, arriving in January 1938. He dropped off the children with their nanny and headed south for Changsha, which had become the temporary residence of Qinghua and other Beijing universities. But before leaving Wuchang, he had a visit from a close family friend, Gu Yuxiu, who had just been appointed vice minister of education. Gu invited Wen to stay, offering him an official position in the ministry that included a good salary and a comfortable residence in Wuchang. When Wen turned down this offer and left for Changsha, Gao was furious. There ensued a hostile exchange of letters, punctuated by long silences from Wuchang, where Gao stubbornly remained with the children.

With Gao threatening divorce, Wen became miserable and frightened. In his letters, many of which went unanswered, he tried to explain that he really belonged in the quiet atmosphere of a university, where he could teach and contribute to the war effort in the old-fashioned way, by educating young elites about the classics of Chinese and Western literature. The conditions were hard, as the universities moved their campus again in mid-1938 to Kunming to form Lianda (United Colleges). Wen acknowledged that life in Wuhan would be more comfortable, at least for a while, and of course he would enjoy the prestige of an official position. Still, he pleaded, he was simply not suited for the political world of

Wuhan—where great pressure existed for cultural conformity on the issue of popularizing learning for the masses.[46]

Wen Yiduo's experience epitomizes the conflict that Chinese intellectuals felt between the ideals of the May Fourth Movement and the aims of wartime cultural mobilization. The choices they faced were too painful and complicated to be framed in retrospect as either/or propositions: either submit to vulgarization for the masses or pursue the cultural renaissance started by the May Fourth Movement. Things were different now. In 1919 Japanese imperialism had been only a threat; in 1938 the nation's very existence seemed in peril. For Wen Yiduo, the decision to avoid Wuhan and retreat to university life was painful. It was also a decision he would reverse at the end of the war.[*]

The cultural norms and propaganda points that the proponents of popularization were introducing at Wuhan in 1938 remained salient throughout the war. And today many scholars argue that during the later war years the movement lost its moorings amid the demands of competing authorities in Chongqing and Yan'an. Thus, for better or worse, the Wuhan experience shows how demands for intellectuals to respond to the horrors of the war altered Chinese culture permanently.[47]

---

[*] After the fall of Wuhan, Gao relented and joined Wen in Kunming, where the couple remained for the rest of the war. Ironically, as the war was ending in 1945, Wen Yiduo, against his wife's advice, dropped inhibitions about pandering to the masses and became politically active in third-party democratic movements. He paid the ultimate price, falling to an assassin's bullet on the streets of Kunming in early 1946.

Other May Fourth intellectuals were equally unable to adapt to the fast life in Wuhan, but for different reasons. The renowned poet and essayist Yu Dafu worked for Guo Moruo in the Third Section (on cultural propaganda) during the spring of 1938 but became so depressed and humiliated when his wife publicly left him for another man (an official in the Wuhan government) that he fled to Singapore. Qian Zhongshu, the great classical scholar and novelist, rejected movements of the *tongsu wenyi* type and returned to occupied Shanghai to care for his frail and enfeebled parents. The great painter Xu Beihong avoided Wuhan after his wife left him for another man (likewise, an official serving in Wuhan). The promising young playwright Chen Baizhen left the tricity after his lover's aggrieved husband shot and wounded him on the streets of Hankou.

SIX

MOBILIZING YOUTH

OVER ONE HUNDRED THOUSAND student refugees passed through Wuhan in early 1938. The streets of the tricity throbbed with the energy of their patriotic speeches and wall posters. As the young journalist Israel Epstein wrote, "The sober commercial city of Hankou began to wear a different aspect. . . . On its walls were countless posters, wall newspapers, and proclamations. Daily they changed, reflecting events in China and in the world. The walls of Hankou were the platform of the people. . . . When the Chinese air force won a victory vivid placards announced the fact. When Hitler spoke in favour of Japan, the walls bore his features in fierce caricature. When Australian dockers refused to load iron for Japan, proclamations signed by the Hankou Seamen's Union shouted their thanks."[1] How to harness this energy for the war effort became one of the most contentious political issues of the Wuhan spring.

During the first few months of the war, as north China and then Shanghai fell to the Japanese, the majority of Chinese students were forced out of secondary schools and universities. Of China's 108 institutions of higher learning, 94 closed or relocated during the war; some moved as many as five times. Comprehensive statistics on secondary schools are not available, but the situation was undoubtedly just as severe.[2] In socioeconomic terms students represented the small privileged elite of the Chinese population. Between 1935 and 1937 only 46,758 students, or about 0.01 percent of the population, were enrolled in institutions of higher learning each year, and 546,212 students, or 0.1 percent, attended secondary schools. Education was expensive, so students came overwhelmingly from the families of businessmen, government officials, and educators. Being so wellborn and seemingly assured of future elite status made them an even more precious group than their counterparts in the West. Since the turn of the century the concerns and enthusiasms of the student class had shaped Chinese politics and anticipated social change.[3]

Thus, in 1938, as earlier, the press and the military leaders who were running Wuhan took student voices very seriously. The convergence of students on Wuhan produced a movement that differed in character from that of its predecessors but had an equally important impact on politics. For the first time, students from all over China were thrown together in one place, Wuhan. Cut off from family support systems, they lived in subsidized housing on the semideserted campuses of Wuchang. Clinging to one another for support, they established bonds that transcended regional and school ties. Their energy and patriotic enthusiasm was the inspiration for the prose and poetry of senior intellectuals like Guo Moruo, Mao Dun, and Lao She.

Braving Japanese bombs, students ferried back and forth across the Yangzi almost daily from Wuchang to participate in rallies and put up fresh wall posters on the Hankou side. Those with local connections, like Hu Qiuyuan and Hu Sheng, borrowed money from relatives and launched publications such as the periodical *Shidai ribao*. More concretely, these young men and women signed up by the tens of thousands as volunteer health and social workers to meet the refugee crisis of the city and surrounding countryside. Others joined the drama troupes being organized by Tian Han and Hong Shen or toured the war zones under the auspices of Guo Moruo's Third Bureau of cultural propaganda. Hundreds with "connections" worked directly under Guo at his Wuchang headquarters as interns. Much of this frenetic activity was disturbing to parents, university administrators, and Ministry of Education officials, who urged students (with little success) to return to the classroom and study hard.

Since the early twentieth century, Chinese student organizers have shown a strong theatrical sense, choreographing demonstrations or rallies and designing wall posters to appeal to foreign as well as domestic audiences. The students in Wuhan in 1938 fit this pattern, but with an interesting twist: they did not direct their rallies against the government. Chiang Kaishek actually attended some of these events and, in return, received at least nominal student support for the new United Front government that was running Wuhan and its defense.

Wasserstrom and other historians have argued convincingly that because the student marches and demonstrations of the twentieth century were so consciously staged, they acquired a symbolic or ritual power that gave educated youth special status as the conscience of the nation.[4] Such student activism had gained a foothold by the May Fourth movement in 1919, and it had shaken the political establishment in Beijing and Shanghai as recently as the December Ninth campus movements of 1935. Wuhan's youth movement built on this tradition of moral outrage choreographed as street theater. Another characteristic of the Chinese student movement since the turn of the century has been the inability of the state to control it. In political terms, power holders have rarely trusted the students. This statement applied to Yuan Shikai and Sun Yatsen when they founded the Republic of China in 1911–12; it applied to Chiang Kaishek, who vigorously suppressed demonstrations during the apogee of his rule in the mid-1930s; and it applies to the government leaders of the twenty-first century, who exhibit similar paranoia about student unrest. PRC authorities typically believe that unbridled student enthusiasm will bring chaos and disaster: witness the rampages of the Red Guards during the Cultural Revolution, the Tiananmen Square demonstrations in 1989, and the anti-Japanese demonstrators who left campuses to storm embassies in 1985 and 2005.[5]

Wuhan in 1938 presents an interesting variation on this theme. Although youth rallied in support of the United Front military council that was conducting the war under Chiang Kaishek's titular leadership, this relationship that should have been mutually supportive remained uneasy. The biggest problem was that neither the Guomindang nor the Communists provided effective leadership for youth. As a result, student leadership fragmented and could not agree about what direction to take. In this situation, the figures who gained the greatest influence with students were the few who exhibited missionary zeal in projecting a consistent vision, whether conservative or liberal, of the ways in which young people could make a responsible contribution to the war effort. One such figure was the minister of education, Chen Lifu, who launched an energetic and ultimately quixotic campaign to motivate students to serve the war effort by rejecting libertine Western models and returning China to Confucian strength.

THE DECEMBER STUDENT PETITION

Wuhan has a long tradition of student activism. During the first decade of the twentieth century, the Tongmenghui [Alliance] student movement in the city—organized mostly from Japan in alliance with mutinying young military officers—plotted the October revolution at Wuchang, which helped topple the Qing dynasty in 1911–12. A decade later, in the mid-1920s, Wuhan was a battleground for student and labor politics—depicted romantically for the Western audience in André Malraux's novel *Man's Fate*—which culminated in the revolutionary experiment and brutal crackdown of 1927. With the Wuhan student movement crushed by 1930, the government reorganized education under the firm hand of Nanjing. Except for a small missionary college (today's Huazhong University), all existing universities were closed and replaced by Wuhan University, built (as we saw in chapter 1) on the outskirts of Wuchang in a monumental Chinese renaissance style. At the new university, students and faculty underwent careful screening, and once admitted, they were subject to the state's watchful eye and control. As a result, Communist Party organizers had only a weak presence on campus. Such was the situation going into the winter of 1937–38, when large numbers of students from Beijing, Tianjin, and Shanghai began to descend on Wuhan.[6]

By late 1937 General Li Zongren (commander for the Xuzhou, southern Henan, and northern Anhui region) had begun to organize patriotic youth in the Fifth War Zone in the north into protomilitary units assigned to propaganda work and some fighting. The most cohesive of these units was General Li's Youth Corps *(qingnian tuan)* of more than five thousand young men and women who had left school to join the war effort.[7] At about the same time, the head of the military council, General Chen Cheng (also commander of the Ninth War Zone), began training a student army *(xuesheng jun)* of six thousand refugees.[8] But these efforts were uncoordinated and only scratched the surface of the drifting student population. Not until December 1937, after the fall of Nanjing, when young people began converging on Wuhan in large numbers, did the students undertake a more concerted effort to organize themselves.

In November 24, 1937, a meeting of educational, student, YMCA, and intellectual leaders convened at Christian College in Wuchang (on today's Huazhong University campus) to form an alliance and recommend strategies for youth mobilization to the government. Here, for the first time, student leaders met National Salvation Association activists from Shanghai and Beijing-Tianjin, who had formerly operated in isolation or with only loose coordination.[9] On December 1 a larger follow-up meeting at nearby Wuhan University was attended by some of the "seven gentlemen" *(qijunzi)* activists from the National Salvation Association who had been arrested in 1936—Shen Junru, the publisher Zou Taofen, and Li Gongpu. Participants debated how best to reorganize education so that youth could participate fully in the war effort. Should students leave school and form military units (as General Li Zongren and others urged), or should they stay in school and receive basic military and logistical training as part of the curriculum (along the lines of General Chen Cheng's training program)?

The initiative for these meetings came from various youth organizers who were in the middle of the road politically: they were neither Communist nor Guomindang activists.[10] The conference delegates represented a variety of newly formed groups, such as the Research Association on Education for the War Resistance *(kangzhan jiaoyu yanjiuhui)*, the Association of Wartime Education *(zhanshi jiaoyu she)*, the Life Educational Association *(shenghuo jiaoyu she)* and the Combat Association *(zhandou xunkanshe)*. Two driving forces behind the proposed alliance were the veteran educational reformer Tao Xingzhi and the Shenghuo publishing house headed by Zou Taofen, which published journals that were at the center of the youth mobilization movement, such as *Zhanshi jiaoyu* (edited by Tao) and *Kangzhan* (edited by Mao Dun).[11]

In a widely publicized petition to the government, the Wuhan University conference delegates called for a unified association to organize youth for the war effort. They argued that continuing the kind of heroic and uncoordinated individual organizational efforts of various groups that had supported the defense of Shanghai would be counterproductive. To support the long war of attrition that Chiang Kaishek was calling for, the reformers wanted to see youth mobilized in mass campaigns to convince rural as well as urban citizens of the need to sacrifice and join in the war effort. Young people needed to acquire basic knowledge of air defense, poisonous gas, hygiene, and first aid and then pass on the information in publicity campaigns. The government needed to open up traditional classrooms and organize youth into performing arts and drama propaganda teams that would go to the villages to perform as well as to provide technical skills. Finally, the activists called for "collective life and self-education" *(jiti shenghuo yu ziwo jiaoyu)*—a new approach that would bring teachers and students together in a kind of wartime collective. Most emphatically, they denounced the status quo in education: simply moving educational institutions inland without reforming them, as the government seemed to be doing, was unacceptable.[12]

THE GOVERNMENT RESPONSE

The central government's initial response went in two directions, reflecting deep divisions within the Guomindang about youth and educational policy. In the first response, a reformist wing led by Peng Wenkai and allied to General Chen Cheng advocated sweeping curricular changes and a revitalized Guomindang-led youth movement. In a new journal, *Qingnian qianxian,* Peng seemed to endorse the reforms called for in the December Wuhan petition: replacement of regular schoolwork with propaganda training for organizing the masses, as well as instruction in guerrilla warfare, first aid, firefighting, and so forth.[13]

To seize the initiative, in early February Peng and others organized a week of citywide rallies under the banner Propaganda Week for the International Anti-aggression Movement, to take place in Zhongshan Park in downtown Hankou. Each day focused on a different sector of the population: women on the first day (Sunday), youth on the second, workers on the third, merchants on the fourth, then a day for refugees and wounded soldiers, and on the last day an extravaganza organized by cultural workers. According to a young United Press wire reporter who was in Zhongshan Park and on the streets every day, the rallies inspired the crowd and brought the tricity together symbolically:

> Early in February, a series of meetings and demonstration were held to support the London Conference of International Peace Campaign. On February 7, thousands of women marched with banners through the streets of the city. . . . February 8 was Youth Day. Five thousand boys and girls gathered at Zhongshan Park for a mass meeting. "Fascist aggression is the enemy of world youth," "Down with Japanese Imperialism," "Long Live the Chinese Air Force," they shouted. . . . On February 12 cultural workers marched to protest against the Japanese destruction of schools and universities. Plays, specially written for the day, were performed. Posters and leaflets drove home the necessity for struggle, the inevitability of China's victory.[14]

The largest rally was on Youth Day. It represented the diversity of the United Front spirit. Speakers included figures from Guomindang headquarters, the local Garrison Command, the Wuhan Young Women's Command, and the Shanghai Buddhist Priests' First Aid Team. Peng Wenkai chaired the rally, and luminaries on the podium ranged from Wang Jingwei to a leading Communist student organizer from Xi'an, Li Chang. As the rally began, an air-raid warning interrupted it and the park was cleared. In a few hours the crowd reassembled with cheers for the defending Chinese air force fighters who were circling overhead. At the end of the rally, participants marched out singing in military formation. As they passed a statue of Chiang Kaishek, they broke into goosestep and cried, "Support the leader in the fight to the end."[15] Indeed, the overtones of European-style fascism displayed by the marching youth groups illustrated the emphasis that Guomindang and military leaders like Peng and Chen Cheng placed on blending ideological training, nationalism, military discipline, and unity of organization.[16]

However, others within the Guomindang leadership were deeply disturbed by the rallies and the emphasis on military training by Peng and his allies. The clearest and most irate voice among them was that of Chen Lifu, the newly appointed minister of education for the central government.

Since the 1920s Chen had been a figure of importance in the Guomindang party apparatus. Although Western educated as an engineer, Chen had a classical Confucian educational background. His uncle, Chen Shimei, was one of the closest associates of Chiang Kaishek and Sun Yatsen. Through this connection, Chen Lifu joined Chiang Kaishek's inner circle as a personal secretary in the 1920s. When I interviewed him in 1992 in Taibei, I found Chen to be a small, serious man of unusual intelligence and determination; though over ninety years of age, he radiated intensity and quiet self-confidence. I could not easily imagine this elegant Confucian gentleman as the ruthless Machiavellian tactician who had reshaped the Guomindang in the late 1920s and early 1930s into a loyal instrument of Chiang Kaishek (in the process outmaneuvering Wang Jingwei in the contest for party leadership).[17]

Chen and his brother, Liguo, led the powerful CC Clique of apparatchiks and bureaucrats that dominated the central government in the 1930s and competed viciously for appointments and influence with rivals like the Whampoa (Huangpu) military clique (of which Chen Cheng was a member) and the weaker Political Study Clique of bureaucrats (which included T. V. Song [Song Ziwen] and others). To stay in charge, Chiang Kaishek cleverly played the cliques off against one another. Critical to Chen's initial success was an alliance with the increasingly powerful secret police (juntong) headed by Dai Li. After the shake-ups and weakening of the Guomindang party structure in the wake of the Xi'an Incident of December 1936 and the declaration of war the next summer, Chen wanted a cabinet position in the central government. Moreover, he did not want just any position; he wanted the education portfolio. He received the appointment in January 1938, and, unlike any education minister before him, Chen tackled the job with passion. His commitment went

beyond politics; he saw the appointment as the opportunity of a lifetime—
a chance to put into practice his personal philosophy of education and
life. Years later, in memoirs and interviews, he called the years as education minister the finest of his career.

As a government minister, Chen Lifu acted like a strict Neo-Confucian
ideologue. He was Confucius in modern dress, with views resembling in
more contemporary terms those of former president Lee Kwanyu of Singapore. In the mid-1930s Chen had been a passionate anti-Communist
and a strong supporter of Chiang Kaishek's New Life Movement.[18] In 1938
his mission was to restore Neo-Confucian standards to the Chinese educational system as the best preparation for a nation at war. Needless to
say, he was no friend of the liberal educational reformers from Shanghai—
men like Tao Xingzhi and the "seven gentlemen," whom he saw as insti-
gators of the petition and student-union initiatives of December. He was
also alarmed by the approval of paramilitary training for youth and the
emphasis on mass rallies by General Chen Cheng and the reformer Peng
Wenkai; to Chen Lifu, such ideas were wrongheaded and a dangerous imitation of foreign models (in this case fascist European practices).

In short, Chen Lifu wanted to give educational policy and youth organizations a firmly traditional stamp—a Neo-Confucian character, as
he called it later in interviews and memoirs.[19] Characteristic of his conservative approach was a long article by his intellectual alter ego, Tao
Xisheng, in *Xuelu*, as well as his own speeches in January and February
of 1938. Tao and Chen did agree with liberal education reformers like
Tao Xingzhi on one general point: China needed more activist reform
policies in the education field. But they saw no need for a basic transformation of the educational system to place it on a wartime footing. Instead, they believed that educational reform should reemphasize science,
Chinese traditional civilization, and nationalism. Students should remain
in school and contribute to scientific progress and industrial production
for the future. Continuity in education, especially at the higher levels (senior high school and university), was critical to strengthening the nation
economically and enhancing its military capabilities for the war of attrition ahead. Discipline problems on campuses should also be dealt with
swiftly and firmly. Activists were abusing freedoms, and a climate of per-
missiveness was resulting in too much Western cultural influence and a
rejection of Chinese traditions.[20]

Chiang Kaishek's response to this controversy over education and
youth was at first ambiguous. In a speech in February 1938 he emphasized that mass mobilization of the populace was essential to surviving

a long war of attrition and that the goal should be to mobilize students
and youth in general and channel young people's energies productively
into the war effort.[21] Chiang realized that the Guomindang needed to
act in this area to preempt the efforts of Shanghai activists like the "seven
gentlemen" and to prevent Communist use of a united student association to recruit the young. He also sought organizational vehicles with
which to rebuild the Guomindang party from the ground up. At the same
time, however, Chiang continued to share the culturally conservative out-
look and Neo-Confucian vision of Chen Lifu.

The debate came to a head at the Special Congress of the Guomindang *(Guomindang linshi quanguo daibiao dahui)* at the end of March,
which was to be a forum for party decisions on a broad range of wartime
policies that the United Front government would then implement. On
March 25, four days before the big party meeting, an All China Student
Conference *(Zhongguo xuelian daibiao dahui)* took place to formulate
and submit proposals on education and youth mobilization. The meeting was the largest and most unified student gathering of its kind in modern Chinese history. Over five hundred delegates attended, representing
eighteen provinces and sixty-five colleges and universities. The leading
theater commander and head of the Military Council, General Chen
Cheng, presided, and Zhou Enlai, Wang Ming, and others from the Communist side also addressed the meeting. The conference called for all students to unite in a single student union under the leadership of the Guomindang. Attendees called for redesigning wartime education to be more
relevant to national defense, with shortened courses of study that were
practical in nature and provided more military training for students.[22]
The conference report and the thrust of its proceedings reiterated messages from the December meetings and petitions. But this time the documents had more input from recently arrived Communist student activists
from Yan'an—notably Huang Hua, a December 9 Beijing student leader
in 1935 (and PRC foreign minister in the 1970s).[23]

The Special Congress of the Guomindang opened four days later, on
March 29, with a major speech by Chiang Kaishek in which he emphasized the need for unity of purpose and organization of youth in the war
effort. The educational policies that the Congress endorsed were conservative and represented a victory for Chen Lifu. Reforms were to be along
traditional lines, and participants offered only vague principles for changing the existing system.[24] In the area of youth mobilization, however, the
Congress showed some responsiveness to pressures from the All China Student Conference of a few days earlier. After General Chen Cheng reported

to the Congress that in touring battle zones he found that the Guomindang was seen as having "no sacrificial spirit and being no longer revolutionary," plans were set in motion for his Military Council to bring all existing youth and student groups into a single organization, to be called the Three Peoples Principles Youth Corps *(sanmin zhuyi qingniantuan)* or Sanqing.[25]

Chiang Kaishek intended to use the Sanqing to neutralize internal factional fighting that had gripped the Guomindang party since the early 1930s, and he wanted it to become the chief vehicle for party recruitment in the future. The Congress passed a constitutional amendment with a clause that positioned the Youth Corps as a replacement for the two-tier party membership system that had been functioning since 1929.[26] Thus Chiang's two motives for establishing the Sanqing were clear: to reinvigorate the Guomindang party by breaking down its clique structure and to co-opt or blunt the youth-organizing efforts of the Communists and others on the left.

The Sanqing Youth Corps was formally launched in June 1938 in a message from Chiang Kaishek in which he described youth as "new corpuscles" *(xin xibao)* for the reinvigoration of the antiwar effort. He studiously avoided mention of the Guomindang directly, emphasizing again the open, inclusive nature of the Youth Corps as a national organization.[27] General Chen Cheng was the first secretary-general of the corps, and the group's organizational principles were left purposely vague, a formula that seemed to work well at first. The Youth Corps grew rapidly as a nationwide organization, enrolling over one hundred thousand members by the fall of 1938.

The overnight success in enrollment was deceptive. A large portion of the new membership came from preexisting groups that merged with Sanqing, as Chiang Kaishek had asked. Although most groups did so voluntarily, some small groups felt coerced.[28] Furthermore, many recruits to Sanqing were hardly aspiring "youth." Leadership positions often went to veteran Guomindang party members like Kang Ze, who were exempt from the age restriction of thirty-eight; indeed, loose application of the restriction was common for ordinary membership as well. Thus when Chiang Kaishek spoke of "new corpuscles," he was really speaking of bringing new life to the party faithful. The creation of the Sanqing had more to do with party rebuilding than it did with controlling student activism, as some historians have asserted.[29]

Using the Sanqing Youth Corps as a vehicle for reinvigorating the party seemed to work at first.[30] Chen Lifu and other Guomindang party leaders fell in step, declaring an end to factionalism. Chen and his brother called a meeting of the CC Clique in April and publicly dissolved its organizational structure. The rival Whampoa (Huangpu) Clique took similar actions in June. But the cease-fire in factional politics lasted only as long as Wuhan did. By the end of 1939 competition between cliques had returned in Chongqing and was as ruthless as ever. The major struggle was between the Youth Corps run by Kang Ze and the Whampoa Clique in an alliance with the secret police headed by Dai Li. Attention to youth recruitment and the provision of services for students was at a minimum, even during the Youth Corps' first year. Thus, despite the creation of the Sanqing Youth Corps in the spring of 1938, the Guomindang never genuinely committed itself to mobilizing youth into a mass movement.

THE CHINESE COMMUNIST PARTY RESPONSE

Perhaps more surprisingly, through the summer of 1938 the Communist Party at Wuhan was as ineffective as the Guomindang in mobilizing students; it seemed almost reluctant to organize them in any overt way. The leaders Zhou Enlai, Wang Ming, and Bo Gu had come from Yan'an in January of 1938 chiefly to establish the central Yangzi branch of the party, to start a Communist daily newspaper *(Xinhua ribao),* and to participate in the United Front military government. In implementing the United Front line, Wang Ming and the Communist leadership in Wuhan bent over backward to accommodate Guomindang positions, as did Moscow, in part because at this time the Soviet Union was the only foreign power giving Chiang Kaishek significant aid: one hundred planes and pilots for the defense of Wuhan.[31] The party was active in United Front propaganda (Guo Moruo), foreign relations and political work (Zhou Enlai), and publicity (Bo Gu ran *Xinhua ribao).* Wang Ming and Dong Biwu tended to the inner workings of the party (overall, Wang Ming was the most senior figure, with authority equal to that of Mao Zedong in Yan'an).[32] Indicative of the party's accommodating spirit was the resolution of a dispute about what song to sing at a large May Day (May 1) rally in Hankou. Instead of the Communist "International" or the Guomindang Three People's Principles anthem, planners found a compromise in a newly minted marching song, "Defend Madrid."[33]

In retrospect, one can see that the Chinese Communist Party was slow to take the lead in organizing the floating student-refugee population. Huang Hua and Li Chang, two prominent student organizers from Beijing and Xi'an who were connected to the party, did not arrive in Wuhan until March and June respectively—just as student and youth groups were dissolving and joining the Sanqing Youth Corps. Huang and Li seemed relatively ineffective at organizing youth during the summer and fall.[34]

At a big rally on the Wuhan University campus in late May welcoming a young delegation from the World Youth Congress, Wang Ming stressed unity with Chen Cheng, Kang Ze, and others with whom he shared the podium. He asked Communist-led student groups to acquiesce and join the Sanqing. A few left-oriented student groups with longer organizational histories—notably the Yishe [literally, "ants"], made up of Shanghai students; the Youth National Salvation Corps *(qingnian jiuguo tuan);* and the Wuhan branch of the National Liberation Vanguard *(minzu jiefang xianfengdui)*—initially resisted incorporation into the Sanqing Youth Corps. But in August the government disbanded and officially outlawed these groups as well, again with little protest from the Communist side. At a large, officially organized demonstration at Hankou in August, Wang Ming and Zhou Enlai joined Chen Cheng and Wang Jingwei in speaking. Again the emphasis in "Defending Wuhan to the Death" was on unity and on connections to the battle for Madrid.[35] Foreign observers were shocked by the reluctance of radical youth to criticize the government and its repressive tactics. Freda Utley wrote: "The same timidity and fear of splitting the 'united front' was evidenced by the youth organizations. These young men and women I talked to were the leaders of the semi-Communist 'ANTS,' which had just been suppressed (mid-August), but were carrying on in spite of the suppression in hope that they would in time 'win the confidence' of the Government. The Government, they said, has suppressed them on account of a 'misunderstanding.' They believed, or professed to believe, that the Government 'wants a mass movement to defend Wuhan.'"[36]

One reason for the Chinese Communist Party's inattention to student recruitment, besides its participation in the People's Political Council, was its obsession with the "problem" of heterodox Communists (mostly Trotskyites) and the renegade former party leaders Chen Duxiu and Zhang Guotao, whom the leadership desperately wanted to muzzle. Both Chen and Zhang, as we saw in chapter 5, had arrived in Wuhan in the spring of 1938 (Chen from a Guomindang prison and Zhang from Yan'an), and within weeks of each other had published separate denunciations of the Communists, much to the delight of Guomindang loyalists. Among the party leaders most obsessed with Chen Duxiu, Zhang Guotao, and Trotskyites were Wang Ming and Kang Sheng (in Yan'an), both recent arrivals from Moscow, where Stalin was in the final stages of consolidating his power with show trials and purges.[37]

At about the same time, however, the Communists were mobilizing youth in rural areas like southern Henan, Xi'an in the northwest, and Guiyang in the southwest. Moreover, and very important in the long run, during 1938 individual student refugees and other young people—like young journalists Hu Sheng and Ge Baoquan and the artist Yu Feng—were joining the party in Wuhan by the thousands.[38]

The irony of ironies was that the party was recruiting new members almost without trying, without a concerted organizational effort. More educated persons joined the Communist movement in 1938 than at any other time before 1949. The key to attracting this group of young people to the party was the soft sell, and many more students later made the pilgrimage to the party's guerrilla headquarters at Yan'an, because of the propaganda campaigns that big-name intellectuals like Guo Moruo, Tian Han, Mao Dun, and Lao She (see chapter 5) were organizing under the United Front banner. The young people were eager to be mobilized and contribute to the war effort, and these propaganda operations brought them into contact with senior Communist-oriented intellectuals. Thus the Communist Party's United Front commitment at Wuhan certainly bore fruit, in important if unexpected ways.[39]

Youth and students were the heart of the "defend Wuhan" spirit—manning the refugee shelters and health clinics; performing and writing patriotic plays, poetry, and songs; and making weekly marches and putting up fresh wall posters daily. They needed no prodding or direction from Guomindang or Chinese Communist Party apparatchiks. They fully believed their own propaganda: Wuhan was linked to Madrid in a global fight against imperialism, a term that was now interchangeable with fascism; and in this heroic struggle, which would change the course of Chinese history, they saw themselves playing a key role. The students had an innocence about them—a naiveté about political realities. But this idealistic spirit was what motivated educated youth to join the Communist Party, whose promise they believed was articulated in publications like the *Xinhua ribao* rather than in the party's leadership or recruitment efforts.*

Caught up in opposition to this trend was Chen Lifu, the minister of education. By the late summer of 1938, while preparing for the retreat to Chongqing, he worried about the leftist seduction of youth. He saw Wuhan as a historic turning point, an opportunity to reorganize and re-

---

* The road ahead was not smooth. Many of the young intellectuals who joined the party in 1938 became vulnerable, labeled "rightists" later because of their middle-class family backgrounds, and thus targets of party purges in the 1950s and 1960s.

structure Chinese society, politics, and culture around traditional, authoritarian Neo-Confucian principles. Otherwise, the Communists would take advantage of the situation, exploit the patriotic zeal of the people, and establish a Moscow-controlled dictatorship—and install probably the bloodiest and most draconian regime in Chinese history. For Chen the key to preventing this outcome was to preserve and reinvigorate the education system, as well as the Guomindang party.

By September 1938 the writing was on the wall. At the end of the month, the Japanese broke through at Tianjiazhen and Xinyang and began to move more rapidly up the Yangzi toward Wuhan as well as overland down the Beijing-Hankou railway from the northeast. Bombing raids were increasingly heavy. Half the population of Wuhan, it seemed, had been evacuated. Yet the rallies and the rhetoric continued.[40] Leaders on the left and the right, from Zhou Enlai to Chen Cheng, as well as Chiang Kaishek himself, remained in Wuhan to the last day. In part, the heavy bombing had strengthened their commitment to resistance. But more complex forces were at work as well. The Wuhan experience had changed China's collective consciousness—reshaped politics, society, and culture. Change was in the air, captured by poets like Wang Tongchao:

> A country four thousand years old has a life undying:
> The winding Yellow River, the fertile Yangzi River, so many miles of land,
> So much riches, and so many historic heroes.
> Their ancestors have left clear milestones on this land,
> And never have they halted in their march, not even in severe storms.
> As we came from the north, we saw all these milestones,
> Now, the brave ones shout aloud the angry cries of an all-consuming war.
> China! Once again this poignant word comes alive, throbbing,
> Irresistibly plucking the chord of everyone's heart.
> What matters if the devil plays tricks,
> What matters if we bend under the strain,
> For this word—China—we have our mission.
> Can you resent us, though we are a gust of stench in the wind?
> You can resent us, but not avoid us, like a stench gusting in the wind![41]

SEVEN

ROMANTIC HANKOU:
THE INTERNATIONAL DIMENSION

THE YEAR OF 1938 WAS pivotal internationally—a time when most of the news in the Western press was ominously grim: the failing defense and factional infighting at Madrid, concessions to Hitler by the major powers at Munich, and Stalin's bloody purge of Soviet leaders and intellectuals. For this reason perhaps, the heroics of the defense of Wuhan seemed to sparkle by contrast, attracting more attention from Western governments and press than the occupation of Manchuria in 1931 or the Marco Polo Bridge incident of 1937. No tribute was more eloquent than the poetry and prose sent home by two of the West's most important writers, the poet W. H. Auden and the playwright Christopher Isherwood, who arrived in the spring of 1938 to bear witness to the unfolding drama. Here is their diary entry for March 8:

> Today Auden and I agreed that we would rather be in Hankow at this moment than anywhere else on earth. Stark and blank along the northern shore, the buildings of the old treaty port present their European facades to the winter river . . . There are consulates, warehouses, offices, and banks; British and American drug-stores, cinemas, churches, clubs; there is a good lending library, a Y.M.C.A., a red-light street of cafes—Mary's, the Navy Bar, The Last Chance. Around all this the Chinese city stretches for miles, a warren of ramshackle, congested streets, out to the race- track, the air-field, and the snow covered Hu-Peh plains. . . .
>
> This is the real capital of wartime China. All kinds of people live in this town—Chiang Kaishek, Agnes Smedley, Chou Enlai; generals, ambassa-

dors, journalists, foreign naval officers, soldiers of fortune, airmen, missionaries, spies. Hidden here are all the clues which would enable an expert, if
he could only find them, to predict the events of the next fifty years. History,
grown weary of Shanghai, bored with Barcelona, has fixed her capricious
interest upon Hankow. But where is she staying? Everybody boasts that he
has met her, but where nobody can exactly say. Shall we find her at the big
hotel, drinking whiskey with the journalists at the bar? Is she the guest of
the Generalissimo, or the Soviet Ambassador? Does she prefer the headquarters of the Eighth Route Army, or the German military advisers? Is
she content with a rickshaw coolie's hut?[1]

When the Chinese generals gathered in Wuchang in mid-January 1938
to decide the fate of General Han Fuju, public opinion in the West had
written off the war in China as a lost cause. Western diplomats and correspondents were impressed by the speed with which the Japanese army
had swallowed up China's coastal provinces. And despite strong Chinese
resistance around Shanghai and elsewhere, they tended to accept the
Japanese view that China's remaining defenders were demoralized and
disorganized. Thus, after the fall of Nanjing in December, most foreign
military observers and diplomats expected the surrender of Wuhan to
come within a month or two.[2] They knew that Chiang Kaishek had sent
representatives to carry on talks in Hong Kong with the Japanese through
intermediaries, including German diplomats. Militarily speaking, besides
having the advantages of overwhelming firepower, the Japanese generals were seen in the West as superior to the Chinese in training and ability to coordinate troops. The survival of a single military command structure on the Chinese side—one that could hold a unified strategic vision
or even coordinate tactically—was seen as highly unlikely, given the country's fractious political history. And, finally, the troops who were left to
face the Japanese at Wuhan were considered inferior and untried.[3]

Furthermore, most people believed that little love was lost between
Chiang Kaishek and his generals in the field (as well as among the generals). After all, regional commanders had kidnapped Chiang in December
1936 and forced him to go to war against the Japanese. In addition, the
conflict between Chiang and the Communist forces to the northwest was
available for the Japanese to exploit. ("The Communists are a disease of
the heart—the Japanese a disease of the skin" was a well-known Chiang
quote.) Finally, many agreed with the *New York Times* bureau chief, Hallett Abend, and the Associated Press bureau chief in Tokyo, Miles
Vaughn, who thought Japanese domination of the northeast could lead

ultimately to the modernization of the country as a whole and produce a more stable political environment for foreign investment.[4]

However, by the time Wuhan fell ten months later, in October 1938, Western correspondents and government observers (military and otherwise) were much more optimistic about China's chances to prolong the war. In retrospect, this reversal of international opinion was critically important. It raised the morale of the Chinese military at a crucial point and served to seriously isolate the Japanese internationally. It also seemed to hold out the promise that significant military aid might soon arrive from the West. And in fact, by the winter of 1938–39, President Roosevelt began to promise aid and approved Washington's first loans, although significant Western aid to the beleaguered Chinese military would not come until after the bombing of Pearl Harbor in December 1941.

What happened in Wuhan in 1938 to shift international opinion so sharply? The objective realities in the field, one could argue, remained rather negative for China throughout the year. Month after month the Japanese ground out victories as the Chinese sustained huge casualties; and of course Wuhan did finally fall to the Japanese in late October. The situation became so dire that major figures on the civilian side, led by the Guomindang's general secretary, Wang Jingwei, decided in late 1938 to negotiate the establishment of a puppet regime in Shanghai under the supervision of the Japanese military. So what can account for the optimistic turn in foreign opinion about the course of the war in 1938? As we can now see, the shift was in part serendipitous—a fortunate confluence of people and events—and in part the result of brilliant propaganda work by the Chinese.

AGENTS OF CHANGE

A new breed of Western correspondents arrived in Wuhan during the spring of 1938 to report on the war. Like many of the Chinese refugee intellectuals around them, these men and women had migrated to the wartime capital from more comfortable bases in Shanghai and Beijing. More important, they also were a larger, more sophisticated, and younger group than those reporting earlier from Nanjing, Shanghai, and Beijing. And the influence of the "old China hands" who had been reporting from Beijing and Shanghai since the 1920s (and before)—Reginald Johnston, G. E. Morrison, Thomas Millard, and Hallett Abend—was fading. In fact, no members of the old guard were present at Wuhan.[5]

In the new group were adventurous young men and women who were willing to live modestly and dangerously, braving the regular bombing raids over Wuhan and later over Guilin, Kunming, and Chongqing. Many of the people writing in English—Edgar Snow, George Taylor, Jack Belden, A. T. Steele, Mac Fisher, Michael Lindsay, Harold Timperley, Freda Utley, Agnes Smedley, and Tilman Durdin—were refugees from the Great Depression. They came to China as freelance journalists and then worked their way into full-time positions as agency and newspaper correspondents. In Wuhan they worked with a handful of more experienced war correspondents fresh from the Spanish Civil War, a group that included the famous Hungarian-born photojournalist Robert Capa and the Russian V. Rogov. A few, like Peggy Durdin and Maurice Votaw, had come from missionary backgrounds and had some facility with spoken Chinese. The distinctive feature of these journalists was their youth: all were in their thirties or younger.

Finally, the drama of the battle for central China attracted several major literary figures from the West. W. H. Auden and Christopher Isherwood toured both occupied and free China in the spring of 1938; together they produced a book of prose and poetry entitled *Journey to a War*, which was widely reviewed and noted in literary circles around the English-speaking world. The biggest foreign celebrity at Wuhan—and the most senior—was the Danish film director Joris Ivens, who arrived to much fanfare in the Chinese press in early March. Already famous for *Spanish Earth*, a film he made with Hemingway about the Spanish Civil War, he flew in from Hong Kong along with the photojournalist Robert Capa and a Dutch cameraman, John Fernhout.[6]

China suddenly had a high profile, with the international jet set (before jets) rushing to Wuhan to write or film the nation's heroic defense. The visitors were welcomed by the Chinese head of the information ministry, Hollington Tong, who was smart enough to place few restrictions on the international press, encourage interviews with high officials, and organize trips to the front. The result was salutary: a stream of in-depth and firsthand reporting that was increasingly sympathetic to the Chinese cause.[7]

Among the foreign visitors to Hankou, the young journalists were the most active. They showed up everywhere—covering demonstrations, bombing raids, and refugee-relief stations; and interviewing Madame Chiang, Zhou Enlai, and the man in the street.

Members of the diplomatic corps, by contrast, rarely ventured out from their compounds. A few clung to the primary concern of the 1920s and early 1930s, which was protecting foreign treaty-port rights as much as possible. And being by training more keenly aware of how domestic politics and international commitments were affecting their home governments, they tried harder than the journalists to stay neutral in their cables about the course of the war. The American ambassador, Nelson Johnson, was from this old school, as was his boss in Washington, Stanley Hornbeck (special adviser to the secretary of state for political relations in the Far East). Despite some optimistic assessments by junior officers, both men remained skeptical about China's chances of prolonging the war.

The British were not particularly popular in Wuhan. For one thing, the British ambassador, Archibald Clark Kerr, a Scotsman and seasoned diplomat, spent more time in Hong Kong with his beautiful new Argentinean wife than he did in Wuhan or later in Chongqing. More significant, the British had an alliance with the Japanese that dated back to 1902, and they seemed to be honoring it: in April 1938 London permitted Chinese customs receipts from Shanghai and elsewhere to be held in a Japanese bank under a complicated agreement that the Chinese saw as an act of betrayal.

The Germans were a special case. Formerly the leading military advisers to Chiang Kaishek, they kept a large military and diplomatic presence in Wuhan until the summer of 1938. Allied with the Japanese through the Anti-Comintern Pact, they had been trying to persuade the Chinese to accept peace terms through the good offices of Ambassador Oskar P. Trautmann—terms that were completely unacceptable to the Chinese.[8] In other words, both the British and German policies toward China at the time were complicated by alliances with the Japanese. In 1938 both nations actively sought to facilitate peace negotiations to end the war (through intermediaries in Hong Kong, Hanoi, and other places).[9]

In the provision of aid and moral support, the Wuhan government's strongest ally in 1938 was the Soviet Union. Stalin was worried about the Anti-Comintern Pact (signed by Germany, Italy, and Japan) and wanted to see the Japanese tied down in China. The Soviets signed a nonaggression pact with China, involving a secret clause that promised military aid, on August 21, 1937, in Moscow. But in subsequent months, as border tensions in Manchuria between Japan and the Soviet Union grew, increasing amounts of Soviet materiel and technical aid began arriving in China. By the summer of 1938, the Chinese switch from German to Soviet aid (with credits to finance it) was visible. On July 5, 1938, Robert Capa photographed the German military-aid mission as it pulled out of Wuchang in special train cars clearly marked with swastikas on their roofs to alert Japanese bomber pilots. A few months earlier, twenty-seven Russian officers, under Lieutenant General A. I. Cherepanov (an adviser and teacher at Chiang's Huang Pu or Whampoa Academy in 1924–27) had arrived to replace the Germans as military advisers.[10] The Russian focus was technical: how to use the tanks and artillery that the Soviets were bringing in over a long, tortuous route through Lanzhou. More important and visible were Russian volunteer pilots in more than two hundred Soviet fighter planes. Almost every day in August, crowds came out into the streets to watch Russian and Chinese pilots in Soviet- or American-made planes duel in dogfights with the Japanese Zeros that were guarding bombing squadrons. Dozens of Russian pilots were shot down; their sacrifice was memorialized elaborately at the time and is still remembered today.[11]

Moreover, along with planes, advisers, and a new ambassador came seven correspondents from the Tass news agency to cover the war. Heading the group was an old China hand, V. Rogov, who was well-known and appreciated in the international community as a source of information and good contacts. Drawing on reports from his six correspondents, who were following Soviet advisers in the field, and on previous connections with the Nanjing government, Rogov traded information with the younger Western journalists as they streamed into Wuhan.

The Soviet replacement of the Germans as lead advisers to the Chinese military was a major change from the Nanjing period (1929–37). More than the Germans before them, twenty-seven military advisers and seven Tass agency correspondents were gathering intelligence on the Japanese and Chinese military that went straight back to Moscow. Chiang Kaishek understood this fact, which explains why he gave the Soviets limited advisory access at a high level. The Soviets used intelligence on the Japanese military in central China to defeat Japanese divisions in the famous battle at Nomonhan (Mongolia) in 1939. Stalin also received reports on the military situation in China from a Japanese perspective through Richard Sorge and Osaki Hotsumi in Tokyo.

Another significant difference was in the new crop of young military attachés who were dispatched to Wuhan in 1938 to act as special observers and advisers to Western governments. These young officers were launching their careers in China and were eager to have an impact on policy back home. The level of violence and destruction they witnessed in the field made them increasingly frustrated with their home countries' lack of preparedness for this obviously looming world war in Europe and Asia.

The most numerous group of observers were Americans—notably
Evans Carlson (U.S. Marines), Joseph Stilwell and his assistant David
Barrett (U.S. Army), Frank Dorn (also U.S. Army), and Claire Chennault
(U.S. Air Force). The French received well-crafted reports from Beijing
by Jacques Guillermaz, a young military attaché who, after his assistant
died of malaria in Wuhan, had to rely on reports passed on from the Americans, Carlson in particular.[12] Also present was a well-informed Dutch
observer, Henri de Fremery, who was especially close to Chiang Kaishek's
chief of staff, He Yingqin.[13] None of these young officers had the experience or perspective of A. I. Cherepanov, the leader of the Soviet mission,
but their energy and hard work produced results. The detailed reports they
sent home still serve historians as useful third-party sources on the battle
of Wuhan.[14] In general—aside from the Germans—the young military attachés worked together, across national lines, sharing reports on battles
and troop movements. They had a common mission: to convince their su-
periors in Europe and North America of the strategic importance of the
China theater. They argued that the Japanese, in their sweeping use of air
power followed by highly mobile assaults on the ground, were making
China a laboratory for working out the future of modern warfare—a process that called for careful and detailed reporting.

Indeed, the reports of these military observers clearly had an impact
on policy in Washington, London, Moscow, and Paris; historians have
argued that their dispatches often had greater influence on policy than
did cables from ambassadors. Most of Evans Carlson's reports, for example, went directly to President Roosevelt (whom he had once served
as a personal guard). After receiving Carlson's long personal account
of the Chinese victory at Taierzhuang, Roosevelt opened a dialogue with
the State Department and his secretary of the treasury, Henry Morgenthau, about how best to aid the Chinese cause.[15] In their deliberations
about China policy throughout the rest of the summer, these men continued to refer regularly to dispatches from Carlson, Stilwell, and others. Historian Sun Youli has shown conclusively that these reports provided a rationale for the beginning of the U.S. lend-lease aid program for
China.[16] One could argue similarly, although with less documentation,
for the influence on Stalin of Cherepanov and Ambassador Smirnov (who
was also a military figure) as well as for the impact of the secret radio
messages from Richard Sorge in Tokyo.

Moreover, the young journalists and military officers had considerable social and professional interaction. Jack Belden and Joseph Stilwell,
for example, worked closely together, sharing and quoting each other's

dispatches about battles. And this group of young journalists, diplomats, and military officers—who called themselves the "Last Ditchers"—would gather weekly for dinner at a round table on the second floor of a local restaurant, Rosie's, in the old concession area of Hankou. Together, during the steamy summer of 1938, they celebrated with food and drink the coming of new arrivals and the departure of old friends while they waited for (and placed bets on) the fall of Wuhan.[17] One of the regulars, Tilman Durdin of the *New York Times,* had this recollection: "Very pervasive at Hankou was close collaboration and friendship between correspondents and American officials. I have mentioned Stilwell, but John Davies was also in the consulate at the time. He and others were eager to get information we had and vice versa. . . . At the time we felt we were all in this together and in the right. China, after all, was being invaded and brutalized by the Japanese, and we had deep sympathy for the Chinese side. This created a spirit of mutual sympathy and cooperation among us."[18]

CHINESE PROPAGANDA

The behind-the-scene details of the makings of the international success of Chinese propaganda management in 1938 are available today in the No.2 Archives in Nanjing, housed in the dusty corners of a once-grand 1930s-era government building. The effort to control and manage news about the Chinese war effort was largely the work of the Nationalist government's Ministry of Information *(xuanchuan bu)* and its remarkable vice minister, Hollington Tong. The story of this effort is an interesting one.

Hollington Tong (Dong Xianguang), whom we met in chapter 5, and Chiang Kaishek were both from Zhejiang Province, where they knew each other as young men in Ningbo. By the 1930s, after years abroad, Dong was back in Shanghai and had forged a close association with the Guomindang party. He was the managing editor of the party's principal English-language paper, the *China Press* of Shanghai, owned by H. H. Kong (Kong Xiangxi) and others. Among the fledgling foreign journalists he hired to work on the paper was a future correspondent for the *New York Times,* Tilman Durdin, as well as Harold Isaacs (later with *Newsweek)* and Harold Timperley (later with the *Manchester Guardian).* Durdin once described Tong as "without official stuffiness or arrogance"—high praise for a government official. His knowledge of Western reporting methods and preferences, his personal rapport with the Generalissimo and Mme. Chiang Kaishek, and his contacts in the United States and Britain made him the obvious choice to oversee and shape the government's message for the foreign press corps that was gathering at Wuhan.[19]

In a series of written exchanges between Tong and Chiang Kaishek during the spring of 1938, the archival record makes clear that the two men made a conscious decision to let the story of China's heroic struggle against the Japanese seem to tell itself—for maximum impact, through the voices of foreign reporters and missionaries. The government's role in Wuhan and abroad was simply to facilitate the telling of it from behind the scenes. In this effort, the Chinese devoted the most attention to the United States. This drive to tell the Chinese story was the origin in New York and Washington of the famous China Lobby, as it became known in the late 1940s. In March 1938, a New York office of the Xuanchuan Bu opened under the name of Chinese News Service. A former Associated Press reporter, Earl Leaf, along with a colleague from Shanghai, Maurice Votaw, and returned missionaries Frank Price and George Fitch, led the U.S.-based bureau. Its operating budget came from the Chinese government, and its purpose was to disseminate positive stories about China in the U.S. press—regional as well as national.

Receiving special emphasis at the time were stories by Western journalists about the atrocities being committed by the Japanese. The Nationalist government financed the publication of *Manchester Guardian* reporter Harold Timperley's influential book about the massacre at Nanjing. But Tong wanted to get out a larger message than one of China's victimhood. The Chinese were fighting back, and the victory at Taierzhuang was worthy of celebration. The Chinese News Service in New York and its small branch in London, run by Timperley, publicized the government's massive effort to move factories and schools upriver from Wuhan to Chongqing as part of a new strategy of protracted war.[20] And in June 1938, when the Japanese appeared poised to buy arms from the Du Pont Corporation, Hollington Tong and Earl Leaf organized a sizable publicity campaign to expose the deal.[21]

Another part of the strategy was to give the foreign correspondents in Wuhan freedom to go wherever they wished and to talk to anyone they chose. Chinese officials made little effort to censor the reports that writers wired to foreign newspapers and governments. Thus, for the most part, representatives of the international press and foreign military observers enjoyed relatively unrestricted movement and good access to leaders in Wuhan, including Communists and their allies among the intellectuals.*

With the United Front at its height, both the Guomindang and the Communists seemed to bend over backward to hide their differences from foreign eyes and ears. The Communists especially seemed eager to cooperate and to work through Guomindang operatives like Hollington Tong. At Wuhan they were content to limit their organized international propaganda effort to interviews with Zhou Enlai, Wang Ming, or Bo Gu. *Xinhua ribao,* the Communist daily (and later the name of the news agency), began publication in Wuhan under the United Front banner. The Communists made no effort to publish or promote their own foreign-language publications. Most effective in the long run, however, was the considerable contact that foreign journalists had with Communist-leaning writers, playwrights, and journalists: Mao Dun, Liu Zunqi, Xiao Qian, Guo Moruo, Lao She, Shi Liang, Hu Sheng, Qian Junrui, Ge Baoquan, Zou Taofen, Zhang Hanfu, and many others. Of considerable help in this regard were leftist members of the Western press corps who were sympathetic to the Communists; Agnes Smedley and the "Red Bishop," Logan Roots, were especially active in facilitating interviews and contact.

The year 1938 also saw the publication of Edgar Snow's *Red Star Over China,* the first personal account by a Western journalist of the Chinese Communists and the Eighth Route Army from a visit to their headquarters near Yan'an. Snow's straightforward reporting and lack of ideological bias was convincing; *Red Star* was translated into Chinese almost immediately and gave a tremendous boost to the image of the Communists, domestically and internationally. Snow himself passed through Wuhan during the summer of 1938, and, as if to balance his portrait of the Communists, he dashed off an influential article, "China's Fighting Generalissimo (Chiang Kaishek)," for *Foreign Affairs.* Echoing *Time* magazine's logic in choosing Chiang as Man of the Year (1937), Snow portrayed the humorless Generalissimo as nonetheless the right leader for China at the time: "Chiang Kaishek is more than ever the focal point. Objective circumstances under which men act can change the character and significance of their role. Chiang's role is as fluid as Chinese society; no more reactionary and no more progressive than the sum total of forces. The objective conditions which are the instrument of Chiang's fate to-

* Overt control of foreign news came later (after 1940) with the organization of news conferences, the establishment of an international press hostel, and heavy government censorship of foreign wire stories by the Nationalist government in Chongqing.

day are relatively dynamic and progressive, and it is because he continues to reflect their nature that his leadership remains secure."[22]

Snow's roommate that summer was the New Zealand social worker Rewi Alley. Alley, a former factory inspector for the British Concession in Shanghai, was absorbed in a new government-backed effort to industrialize the Chinese countryside in support of the war effort. The Chinese Industrial Cooperative Movement, or Indusco (also known as the Gongho or Gonghe movement), was established with much fanfare in August 1938 to develop and fund small industrial enterprises in northwestern and southwestern China.. The central government supplied a small budget to the organization but expected Indusco to raise the rest of its funding abroad. Hence the fanfare that surrounded the establishment of industrial co-ops set rather extravagant goals for industrializing the hinterland and fortifying resistance to the Japanese. The Indusco program pitched itself internationally as the engine for bringing a kind of New Deal in light industry to the Chinese countryside. The idealism of the project was seductive, and for the first few years, 1938–41, funds flowed in and the movement spread rapidly in nonoccupied areas of the northwest and southwest.

The idea for the organization—as a kind of microfinance program for the rural poor—apparently originated with Alley and Kong Xiangxi (HH Kong), the head of the Executive Yuan and later finance minister, who also was one of the Generalissimo's brothers-in-law. Kong's steadfast support was the key to the success of cooperatives in the early years. The Indusco movement put an idealistic emphasis on self-reliance, which was the aspect of the program that initially attracted the strong endorsement and financial support of Kong's sometime rival Weng Wenhao, the dynamic minister in charge of rebuilding the industrial infrastructure for war in the hinterland after the fall of Nanjing and Shanghai. In the first few months of Indusco's existence in 1938, it established three industrial cooperative bases to oversee hundreds of projects that were up and running in the northwest (Gansu), southwest (around Chongqing), and around Hengyang in Hunan Province.[23]

From the beginning, the orientation of the Indusco organization was international. By the end of 1938 Indusco had opened offices in Hong Kong and New York to raise money and generate publicity. It established an international board that combined overseas Chinese engineers and scholars with foreign journalists and philanthropists. The movement attracted the support of Henry Luce, the publisher of *Time* and *Life*, and received considerable attention in the U.S. and British media. Rewi Alley and others, such as Ida Pruitt and Helen F. Snow (Edgar's estranged wife), spent the war years speaking and churning out promotional pamphlets for distribution all over the world. By the war's end, the Indusco movement had made Rewi Alley an international celebrity of sorts, and he became probably the most famous of the "old China hands" still residing in the country.[24]

Through three changes of leadership at the Ministry of Information, Vice Minister Hollington Tong kept a firm hand on the government's domestic and international propaganda efforts, including publicity for the launch of the Indusco program. In Wuhan itself, besides conducting press conferences and making speeches, the Nationalist government mostly focused its international propaganda effort on organizing large mass rallies in support of victories on the battlefield and mobilization of the citizenry. At these rallies, Tong often used the resident international community for domestic propaganda purposes: he gave foreign officials and journalists prominence of place and often asked them to speak to the assembled crowds. For example, the British journalist Freda Utley, who had just published a book condemning Japan, frequently received invitations to speak to crowds for the purpose of convincing the Chinese public that international support for the Japanese was shrinking.

For the same morale-boosting reasons, the government was eager to publicize international efforts at medical relief—most prominently the contribution of overseas Chinese supervised by the Health Ministry's Dr. Robert K. Lin (Lin Kesheng).[25] Again, the Chinese made effective use of foreigners at rallies. Fifteen years later a YMCA worker named Liu Liangmo recalled hearing the American journalist Agnes Smedley speak at a large fund-raising event organized by Dr. Lin in Changsha: "Smedley spoke quietly at first about victories over the Japanese. Then, her voice rising gradually to a passionate intensity which seemed to transform her physically, she described the desperate needs of the Chinese wounded, ending with a dramatic appeal for funds. She sat down abruptly, exhausted, and there was a long silence. Then the crowd stirred and began donating money, in large amounts. . . . It was the most successful fund-raising event of the year."[26]

Hollington Tong and his staff often carefully choreographed special events involving foreigners. For example, in June 1938 an international youth delegation, made up mostly of European and North American antifascist youth leaders, visited Wuhan. The government's top leaders (Communist and Nationalist) attended the rallies that planners had organized to welcome the delegation. The anti-Japanese rhetoric of the visitors, and the connecting of the sieges of Madrid and Wuhan as part of a global anti-Fascist struggle, received wide coverage in the domestic press (even though the international press corps largely ignored the story).[27] The key aspect of the Chinese effort to manage international propaganda in 1938 was Hollington Tong's deliberately indirect approach: the very absence of controls and overt propaganda campaigns aimed at foreigners were the elements that made the program so effective. Because international correspondents' reporting was relatively uncensored by the Chinese government, they believed that they were choosing the stories and could write as they saw fit. As a result, the foreign press became genuinely enthusiastic about and sympathetic to the justice of the Chinese cause and gave enthusiastic support to calls for sanctions against the Japanese. Relatively few negative stories about government corruption or mismanagement appeared in the Western papers in 1938. Even Edgar Snow praised Chiang Kaishek. Nor did correspondents report much on political differences or struggles between the Communists and the Guomindang. Ironically, the avoidance of heavy-handed control of propaganda in 1938 produced the largest propaganda victory of the war for the Nationalist government.

WUHAN AS PARADOX: UNINTENDED INTERNATIONAL CONSEQUENCES

The fall of Xuzhou in May 1938, the rout at Madang on the Yangzi, and the breaking of the dikes and flooding of the Yellow River at Huayuankou in June were also reported in diplomatic dispatches and the Western press. But these negative developments did not provoke a return to pessimism about China's chances in the war. Negotiations for a major U.S. loan to the Chinese government for the purchase of armaments had already begun in July 1938. At the time, the Western press widely reported that Chiang Kaishek had flatly refused Japanese "peace" overtures despite meditation efforts by the Germans and others. Thus, when Canton and Wuhan fell in October 1938, and shortly thereafter Wang Jingwei defected and accepted separate "peace terms" from the Japanese, Western opinion about China remained positive. Despite China's battlefield defeats, foreign military observers predicted that the Chinese might ultimately prevail with their strategy of prolonging the war.[28] In the Western press, the orderly nature of the retreat to Chongqing in October and November of 1938 received as much attention as the military defeats. In Washington, Roosevelt and Morgenthau responded to the fall of Wuhan by finalizing in December the first $25 million commodity loan to China, marking the beginning of direct U.S. aid to the Chinese war effort. (The Soviets had supplied $100 million in credits earlier but abruptly terminated them in 1939). Certainly a fear of Japanese hegemony in East Asia influenced the U.S. decision, but growing public support for China in the West was also a key factor.

Put another way, the outcome of the ten-month battle for Wuhan in 1938 was paradoxical: by losing battles, the Chinese gained political strength. The Chinese lost Wuhan after a long siege, but the resistance effort boosted morale and turned international opinion against Japan. This result still befuddles Japanese historians, just as it did Japanese generals at the time.[29]

Before long, however, the international propaganda victories of 1938 raised unrealistic expectations in both China and the West. After 1938–39 the Chinese public (as well as Chiang Kaishek) began to expect an outpouring of Western aid in amounts that never materialized. As for public opinion in Western countries, it too became disillusioned with the Chinese war effort, as reports accumulated about corruption, Guomindang-Communist disunity, poor military leadership, and lack of progress against the Japanese.[30]

CONCLUSION

ON NOVEMBER 25, 1938, Chiang Kaishek convened a major military conference at Hengyang (on the railway line south of Changsha). The meeting was comparable to the one at Wuchang the previous January, at which top field commanders met for serious planning and strategizing, but this time Chiang acted with less bravado. He was humbled in particular by the scandal brewing around the tragically bungled torching of Changsha a few weeks earlier (for which he denied direct responsibility). The continuing influence of the Baoding group of generals was palpable. At the meeting, they mourned the loss of their mentor, Jiang Baili, recently appointed commandant of the Army Staff College, who had died a few weeks earlier in the hills of western Hunan while leading students and faculty in retreat.*

The conference opened with muted self-criticism about the conduct of the war (including decisions made by Chiang). Attendees endorsed greater attention to guerrilla warfare. At the end of the meeting, Chiang summarized the results and called for a strategic defense of the Nanyue region, laying out elaborate plans for recruitment, deployment, and training. The blueprint was impressive and detailed, closely following ideas

---

* On November 4, 1938, shortly after the fall of Wuhan, Lieutenant-General Jiang Baili was on foot in the mountains of southwestern Hunan Province when he was struck down by a heart attack at the age of fifty-six. His intention had been to reestablish the elite officers' training school at Guilin, the picturesque mountainous capital of Guangxi Province, under the protection of General Bai Chongxi, a Baoding graduate.

put forth in the recently published works of Jiang Baili.[1] Probably more important were the things Chiang did not say. From the military engagements that followed, one can see that Chiang, Chen Cheng, and General Bai Chongxi had learned to be more aggressive, often ordering counterattacks during sustained engagements with Japanese forces. They also had a better idea of who their most reliable generals were. Over all, the Whampoa graduates had not performed well; the Japanese-educated Tang Enbo, one of the heroes of Taierzhuang, was an exception. For the key engagements that lay ahead in 1939 and 1940, namely the defense of the Nanyue region, they agreed that the senior Baoding generals—Chen Cheng, Xue Yue, and Luo Zhuoying—would be in charge.

Over the next five years under Japanese occupation, Wuhan and its environs remained relatively undisturbed. The tricity faced no massacres, Nanjing style. A reasonably effective collaboration regime formed under Zhang Renli (1900–51), the Japanese-educated youngest son of the legendary nineteenth-century governor-general, Zhang Zhidong, whose reform efforts I discuss in chapter 1. Once installed as the new mayor of Wuhan, Zhang and a hand-picked cabinet of Japanese-educated officials were successful in maintaining order, reorganizing the economy to fit Japanese war aims, and preparing the cities to become launching pads for military operations to the south and west (including extensive bombing raids on Chongqing). The sparse secondary literature about the occupation period suggests a grudging admission that Zhang was an effective administrator. (Near the end of the war he became the mayor of Tianjin, long a Japanese stronghold.) A few leaders from the prewar Wuhan merchant community—including members of the Cai clan as well as the real estate mogul Liu Xinsheng and others with previous business ties to the Japanese—openly collaborated (and profited) from association with the "puppet" government. (The Japanese had been the largest foreign community in Hankou before the war.) Returned to power as the governor of Hubei was General Ye Peng, who had been notoriously repressive as the security chief for the province in prewar days. Not surprisingly, under General Ye, members of the Yang Qingshan "Green gang" resurfaced to enforce law and order and hunt down resistance fighters.[2]

Sadly, the Japanese use of Wuhan as a command post and airbase for a massive invasion of south China during the spring of 1944 brought a terrible retribution. In one week in December 1944 American B-29 bombing raids from Sichuan destroyed what remained of the tricity's infrastructure and industrial capacity, along with airfields and military bases. Hanyang in particular was left a smoldering ruin. Thus, in the end, Wuhan did not escape the fate of other major inland cities like Nanjing, Jinan, Xuzhou, or Changsha. The tricity area, especially Wuchang and Hanyang, was in ruins by the end of the war—a blow from which it took well over a decade to recover.* For a while, the destruction of the tricity and subsequent events—civil war between 1945 and 1949 and the Communist triumph—seemed to eclipse memory of the remarkable spirit of resistance that gripped Wuhan in 1938.

Thus historians have often dismissed Wuhan's inspirational role as de facto capital in 1938 as inconsequential or at best quixotic, a fleeting anomaly in the otherwise fratricidal politics of the Republican era.[3] Indeed, if we consider only the history of the Guomindang and Communist parties, this conclusion is largely accurate. The ten months of unified governance at Wuhan were an aberration, a time of unusual amity during which internal factionalism subsided and relations between the parties improved. The Guomindang leaders exercised surprising flexibility: they tolerated diversity of opinion, limited police repression, and made deft use of propaganda. The behavior of the Communists was likewise strangely out of sync with the accepted narrative of their rise to power in 1949.

Though leaders like Zhou Enlai and Wang Ming gave stirring speeches that connected Wuhan to Madrid, calling on workers and the army to defend the tricity in the manner of their Spanish brothers and sisters, their organizational initiatives were few.[4] They were slow to respond to others' efforts to organize refugee welfare, students, women, and intellectuals. Most noticeably, the Communists did little to organize the workers who were toiling in the burgeoning war industries of Wuhan and, in the eyes of foreign observers, being badly exploited. The leadership's obsession at the time was with combating Trotskyite influences on students,

---

* Wuhan's economy did not recover and grow until the late 1950s and early 1960s, when the tricity became a center for heavy industry, organized along centralized Stalinist lines, and regained its position as a nexus for regional commerce. Administratively, the three cities were joined under a single municipal government; physically, they were connected by a massive bridge, built in 1957 (a second bridge was completed in the late 1990s). Politically, Wuhan was a center of Maoist politics well into the 1970s. Chairman Mao liked its provincial atmosphere and food, and he spent weeks in a parklike retreat in the center of Wuchang every year during the spring and fall, swimming, relaxing, and holding court. His famous swim in the Yangzi at Wuhan in July 1966 launched the Cultural Revolution. The tricity was also the site of sharp armed conflict in 1968, at the height of the Cultural Revolution. On Wuhan's economic ups and downs during the PRC period, see Gittings, *Real China*, 116–39; as well as the works of Dorothy J. Solinger, most recently *Contesting Citizenship*. On the Cultural Revolution, see Wang Shaoguang, *Failure of Charisma*. Today the public can visit Mao's Wuhan residence as a museum.

intellectuals, and the media of Wuhan. In hindsight, the abnormal behavior of the Guomindang and Communist parties appears secondary
to the much larger story of the refugee population that overwhelmed
Wuhan and surrounding cities during the spring of 1938.

Nationwide, the flight of refugees (or more accurately, survivors), first
to the south and then inland to the west, was an immediate result of the
terrible violence of the early years of the war. The movement of people
was unprecedented, even in Chinese history. Family members who had
survived the killing and destruction of war as well as the rampages of
Japanese troops during the first few weeks of occupation fled in terror.
They had no clear destination in mind and took few belongings with them.
Needless to say, they were also deeply traumatized by the violence they
had witnessed; everyone had a grim personal story to tell. But precisely
because the violence had been so extreme and arbitrary, and the path to
survival so haphazard, the refugee experience became transformative.
When the population of Wuhan doubled within a few months, producing a social and health crisis of grave proportions, refugees found the energy to pull together in new ways. Because their survival to this point
had seemed miraculous, uniting to make a last stand became a moral necessity and, psychologically, a way of facing survivor guilt. Such an at-
titude helps explain the desperately optimistic atmosphere that gripped
Wuhan for ten months in 1938, which stood in sharp contrast to the panic
and chaos that accompanied the fall of Nanjing and Jinan in November
and December of 1937.

The key to understanding why the civilian population pulled together
as it did in the face of a seemingly hopeless situation lies in the military
history of the defense of Wuhan, for the military context was essential
to the social and cultural covenants that people forged there. Shaping
the military history was a group of senior generals—most of them Baoding graduates—who came together and took charge at Wuhan. Chiang
Kaishek's leadership remained symbolically important, but decision
making and leadership on the battlefield were in the hands of generals
like Chen Cheng, Li Zongren, Bai Chongxi, Xue Yue, and others. Initial
victories at Taierzhuang in April during the battle for Xuzhou boosted
morale and made overnight heroes of the commanders. They also
strengthened the Baoding generals' ability to exercise civil authority over
Wuhan through the Military Affairs Council led by General Chen Cheng.
In other words, the concentration of military and political power in the
hands of these generals created an atmosphere of tolerance for experi-

ments in social and cultural affairs that was unique for a Chinese capital. Of key importance politically was the leaders' encouragement of a free press. To promote unity and political participation, the new media of Wuhan publicized major changes in social organization and cultural activity as part of the war effort.

In these ways, the Wuhan experience of 1938 anticipated broad patterns of change, such as the unprecedented mobilization and politicization of the populace, both urban and rural, during the rest of the war period (and well into the 1950s). While defending their city for ten months, the activists of Wuhan initiated changes in Chinese society, culture, and politics that were as far-reaching as those that transformed Europe during the First World War.

Wuhan in 1938 became a laboratory for cultural experimentation. The intellectuals who gathered at Wuhan—a group that included the nationally prominent figures in most fields—shared a consensus that their nation needed to turn culture into a potent weapon in the war against the Japanese. They sought to reshape arts and letters to reach the masses—especially the rural masses—and persuade them, at the least, to cease cooperating with Japanese occupying forces. The writers disagreed about how to accomplish this goal, as we have seen in the clashes between Lao She and Feng Xuefeng. Should cultural leaders reshape traditional folk forms and styles (as new wine in old bottles), or should they try completely new forms of art? Many people have criticized the overall result of the war effort in the cultural sphere as a tragic watering down of the New Culture experiments that grew out of the "renaissance" period of the May Fourth Movement. But to see the Wuhan effort simply as a process by which intellectual elites were co-opted by the state would be a mistake. At Wuhan state power was fragmented; the authority of the central government was relatively weak. The embrace of new directions in cultural production at Wuhan was clearly voluntary, elite inspired, and enthusiastically pursued at the time. When dissenting figures like the writers Wen Yiduo and Qian Zhongshu or the painter Xu Beihong retreated, feeling isolated by the strength of the popularization movement, they did so in reaction to pressure from their peers, not from the state.

The long-run impact of the popularization movement on Chinese culture was profound. The movement was later picked up and magnified skillfully by cultural commissars in Yan'an—led by figures like Zhou Yang—and badly distorted by Mao in his talks at the Yan'an Forum of

1942. Can we blame the Communist Party's seduction by the late 1940s of leading cultural figures like Lao She, the painter Xu Beihong, the cartoonist Feng Zikai, the philosopher Feng Youlan, and others on enthusiasms generated at Wuhan? Perhaps. But to blame the enthusiasms of the Anti-Japanese War period for the repression of intellectuals during the 1950s and the excesses that culminated in the Cultural Revolution of 1966–76 would certainly be ahistorical.

Other, more positive interpretations of the cultural impact of the war are possible if we look at the Wuhan period through the lens of Chinese journalism.[5] Wuhan showed what can happen to modern Chinese media when the exercise of central government authority is suddenly weakened. The usual Leninist-inspired controls on the media by either the Guomindang or Communist Party were not present at Wuhan. The result was a remarkable blossoming of voices in the daily newspapers and periodicals, as well as in the arts. Not a single publisher or journalist was arrested or murdered in 1938, a record for a Chinese capital. Also contributing to the vibrancy of the Wuhan media scene was the decision of the more adventurous treaty-port mass-media barons of Tianjin and Shanghai to relocate, finding new homes and audiences in inland China.

Granted, the moment of press freedom and experimentation at Wuhan was fleeting. After 1938 the Ministry of Information and its Communist counterpart reasserted controls from Chongqing and Yan'an. But on the fringes, in Guilin, Kunming, and Hong Kong (until 1942), the free-press spirit of Wuhan flourished. Thus *Dagong bao* was able to continue to publish from Guilin as the independent paper of record. Major figures like Mao Dun, Zou Taofen, and Wen Yiduo found refuge and outlets for their work. After 1945, during the civil war, Hong Kong bounced back and echoed Wuhan as a media center for relatively free expression.

Much later, at the end of the century, in Taiwan and under the PRC, the Wuhan experience repeated itself. When state controls broke down or were cut back—even if only briefly—the Chinese media quickly grasped the opportunity for free expression and offered unflinching criticism of government leadership and corrupt practices. This resurgence happened during the Beijing Spring of 1989, before the leadership struggle at the top took a tragic turn and ended in the calamity of June 4 at Tiananmen Square. In Taiwan at about the same time, expansion in the freedom of the press, during the last years of the reign of President Chiang Chingkuo, began the political process that has led to the island's muscularly democratic politics of today. Thus, for good or ill, one lesson from Wuhan is never to underestimate the power and ingenuity—

including the speed of response—of Chinese publishers and journalists when censorship is reduced.

More obvious and concrete was the legacy of Wuhan in the realm of social services (see chapter 4). The state-sponsored public health campaigns for both the rural and urban populations proved to be building blocks for the national health systems erected later in the People's Republic of China and Taiwan. Similarly, the organization of refugee welfare centers and relief way stations at Wuhan paved the way for the state to take major responsibility in such matters and trained those who would lead in these fields during the second half of the twentieth century. Most visible at the time was the concerted effort at Wuhan to rescue children orphaned by the war. Madame Chiang Kaishek herself led the charge, pushed by remarkable activists like the Shanghai lawyer Shi Liang. The state's assumption of major responsibility for orphans was new and has remained a pillar of the Chinese welfare state ever since.

More difficult to describe with precision is the changing position of women during the war. Out of necessity, many women had to leave their homes and enter the workplace—often as widows left to fend for themselves and their children as sole breadwinners. Higher education expanded during the war, giving a growing percentage of young women unprecedented (and at times perilous) opportunities for service beyond their hometowns and regions. In other words, family, gender, and class relationships—including regional ties—were shattered by the war. The disruption was drastic, so devastating that it made impossible, even unthinkable, a postwar return to the more traditional elitist social norms of prewar China.

At Wuhan we saw evidence of the desperate social situation in the faces of refugees in Robert Capa's photos and in statistics about the makeup and size of the refugee population. At a more prosaic level, I have tried to explore—through poetry and a look at tensions in the marriages of leading May Fourth cultural icons like Guo Moruo, Yu Dafu, and Wen Yiduo—how the chaos of the times unraveled people's personal lives.

Others have studied and described the wartime state planning that took place at Wuhan, and later in Chongqing.[6] The organization and nationalization of heavy and light industry under Weng Wenhao, the head of the National Resources Commission, set precedents that were followed in the People's Republic of China and in Taiwan. The transport upstream to Chongqing of equipment and workers in Wuhan's and Shanghai's armament industries has received much attention. Weng Wenhao and Zhou

Enlai also made a deal to open up exploration of the Yumen oil fields in the northwest.[7] Although inadequate to meet wartime needs, these efforts were an impressive harbinger of the massive nationalization and economic reorganization that lay in the future.

Finally, the most important impact of the wartime refugee experience on the history of modern China—of which the Wuhan experience is but a poignant snapshot—may be psychological. The scars on the national psyche are a deeply tragic legacy.[8] Diana Lary and I have argued at greater length elsewhere that the unprecedented violence of this long war profoundly brutalized Chinese society.[9] As we have seen more recently in the former Yugoslavia, Rwanda, and Iraq, such sustained experiences of violence breed a profound distortion of social norms.[10] In China the Great Anti-Japanese War produced a survivor mentality—a kind of psychic numbness to violence and ability to endure oppression without protest—that continued well after 1945 and possibly laid the groundwork for sullen acceptance of the horrors of the late 1940s, 1950s, and 1960s.

WARTIME WUHAN, A CHRONOLOGY

1937

JULY

7 The Marco Polo Bridge incident takes place in a Beijing suburb, and the Chinese declare war; Guomindang and the Communists form the United Front.
28 Beijing capitulates.
29 The Japanese occupy Tianjin.

AUGUST

13 The battle for Shanghai begins.

SEPTEMBER

23 Baoding falls.

Chen Lifu, Wang Jingwei, Shi Liang, Dong Biwu, and others visit Wuhan to prepare to move the seat of government; defensive military preparations begin with construction of riverine fortresses at Madang and Tianjiazhen.

NOVEMBER

5 The Japanese land at Hangzhou Bay.
11 Taiyuan is taken.
12 Shanghai falls.
24 The first student organizational meeting takes place at Wuchang.
25 Wuxi falls.

DECEMBER

Lao She arrives in Wuhan and establishes a writers colony in the Feng Yuxiang compound.

1   Wuhan University hosts a large meeting at which the students petition the
    government.
13 Nanjing falls.
27 The Japanese occupy Jinan.

1938

JANUARY

8   Top generals meet with Chiang Kaishek at Hankou for the first strategy
    session in the campaign to defend Wuhan.
11 General Han Fuju is arrested at Kaifeng; the Japanese conduct the first bomb-
    ing raid over Wuhan; Chinese leaders announce the establishment of the Mil-
    itary Affairs Council *(junshi weiyuanhui)*.
19 The reorganized Military Affairs Council meets, with Chen Cheng presid-
    ing; the military trial of Han Fuju begins, concluding on January 21 with a
    death sentence.
24 Han Fuju is executed at Wuchang; the Japanese conduct the first bombing
    raid on Yichang.

FEBRUARY

8   A large Youth Day rally takes place in Wuchang.
18 A major bombing raid and air battle take place over Wuhan.

MARCH

1   Guo Moruo is officially named the head of the Military Affairs Council's
    3rd Section for cultural propaganda.
3   Shi Liang leads a meeting on refugee children.
8   A snowstorm blankets Wuhan.
12 The battle of Linyi begins.
17 Teng *xian* falls (General Wang Mingzhang dies).
22 The battle of Taierzhuang begins.
25 The All China Student Conference takes place.
27 The Japanese conduct a bombing raid over Wuchang; the Writers Union
    (wenxie) is established.
29 The Special Congress of the Guomindang opens.

APRIL

1   The Writers Union meets for the first time with Feng Yuxiang as chair; the
    Special Congress of Guomindang concludes.
3   Chiang Kaishek gives a major speech on unity at a mass rally.
4   Shi Liang establishes the Wartime Refugee Children Welfare Center; young
    journalists call an organizational meeting.
6   The Guomindang announces its wartime constitution (Organic Law).
7   The battle at Taierzhuang ends with a Chinese victory.
8   Six thousand people attend a ceremony at Hankou honoring fallen hero Gen-
    eral Wang Mingzhang.
16 Talks begin between the Guomindang and the Japanese in Hong Kong.
25 Students hold a big meeting in Hankou.

28   Artists and writers hold a summit and debate popularization versus massification.
29   The Guomindang party holds a meeting of the full membership; party members call for establishment of a youth corps; the Japanese launch a bombing attack in honor of Emperor Hirohito's birthday, producing a dramatic air battle in the skies over Wuhan.

MAY
10   The League of Nations discusses the "China Incident."
14   The bombing of Xuzhou commences.
15   General Li Zongren starts withdrawal.
19   General Hata marches triumphantly into Xuzhou.
20   Women leaders meet at Lu Shan.
21   General Li Zongren completes withdrawal.
26   Chairman Mao delivers his War of Attrition (*chijiu zhan*) speech.
21–29 The World Youth Delegation arrives in Hankou and conducts a series of rallies.
31   An air battle takes place over Wuhan.

JUNE
5,7   Chinese generals blow the dikes at Huayuankou, which changes the course of the Yellow River and floods Shandong Province and the Huai River plain.
6   Kaifeng falls.
9   Chiang Kaishek meets with foreign reporters.
12   The battle for Wuhan formally begins.
15   Anqing falls.
24–29 The Madang riverine fortress is encircled and falls on June 29.
29   The National Resource Commission begins to move factories out of Wuhan.

JULY
1   Two hundred thousand people march in a mass patriotic rally.
4   Military Affairs Council chief General Chen Cheng meets foreign journalists.
5   German military advisers, led by Alexander von Falkenhausen, leave Wuhan.
6   The People's Political Council convenes.
7   A big rally at Sun Yatsen park (Hankou) honors war dead.
8   Hukou falls.
9   The Guomindang establishes the Youth Corps (*qingnian tuan* or *sanqing*).
15   The People's Political Council closes with a flurry of resolutions.
19   The first heavy bombing of Wuhan takes place, killing eight hundred people.
25   Taihu falls.
28   Jiujiang falls.

AUGUST

1–31   Heavy, almost daily bombing raids destroy Chiang Kaishek's headquarters at Wuchang.

4   Huangmei falls.

20   The government issues censorship decrees aimed at shutting down mass youth publications; Ruichang falls at the end of the month.

SEPTEMBER

2   Song Meiling (Mme. Chiang Kaishek) leads the largest women's rally to date.

9   Guangji falls; the battle of Wanjialing begins and lasts through October.

17   Guo Moruo leads a mass rally, with a radio broadcast on September 19.

29   Tianjiazhen, a key riverine fortress, falls.

30   The Japanese take Xinyang on the Beijing-Hankou railway line without a fight.

OCTOBER

21   Canton falls after little fighting.

25   Wuhan capitulates.

NOVEMBER

4   Jiang Baili dies in the mountains of western Hunan.

25–28   The 1st Nanyue Military Conference at Hengyang assesses the defense of Wuhan, summarizing lessons learned and ordering reorganization of units.

NOTES

---

1. WUHAN BEFORE THE WAR

1. Rowe, *Hankow: Commerce* and *Hankow: Conflict*. In Chinese, the most up-to-date review of these subjects is in Chen Feng, *Ming-Qing*.

2. Bays, *China Enters the Twentieth Century*.

3. Zhang's reforms have been the subject of much study. See the following good general studies on the local economy: Esherick, *Reform and Revolution in China*; Su Yun-feng, *Zhongguo xiandaihua quyu yanjiu*; Rowe, "Wuhan and its Region, 1736–1938"; and Pi Mingxiu, *Jindai Wuhan chengshi shi*.

4. Chang Ke-ming, "A Study of the Import and Export Trade of Hankow," 293–94.

5. Yang Bingde, *Zhongguo jindai chengshi yu jianzhu*, 145–48; Pi Mingxiu and Yang Pulin, *Wuhan chengshi fazhanjiuyi*, 375–435; *Jianghan wenshi ziliao*, 135–46. On Cai and Liu, see Rowe, *Hankow: Commerce*, 50–51, 66, 395; *Wuhan wenshi ziliao*, no.2 (1985): 130–37, and no.4 (1988): 148–53; Pi Mingxiu, *Jindai Wuhan chengshi shi*, 301–5.

6. Su Yun-feng, *Zhongguo xiandaihua quyu yanjiu*, 82.

7. "Wuhan Industries after the Flood," "Wuhan Commerce after the Flood," and "Industries of Hankou"; Pi Mingxiu, *Wuhan jinbainiansh*, 174–75; *Wuhan wenshi ziliao*, nos. 3, 4 (1990):115–19. For a comprehensive overview of Wuhan's development, see Pi Mingxiu, *Jindai Wuhan chengshi shi*, 271–447.

8. "Wuhan sanzhen zhi xianzai ji qi jianglai."

9. Yang Bingde, *Zhongguo jindai chengshi yu jianzhu*, 145–48; Pi Mingxiu and Yang Pulin, *Wuhan chengshi fazhanjiuyi*, 375–435; on the continuing role of Liu Yinsheng, see Pi Mingxiu, *Jindai Wuhan chengshi shi*, 677, 688–90, 692.

10. Weyl, "The Chicago of China."

11. Liu Wangling, *Heixue jinku*. See also Cai Qi'ao, *Wuhan xinwen shi*, and Fang Hanqi's work for the later period, *Zhongguo Xinwen shiye tongshi*. The

historian Liu Wangling has traced in meticulous detail the rise and fall of 184
publications between 1864 and 1919,with the bulk appearing in the first two
decades of the twentieth century. Most of these publications continued and mul-
tiplied through the 1920s.

12. *Dong Biwu zhuan*, 179–244, deals with his 1926–27 activities. See also
Rowe, *Crimson Pain*, ch. 10, 239–68, for analysis.

13. *Hankou Jiujiang shouhui yingzujie ziliao xuanbian*; and Pi Mingxiu, *Jindai
Wuhan chengshi shi*, 307–31.

14. On the 1927 Wuhan government, see *Wuhan guomin zhengfu shi*; C. Martin Wilbur, *The Nationalist Revolution in China*; and the classic work by Harold
Isaacs, *The Tragedy of the Chinese Revolution*, which originally (1938) had a fore-
word by Trotsky; the great novel inspired by Wuhan in 1927 is André Malraux's
Man's Fate (La Condition Humaine). Rowe, *Crimson Pain,* 239–68, describes
violence in the surrounding countryside.

15. Rowe, "Wuhan and Its Region"; see Chen Feng, *Ming-Qing*, 811–79, for
an excellent comparative analysis of the efforts by Hankou's most progressive
mayor, Liu Wendao, to modernize the city's police, social services, and public
transport system in the 1920s and 1930s.

16. Abend, *Treaty Ports*, 173–74.

17. *Wuhan wenshi ziliao*, no. 9 (1982): 85–112.

18. Ibid., no. 1 (1985): 68–71 and no.9 (1982): 99.

19. Ibid., no. 1 (1985): 126–42 and nos.3, 4 (1990): 237–39.

20. Cai Qi'ao, *Wuhan xinwen shi*, 29–30, 109–25.

21. Yang Bingde, *Zhongguo jindai chengshi yu jianzhu*, 156–57, 186–89;
Wuhan daxuexiao shi, 102–32.

22. Pi Mingxiu, *Wuhan jinbainianshi*, 280–85.

23. Ibid., 283–85, and Pi Mingxiu and Yang Pulin, *Wuhan chengshi fazhanjiuyi*, 332–34.

24. *Dong Biwu zhuan*, 309–15.

2. DEFENDING CENTRAL CHINA, 1938

1. Wei Hongyun, *Kangri zhanzheng yu Zhongguo shehui*, 163–76, and for
a description of civilian panic in Shandong, see Lao She's reports in *Dagong bao*,
December 4–6, 1937, and his January 1938 essay in *Lao She wenji* vol.14 (1989),
96–100.

2. Standard accounts and relevant documents on military campaigns for the
1937–38 period are available in vol. 1 of *Kangri zhanzheng zhengmian zhanchang* (hereafter *Documents from the Frontlines, 1987)*; for references to the fall
of Jinan and Qingdao, see *Kangri zhanshi*, vol. 20, *JinPu Tielu* [JinPu Railway
Campaign], 75–84; and Zhang Xianwen, *Kangri zhanzheng de zhengmian zhanchang*, 86–96.

3. *Dagong bao*, January 20, 24, 25, 26, 1938; Xin Ping, *1937: Shenchong de
cainan yu lishi de zhuanzhe*, 134. People have put forth conflicting accounts of
General Han's actual execution. I have chosen one of the more dramatic versions
heard at the Changchun temple at Wuchang; it finds some corroboration in reports in *Dagong bao*, as cited above. See also Wang Yimin, "Guanyu Han Fuju

tongzhi Shandong he bei busha di jianwen" ; and Sun Dongxuan, "Han Fuju beike qianhou." Also see, in English, Tang Te-kong and Li Tsung-jen, *Memoirs of Li Tsung-jen*, 338–40; and Dorn, *Sino-Japanese War,* 138–45. A definitive recent study of Han Fuju's career and demise is in Lary, "Treachery, Disgrace and Death." In January 1938, Liu Xiang, the most important militarist in Sichuan, who shared with Han Fuju a history of defying Nanjing, died mysteriously in a Wuhan hospital. At a 2004 conference in Hawaii, military historian Liu Feng-han insisted that Feng Yuxiang (Han began as a Feng protégé) had everything to do with the execution of Han Fuju and the death of Liu Xiang. For Feng's view of the matter, see *Feng Yuxiang riji*, vol. 5, 345–57.

4. The Communists did not participate directly in the January 19 tribunal decision, but by the end of the month Zhou Enlai had joined the United Front government at Wuhan as the the the vice head of the political section of the Military Affairs Council under Chen Cheng. See *Kangzhanzhong de Wuhan*, 60–80; and Mao Lei *Wuhan Kangzhan shiyao*, 35–39, 147–51.

5. Wilson, *When Tigers Fight*; Dorn, *Sino-Japanese War*; Ch'i Hsi-sheng, *Nationalist China at War;* Dreyer, *China at War*; Eastman, "Nationalist China during the Sino-Japanese War."

6. A definitive work on this subject is van de Ven, *War and Nationalism.*

7. On the planning for the defense of Xuzhou and then Wuhan, as well as Japanese strategies, see a book by a leading Chinese military historian, Xu Yong: *Zhengfu zhi Meng*, 147–56, 179–228; and an article by Ao Wenwei, "Wuhan kangzhan shiqi Jiang Jieshi de zhanlueshu sixiang," on Chiang Kaishek's battle strategies. *Chijiu zhan* as a modern strategic concept had its roots in the writings of Jiang Baili and others in the 1920s but can be traced earlier, some say to the Song dynasty. See the classic article on the subject by Wu Xiangxiang, "Total Strategy Used by China."

8. Jiang was with Cai E when he died in Japan in 1916. Since the 1900s Jiang had also been closely associated with Liang Qichao, the great late Qing thinker and political activist, with whom he made a much-publicized trip to Europe in 1920. The result was a book on the history of the European Renaissance, *Ouzhou wenyi fuxing shi*. Jiang was shocked by what he saw in Europe, especially the sorry state of Weimar Germany, which he now blamed on the militarism he had witnessed as a student in the decade before World War I. Jiang's connection to the May Fourth intellectual movement has been studied best by Lu Yan, *Re-understanding Japan*, 194–219. Lu explores in detail Jiang's Japanese connections, including his marriage to the Japanese nurse Sato Yato. See also Michael Godley's unpublished essay about the May Fourth period, Jiang's important editorship of *Gaizao* in 1920–21, and Jiang's relationship with Liang Qichao. Today Jiang may be best known for his long introduction to Liang Qichao's survey of Qing dynasty thought. Jiang's military writings, the main corpus of his work, have received much less scholarly treatment. For a recent translation of *Sunzi bingfa*, see Ralph Sawyer's 1994 version.

9. See, for example, two essays by Jiang Baili: "Shijie junshi dashi yu Zhongguo guoqing," on China's situation in the world military context, which first appeared in the journal *Gaizao* in August 1921; and "Zizhi wenti yanjiu," on Chinese autonomy, in the March 21 issue of the journal. See also the selection

of essays reprinted in *Jiang Baili xiansheng quanji*, especially those in vol.1, 89–93, 141–57, and vol. 2, 269–77 (the latter, a 1922 essay on militarism, appeared in *Guofang lun*).

10. *Guofang lun* was published first in 1937 and reprinted in *Jiang Baili xiansheng quanji*, vol. 2, 131–354. Jiang's memos to Chiang Kaishek in 1937 and 1938 are also collected in this work (see vol. l, 303–7, for a widely circulated essay from *Dagong bao* entitled "Quick Decision and Protracted Sustainment (*Sujue yu zhijiu).*" Jiang Baili's wartime essays were reprinted by *Dagong bao* in pamphlet form shortly after his death, in *Jiang Baili xiansheng kangzhan lunwenji*.

11. Xu Yiyun, *Jiang Baili nianpu*, 130–66. For a summary of Jiang's military thought, see Xue Guangqian, *Jiang Baili de wannian yu junshi sixiang*. Xue traveled with Jiang to Italy and Germany in the mid-1930s.

12. In 1934 he founded a journal for specialists, *Junshi zazhi*, to stimulate discussion and study of strategy and tactics; his regular contributions to it included translations of long interviews in Berlin with China's most important German military adviser, the widely respected General Hans von Seeckt. Internationally at least, Jiang was known as "China's Clausewitz."

13. Tao Juyin, *Jiang Baili xiansheng zhuan*, is especially good on these episodes; see also Cao Juren, *Jiang Baili pingzhuan*. For Cao's remarks on how prescient Jiang's early views were on strategy and the need to plan for a war of attrition, see Cao's *Wo yu wode shiji* and Li Juanli's *Junxue qicai—Jiang Baili*.

14. Liu Fenghan, "Wuhan huizhan yanjiu," vol. 1,99–162.

15. Chang Jui-te, *Kangzhan shiqi de Guojun renshi*.

16. See Van Slyke, "Battle of the Hundred Regiments."

17. Liu Fenghan, "Wuhan huizhan yanjiu."

18. Ibid.

19. On the strategic importance historically of Xuzhou as the gateway to the central Yangzi valley, see Lary, "Defending China."

20. Besides the previously cited detailed study by Liu Fenghan, see the classic earlier work by Liu, *Military History of Modern China*, chs. 13 and 17. On the origins of the New Fourth Army, see Benton, *New Fourth Army*, and Ch'en Yung-fa, *Making Revolution*.

21. Van de Ven, *War and Nationalism;* and on the lack of good intelligence, see Dorn, *Sino-Japanese War*.

22. Dorn, *Sino-Japanese War*, 6–10. This assessment has not been contested, even by van de Ven, who is severely critical of Dorn's general approach.

23. Dower, "Lessons of Another Occupation."

24. Peattie, "Attacking a Continent."

25. See the paper in English by Tobe Ryoichi, "Central Yangzi Campaign."

26. Western military observers, whether European, North American, German, or Russian, seemed in agreement on these points. Hans van de Ven discusses their observations in detail in ch. 6 of *War and Nationalism*. Chinese forces under different leadership pursued a similar strategy in Korea from 1950 to 1952.

27. Chang Jui-te, "Chiang Kaishek's Coordination by Personal Directives."

28. See Liu, *Military History of Modern China*, ch. 17; and Ray Huang, "Chiang Kaishek and His Diary."

29. *Baoding lujun junguan xuexiao*, and Lin Dezheng, *Baoding junguan xuexiao zhi yanjiu*; Shi Sheling, "Baoding junguan xuexiao cangsangji," 9–14, 16–21, 35–38.

30. See, for example, Carlson, *Chinese Army*, and Smedley, *Battle Hymn of China*.

31. See *Wuhan kangzhan shi* for the connection between the battles from the Chinese point of view, and see Tobe Ryoichi's paper, "Central Yangzi Campaign," for the Japanese perspective.

3. THE BATTLE FOR XUZHOU AND THE DEFENSE OF WUHAN

1. See the chapters on Xuzhou and Wuhan in Dorn, *Sino-Japanese War*, as well as original reports by Carlson and Stilwell in *U.S. Military Intelligence Reports: China, 1911–41*, reel 10 for the following dates in 1938: March 16; April. 6, 22; May 5, 13, 21; June 25. The leading German adviser, General Alexander von Falkenhausen, expressed the same view in Liu, *Military History of Modern China*, 162–66. See also Liang Hsi-huey, "General Alexander von Falkenhausen," 175–86; for the views of Soviet advisers, see Kalyagin, *Along Alien Roads*. Chinese historians who share this view include Xu Yong, *Zhengfu zhi meng*; and Liu, *Military History of Modern China*, especially ch. 17; and Ao Wenwei, "Wuhan kangzhan shiqi Jiang Jieshi de zhanlueshu sixiang."

2. Tobe Ryoichi, "Central Yangzi Campaign."

3. For relevant documents, see *Documents from the Frontlines*, vol. 1, 558–69; and Ao Wenwei, "Wuhan kangzhan shiqi Jiang Jieshi de zhanlueshu sixiang."

4. Changes in troop allocation and personnel are clear from Tobe Ryoichi, "Central Yangzi Campaign." Determining the politics behind these moves in Tokyo is more difficult. See Kubo Toru, "Koa-Institute and its Research on China." Nevertheless, the minister of war was cashiered in early April and replaced by General Itagaki Seishiro, a veteran of the Shanghai campaign.

5. A balanced, succinct account in Chinese of both the Xuzhou and the Wuhan campaigns appears in *Wuhan kangzhan shi*, 35–175. Documents in *Documents from the Frontlines*, 558–778, are good for individual campaigns. Memoir collections edited by People's Consultative Congress *(zhengxie)* at the provincial level include *Xuzhou huizhan* and *Wuhan huizhan*, as well as Li Zongren's *Memoirs* in English translation. Guomindang- (Taiwan-) based archival documents that focus on Chiang Kaishek and provide the official Guomindang postwar analysis are available in the official Ministry of Defense multivolume publication *Kangri zhanshi*, which includes *Wuhan huizhan* (10 vols.) and *Xuzhou huizhan* (4 vols). Liu Fenghan, the doyen of Taiwan military historians, offers a solid summary of the battle of Wuhan in "Wuhan huizhan yanjiu," 99–162. Liu makes a special effort to evaluate the number of casualties and to document the use of chemical weapons by the Japanese.

6. Wang Mingzhang's heroics are chronicled in *Kangri zhanzheng guomindang zhenwang jianglinglu*, 99–103.

7. Sun Youli, "Chinese Military Resistance."

8. Two years later Zhang Zizhong died in battle defending Yichang and be-

came the most celebrated fallen hero of the war on the Chinese side; streets are named for him in both Taibei and Beijing. The literature on Zhang Zizhong is considerable; for a summary, see Waldron, "China's New Remembering."

9. Hans van de Ven, in *War and Nationalism*, 217–25, provides an alternative version of the battle for Xuzhou that is critical of Li Zongren and complimentary to Tang Enbo and that emphasizes the quality of the overall management by Chiang Kaishek. His discussion of Japanese units and their intentions is also important.

10. Note the careful wording by the best Japanese military historian of the period, Tobe Ryoichi, in "Central Yangzi Campaign," that the Japanese were not defeated at Taierzhuang. The battle for Taierzhuang was well-known. While the city was in Chinese hands, the foreign press corps were invited on a tour. I have based the preceding and following narrative on the fine summary by Diana Lary in "Defending China," and the celebratory Chinese accounts in Miao Fenglin, *Taierzhuang dazhan*, and *Xuzhou huizhan*. Also useful were detailed eyewitness military attaché reports by Evans Carlson and Joseph Stilwell in *U.S. Military Intelligence Reports: China, 1911–41*, reel 10, for the following dates in 1938: March 16; April 6, 22 (Carlson's April 3–10 visit); May 5, 13, 21, 25; and June. For French attaché reports, see *Rapports des attaches militaires*, files 7N3290, 7N3291 (Chine).

11. Lary, "Drowned Earth," and Bi Chunfu, *Kangzhan Jianghe juekou mishi*.

12. For details see Tobe Ryoichi, "Central Yangzi Campaign."

13. Because of pyrrhic victories at Xuzhou, Chinese historians have at times dealt separately with the battles for Xuzhou and Wuhan—distinguishing the more positive story from the more negative one. But, as military history and in the minds of the commanders on both sides at the time, the Xuzhou and Wuhan campaigns were inextricably related and to some degree simultaneous (see the chronology of events in the appendix to this book).

14. See Wu Xiangxiang, "Total Strategy Used by China"; Hsu Lung-hsuan and Chang Ming-kai, *History of the Sino-Japanese War*; and Ao Wenwei, "Wuhan kangzhan shiqi Jiang Jieshi de zhanlueshu sixiang." This view is argued forcefully by van de Ven in *War and Nationalism*, 217–27.

15. Lary," Defending China."

16. Carlson and Stilwell, *U.S. Military Intelligence Reports: China 1911–41*. See also Carlson, *Chinese Army* and *Twin Stars of China*; his and Stilwell's views are echoed in Dorn, *Sino-Japanese War*; for Epstein on touring the battlefield, see *People's War*. Stilwell's May 13–14, 1938, report on Taierzhuang was typical of his dispatches. He especially praised the 31st division commander, Chi Fengcheng, for his bravery and brilliance. General Chi was thirty-four years old, a northerner who worked his way up through the regional armies associated with Feng Yuxiang (graduating from the Nanjing Staff College in 1933). Dorn repeats the accolades in *Sino-Japanese War*, 152–58. Hans van de Ven, in his introduction to *War and Nationalism*, is especially critical of Dorn's analysis, seeing it as almost "orientalist" in perspective.

17. For a book-length elaboration of this argument, see van de Ven, *War and Nationalism*, who also notes Chiang Kaishek's attempts at aggressive pursuit of the enemy—and the reluctance of commanders like Li Zongren to follow orders.

18. What happened to General Li at this point remains a mystery. His leadership of troops and participation in the war were never again at the same level. He did return to command troops in the Dabeishan area before the fall of Wuhan, and he remained there for most of the rest of the war. From 1939 on he directed only relatively light engagements in answer to Japanese probes west of the Ping Han railway. I have benefited from discussions about General Li's malaise with Diana Lary. See Li Zongren's Memoirs and Lary, "Guangxi's Experience of War."

19. For details, see Tobe Ryoichi, "Central Yangzi Campaign."

20. For the relevant documents, see *Wuhan huizhan*, 6–29, and *Documents from the Frontlines*, vol. l, 3–29, 558–68, and 648–749.

21. The best popular history of the battle for Wuhan that describes the personalities and peccadilloes of the commanders is Fang Zhijin, *Jianghan aige*. The most authoritative scholarly text is *Wuhan kangzhan shi*.

22. In May the preparations at Madang were well publicized. International observers and journalists were invited to inspect the defenses, which included cables cutting across the river and the sinking of ships to further block movement upstream; see *Wuhan huizhan*, 30–43; Ao Wenwei, *Hubei kangri zhanzheng shi*, 75–83.

23. The question of Japanese use of chemical weapons is highly controversial. Japanese scholars in general remain skeptical. Chinese scholarship (mainland and Taiwan), in contrast, has dealt at length with the subject, using for the most part Chinese sources. See, for example, an essay on the issue for the Wuhan campaign by Bi Chunfu, "Jinlue rijun wuhan huizhan jijian huaxue zhan shishi jikuang,"which cites Japanese and Chinese sources; as well as Ji Xueren, *Riben luehua zhanzheng de huaxue zhan*, 79–120. A better-documented and influential book on the subject is *Ribenjun zhanzheng baoxing zhiyanjiu* by the Taiwan scholar Li Enhan.

24. See Merker, "The Guomindang Regions of Jiangxi."

25. *Wuhan huizhan*, 94–114; see also Tobe Ryoichi, "Central Yangzi Campaign," on the brief Japanese thrust into Lu Shan. Zhang Fakui was eager to redeem his name for the failed defense of Hangzhou Bay in the 1937 battle for Shanghai.

26. Fang Zhijin, *Jianghan aige*, 246–59; and *Wuhan huizhan*, 184–98.

27. Chinese sources often highlight Wanjialing as a victory on the order of Taierzhuang. See, for example, *Wuhan kangzhan shi*, 106; *Jianghan aige*, 272–94; and Chen Fu'an and Liu Guangming, *Wuhan huizhan yanjiu*, 100–9.

28. *Wuhan huizhan*, 167–83.

29. Ibid., 246–63; *Wuhan kangzhan shi*, 117–19.

30. *Wuhan huizhan*, 1–5 (excerpted from Li Zongren's memoir, a searing attack on Hu Zongnan), also 231–45;a more colorful account appears in *Jianghan aige*, 206–16.

31. *Wuhan kangzhan shi*, 341–48; Ao Wenwei, *Hubei kangri zhanzheng shi*, 145–47.

32. The question of Chiang Kaishek's leadership during the battle of Xuzhou and the defense of Wuhan deserves a long note. Chiang issued elaborate plans and almost daily instructions to commanders, but his control of events in the field was inconsistent. When he did intervene and was listened to, the tactical re-

sults were often disastrous (as with breaking the dikes at Huayuankou or torching Changsha). However, Chiang did demonstrate personal leadership. Courageously injecting himself into the fighting, he would fly anywhere—to Xuzhou, Zhengzhou, Madang, or Xinyang—on the eve of a battle and appear to take command. He was the last to fly out of Wuhan on October 24, before the Japanese storm troopers arrived. Thus Chiang understood that his continuing physical presence was symbolically important, and his Baoding colleagues appreciated this fact. In strategic terms, by negotiating with the oligarchy of senior Baoding-connected commanders as well as his own team of Whampoa loyalists, he was able to place division commanders and their troops in ways that made political and military sense. In short, the defense of the central Yangzi region and Wuhan turned Chiang into a more determined and effective leader and helped him survive politically to the end of the war.

33. Zhang Zhizhong spent the rest of his career trying to live down the Changsha fire. He continued as a trusted associate of Chiang, playing a major role in the mid-1940s in the civil war negotiations; see Yu Jipang, *Zhang Zhizhong*, 43–64; and Zhang Zhizhong, *Zhang Zhizhong huiyi lu*.

4. WUHAN'S REFUGEE CRISIS

1. White and Jacoby, *Thunder out of China*, 55.

2. The generally recognized "great" novel of the period, if not the century, is *Weicheng (Fortress Beseiged)* by Qian Zhongshu, available in a new translation by Nathan Mao and Jeanne Kelly. It is a lyrical farce about soul-searching university elites during the war period and an exploration of the sorry state of Chinese high culture. Qian himself, a classically trained scholar, sat out most of the war in occupied Shanghai.

3. Yuan Shuipai, *Mafantuo de shange*, 13–14, excerpted from a poem titled "Biaoti yinyue" [Headline music] and following a translation by Hsu Kai-yu, *Twentieth Century Chinese Poetry*, 375.

4. Spence, *God's Chinese Son*, 303.

5. Ho Ping-ti, *Studies of the Population*, 236–48.

6. Li Wenzhi, *Zhongguo jindai nongye shi ziliao*, 151.

7. See McCord, "Burn, Kill."

8. Rowe, *Hankow: Commerce*, 40–41; and chapter 1 of this book.

9. See Brook, *Collaboration*, on the Jiading area; and Wakeman, *Shanghai Badlands*.

10. Lary, "A Ravaged Place."

11. Eastman, "Nationalist China during the Sino-Japanese War," 565; his source is Chen Ta, *Population in Modern China*, 61–68.

12. Ch'i Hsi-sheng, "The Military Dimension," 180. In recent years a younger generation of Chinese scholars has begun in-depth studies of the archives, both national and regional, to reexamine questions about wartime shifts in population. So far their work has shown the tremendous complexity of the subject while confirming as roughly accurate the statistics cited above. See Xia Mingfang, "Kangzhan shiqi zhongguo de huozang?"; Cheng Chaoyun, "Kangzhan chuji de nanmin neiqian"; Liu Bing, "Kangri zhanzheng yu zhongguo renkou wenti xueshu

luntan zongshu"; and Bian Xiuyue, "Kangzhan sunshi wenti yanjiu de quyu yanjiu jichu goujian."

13. Wei Hongyun, *Kangri zhanzheng yu Zhongguo shehui,* 164–65.

14. *Dagong bao,* November 21, 1937, and March 23, 1938; Sun Yankui, *Gunande renliu,* 44–45.

15. Wakeman, *Shanghai Badlands,* 7.

16. *Shen bao,* February 11 and 12, 1938.

17. Wei Hongyun, *Kangri zhanzheng yu Zhongguo shehui,* 169. See also
Brook, *Collaboration.*

18. Lary, "A Ravaged Place."

19. Utley, *China at War,* 47–48.

20. On wartime growth of Wuhan's population by at least half a million, see
Wu Chengguo, "Wuhan kangzhan shiqi de nanmin zhouji gongzuo," 100; also
Sun Yankui, *Gunande renliu,* 81–89.

21. Sun Yankui,*Gunande renliu,* 69–71.

22. *Xinhua ribao,* May 22, 1938.

23. Sun Yankui, *Gunande renliu,* 75; see also Cheng Chaoyun, "Kangzhan
chuji de nanmin neiqian."

24. Shen Benwen, *Xiandai shehui wenti,* 261.

25. Liang Kan, "Chinese Intellectuals in the War." In general terms, see Spence,
Gate of Heavenly Peace, 303–26.

26. *Wuhan kangzhan shiliao xuanbian,* 249–58; *Hubei wenshi ziliao,* no.2
(1985): 170–85; Mao Lei, *Wuhan kangzhan shiyao,* 17–22, 377–80; and *Kangzhan shiqi neiqian xinan de gongshang qiye.* Parks Coble argues in a recent book,
Chinese Capitalists in Japan's New Order, that the historical literature has exaggerated the movement of industry upriver to Wuhan and Chongqing. Most of
the industrial base continued to function, and even prosper, in Shanghai under
Japanese occupation.

27. On the leadership of Weng Wenhao, whose career seemed to reach a
peak during the Wuhan period, see Li Xuetong, *Weng Wenhao nianpu,* especially 154–77.

28. Yang Bingde, *Zhongguo jindai chengshi yu jianzu,* 157; *Wuhan kangzhan
shiliao xuanbian,* 249–57; Pi Mingxiu and Yang Pulin, *Wuhan chengshi fazhanjiuyi,* 334–39; Pi Mingxiu, *Jindai Wuhan chengshi shi,* 658–71; Ao Wenwei, *Hubei
kangri zhanzheng shi,* 142–47.

29. Sun Yankui, *Gunande renliu,* 79–80; Lu Fangshang develops these themes
at length in "Lingyizhong weizuzhi" and "Kangzhan shiqi de qiandu yundong";
see also Shen Benwen, *Xiandai shehui wenti,* for rich contemporary data on the
social disruption. After the war, the disruption of the family and marriages became the subjects of feature films.

30. Utley, *China at War,* 47.

31. Eastman, *Seeds of Destruction,* 152–57. On Shanghai, see Wakeman,
Shanghai Badlands, 7; and Feng Yi, "Le problème des refugies."

32. Sun Yankui, "Kangzhan chuqi Wuhan nanmin jiuji zouyi," 43–48.

33. On Shi Liang, see Zhou Tiandu, *Qi junzi zhuan,* 463–590; Shi Liang,
"Wode shenghuo daolu"; and Yang Tianshi, *Renwu shuwang,* vol. 2, 518–27. In
Shanghai the communists were more focused and did effective organizing work

in refugee camps, recruiting new members and troops for the New 4th Army guerillas; see the documentary collection *Kangzhan chuqi de Shanghai nanmin gongzuo* as well as works of Zhao Puchu ("Khangzhan chuqi de Shanghai nanmin gongzuo"), Feng Yi ("Le problème des refugies"), and Patricia Stranahan *(Radicalization of Refugees)*.

34. Sun Yankui, *Gunande renliu*, 142–91.On He Hengfu, see *Wuhan renwu xuanlu*, 307–9; and *Wuhan wenshi ziliao*, no.34 (1988): 173–74. Ho (1888–1968) went from trading *tong* oil to running a power company, textile factories, and coal mines by the 1930s.

35. *Wuhan sanzhen nanmin shourongso yizhanbiao* (June 1938) from No. 2 Archives, Nanjing, as cited in Sun Yankui, "Kangzhan chuqi Wuhan nanmin jiuji zouyi," 44.

36. Rowe, *Hankow: Conflict*, 92–186; and Rankin (1986), for merchant-elite philanthropy in general.

37. On the important role of merchant-organized *tongxianghui*, or provincial associations, in the urban life of early twentieth-century China, see Goodman, *Native Place*.

38. *Wuhan wenshi ziliao*, no.13 (1983): 155–67, and no.48 (1992): 39–45, for fragments of *cishantang* history; for more comprehensive treatment, see *Ge shantang zhuangli yange ji shiye qingguang*. For a good summary of wartime activity, see Sun Yankui, *Gunande renliu*, 198–208.

39. See Sun Yankui, "Kangzhan chuqi Wuhan nanmin jiuji zouyi,"44–45; for the history of the Wuchang YMCA, see *Hubei wenshi ziliao*, no.5 (1982): 188–95.

40. See Feng Yi, "Le problème des refugies"; and Kohama Masako, "The Problem of Refugees."

41. *Dagong bao*, May 2, 1938, 3; see Gu Weiming, "Zhongguo zhanshi ertong baoyuhui shulue"; and Li Xuetong, "Zhanshi ertong baoyuhui de lishi yu zuoyong," on the organizational details and the spread of *Baoyuhui* across western China.

42. Wei Hongyun, *Kangri Zhanzheng yu Zhonggujo shehui*, 174; and Sun Yankui, "Kangzhan chuqi Wuhan nanmin jiuji zouyi," 46; *Wuhan wenshi ziliao*, no.18 (1984): 48–88; Mao Lei et al., *Wuhan kangzhan shiyao*, 220–23. Recent years have seen an explosion of interest in the history of the wartime orphanage movement, including a ten-part documentary shown nationally in 2006 on CCTV (China's national network). One reason may be that the head of state during the late 1990s, Jiang Zemin, was himself a war orphan. Feeding these developments, including scholarship, is a growing memoir literature from the orphans themselves, channeled through their organizational journal, *Baoyusheng tongxun* [Newsletter for children's home alumni], which began publishing in 1995. These writings increasingly recognize the leadership role of Madame Chiang Kaishek (Song Meiling) and Christian missionaries. See Plum, "Unlikely Heirs," as well as Gu Weiming, "Zhongguo zhanshi ertong baoyuhui shulue" and "Song Meiling quanjiu kangzjhan zhong de nantong."

43. Smedley, *Battle Hymn*, 227. For a new work attempting to draw a comprehensive picture of the relief effort, see Liu Lu, "A Whole Nation Walking: The Great Retreat in the War of Resistance, 1937–1945."

44. *Wuhan wenshi ziliao,* no.2 (1985): 58–60; Mao Lei et al., *Wuhan kang-zhan shiyao,* 217–19; *Zhongguo funu yundong lishi ziliao,* 44–135.

45. In the early 1930s, before becoming minister of health in 1933, Dr. Liu headed the Peking Union Medical College.

46. Perhaps because Dr. Lin went to the United States after the war, his wartime work has yet to receive the attention it deserves in China. The best eye-witness accounts seem to be in English; see the lengthy chapters in Utley, *China at War,* and Smedley, *Battle Hymn,* as well as the U.S. military attaché reports discussed in chapter 3.

47. On Dr. Lin's Red Cross work, see *Wuhan wenshi ziliao,* no.13 (1983): 170–73. Dr. J. Heng Liu's papers in the manuscript division of Butler Library, Columbia University, are disappointing for the war period. For prewar background and an excellent bibliography, see Yip, *Health and National Reconstruction.* On malaria epidemics and survival rates, see Wu Renshu, "Kangzhan yu jiyi"; also Yip, "Disease and the Fighting Men." Demographically speaking, within the civilian population, adult males seemed to have survived the war in greatest number.

48. Ao Wenwei, *Hubei kangri zhanzheng shi,* 151–55.

49. This point receives greater attention in MacKinnon, Lary, and Vogel, *China at War.* Moreover, historians and sociologists of the global wartime refugee experience have neglected the Chinese case. See, for example, the influential, prize-winning study by Peter Gatrell, *A Whole Empire Walking,* especially the theoretically oriented introductory chapter defining "Refugeedom" as a state of involuntary displacement. The Chinese case stands with the Russian one as an equally forceful example of how a huge refugee movement profoundly changed the larger society and culture.

5. CULTURE AND THE PRESS

1. In the judgment of these scholars, leading May Fourth figures from the 1920s like Mao Dun, Guo Moruo, Zhang Shenfu, Feng Youlan, Ba Jin, and Xia Yan were swept up in nationalist fervor, which caused them to abandon their inheritance from Lu Xun and Hu Shi and naively embrace the cultural norms of the refugee societies in which they were living. In the name of outreach to the masses (*qunzhong*), they wasted their talents and careers pandering to the uneducated. The result was a mediocre cultural product that was of little interest even to its intended beneficiaries: peasants and workers whose milieu was folk culture and traditions. Even more serious, the cultural loss paved the way for the rise of Mao Zedong and the acceptance of his shallow and authoritarian approach to mass culture, as articulated in 1942 in the talks at Yan'an Forum. In this way, they argue, the Anti-Japanese War established the trends that were to politicize and brutalize all cultural life, solidifying an impoverishment from which the Chinese are still recovering. See Li Zehou, *Zhongguo xiandai sixiang shilun;* Feng Chongyi, *Kangri zhanzheng shiqi zhongguo hua sizhao di miaoshu;* Gunn, "Literature and Art of the War Period," 235–73; and Schwarcz, *Time for Telling Truth* and *Chinese Enlightenment.* A similar critique focusing blame on the Communists and skipping the Anti-Japanese War years appears in popularly written works

on Chinese cultural issues by Simon Leys (Pierre Rickmans); see, for example, *Chinese Shadows* and *Burning Forest*.

2. On the earlier movement toward popularization of culture, see Fitzgerald, *Awakening China*, and Spence, *Gate of Heavenly Peace*; see Alitto, *The Last Confucian*, Charlotte Furth, *The Limits of Change*, for the conservative backlash.

3. Yuan Jicheng, "Kangzhan chuqi Wuhan de baozhi kanwu,"26. This long essay is the exhaustive, definitive study of the subject, running eighty-seven pages. See also Wang Jianhui, "Da Wuhan."

4. On the history of print culture in the 1920s, see MacKinnon, "Toward a History of the Chinese Press"; Weston, "Theory and Practice of Newspaper Journalism"; and in Chinese, Ge Gongzhen's classic history of the Chinese press, *Zhongguo baoxue shi*, and the monumental Fang Hanqi, *Zhongguo xinwen shiye tongshi*, a three-volume work in which vol.2 is on the Republican period. Fitzgerald, "Origins of the Illiberal Party Newspapers," connects the late 1920s crackdown to the rise of Leninist political parties.

5. Cai Qi'ou, *Wuhan xinwen shi.*

6. *Wuhan xinwen shiliao,* no. 1 (1983): 120–24, and no. 2 (1983): 88–92; *Hubei xinwen shiliao huibian,* no.8 (1985): 28–29; Fang Hanqi, *Zhongguo Xinwen shiye tongshi,* vol. 2, 627–34; Yuan Jicheng, "Kangzhan chuqi Wuhan de baozhi kanwu"; Wang, "The Independent Press."

7. See *Ershi shiji Hunan renwu* for more on Huang Shaogu (1901–96). For general treatment of *Saodang bao,* see Fang Hanqi, *Zhongguo xinwen shiye tongshi,* vol. 2, 634–35; and *Kangri zhanzheng shiqi de Zhongguo xinwenjie,* 80–88.

8. Ding was the brother of the mathematician Ding Wenjiang and education professor Ding Wenzhi; today his granddaughter Ding Zilin, a retired professor, is one of China's most important dissident intellectuals.

9. On war reporting in a more general context, see Changtai Hung, *War and Popular Culture,* ch. 4, 151–86; and Gao Tian, "Zhandi tongxun de xin dongxiang," 16; for reporting by Liu Zunqi, see "Zhandi jizhe de yixie yinxing"and a series of frontline reports in *Saodang bao,* April 22 and 23, 1938. In retrospect, see his *Tongxun zawen xuan,* 1–4, 61–74, 81–84; also Yu You, *Liu Zunqi,* and Li Hui, *Jianyu yinying de rensheng.* An important exception was the *Dagong bao* dispatches posted by the dean of war correspondents, Fan Changjiang.

10. The third-party movement has been a subject of much study. See Jeans, *Roads Not Taken,* especially 241–68, for the war period; and Fung, *In Search of Chinese Democracy.* Another typical third-party publication besides *Zaisheng* was *Kangzhan xingdong,* nos. 1–7 (February–June 1938), which called for more democracy. For a documentary collection on the Youth Party, see *Zhongguo qingnian dang*; on the People's Political Council, see the comprehensive two-volume collection of documents, *Guomin canshenghui ziliao,* of which vol. 1 documents the Wuhan sessions. For recent essays analyzing the 1938 meetings, see *Jinian Wuhan kangzhan,* 480–533. A contemporary summary of the Wuhan sessions appears in the following 1938 issues of *Wuhan ribao*: June 30 and July 1, 26; for more thorough contemporary reporting, see these 1938 issues of *Dagong bao*: July 7, 2; July 8, 3; July 9, 2; July 11, 2; July 13, 2; July 14, 2; July 15, 2 (with an editorial); July 16, 2 (also with an editorial).

11. See Ye Qing, "Guanyu zhengzhi dangpai," and his collected essays in

Zhongguo dixian jietuan jiqi jianglai. Chen Duxiu, a major intellectual figure and founding father with Li Dazhao of the Chinese Communist Party (in 1921) was released from prison in July 1937 and ultimately made his way to Wuhan. For his Wuhan essays criticizing the communist movement, see Chen, *Duxiu zhe zuoxuan*, 399–409. In English, see Benton, *Chen Duxiu's Last Articles*; for Zhang Guotao, see Sheng Renxue, *Zhang Guotao wenti yanjiu ziliao*; for a summary of press commentary, see *Xuelu*, no.12 (April 2): 190–92. A good overview is available in Tang Baolin, *Zhongguo tuopai shi*, 207–91. For extensive contemporary discussion, see the following 1938 issues of *Minyi*: no.14 (March 16): 8–9; no.15 (March 23): 14–15; no.16 (March 30); no.20 (April 27): 16; no.21 (May 4): 16; no.22 (May 11): 12–13; no.23 (May18): 16. For *Dagong bao* on Chen Duxiu, see March 3, 1938, 3, March 16, 19383; on Zhang Guotao, see April 24, 1938. *Kang zhan xiangdao*, edited by former Communist Ye Qing, was obsessed with the subject: see nos. 1–12 (April 3–June 30, 1938). For vituperative attacks by the Communist leadership in speeches and articles on Chen Duxiu and Zhang Guotao, see the following 1938 issues of *Xinhua ribao*: March 5 and April 6, 18, 20, 22, 26, and 29; as well as pamphlets by Wang Ming, *Weiduli ziyou xingfude Zhongguo douzheng*; Lo Fu (Zhang Wentian), *Xi shinian lai de CCP*; and *Bo Gu zhuan*, 284–323. As early as January 1938, from Yan'an, Kang Sheng had denounced Chen Duxiu as a traitor (*hanjian*); see also Yang Tianshi, *Renwu shuwang*, vol.1, 99–105.

12. *Wuhan wenshi ziliao*, no.30: 61–63. Mao Lei, *Wuhan kangzhan shiyao*, 200–4; *Zou Taofen nianpu*; Yeh Wen-hsin "Progressive Journalism," 186–238. *Funu shenghuo*, which was edited by Shen Zijiu (China's best-known woman journalist), took a broad view politically of women's issues, making it the most influential journal of its kind.

13. Interview with Hu Qiuyuan on June 21, 1992, in Taibei; and *Hubei xinwen shiliao huibian*, no. 4 (1982): 96; Mao Lei et al., *Wuhan kangzhan shiyao*, 192; and Hu Qiuyuan, "Wo yu Cheng Shewo xiansheng," 54.

14. On the National Salvation movement, see Coble, *Facing Japan*.

15. Interview with Hu Sheng on June 3, 1992, in Beijing; see also *Hubei xinwen shiliao huibian*, no.5 (1983): 6. By the 1950s, Hu Sheng was a major figure in the PRC media establishment, and in the 1980s he became president of the Chinese Academy of Social Sciences as well as the author of standard textbooks on modern Chinese history.

16. Isaacs, *Re-encounters in China*; Yu You, *Liu Zunqi*; and Li Hui, *Jianyu yinying de rensheng*. In 1941 the Americans recruited Liu Zunqi in Chongqing to join their wartime press center as chief of the Chinese staff for the American Office of War Information. From this post, he exerted a major influence on American wartime coverage of China until at least 1945. See MacKinnon and Friesen, *China Reporting*.

17. On Dong Xianguang, see Boorman, *Biographical Dictionary*, vol. 1, 338–40; and Tong, *China and the World Press;* Liu Jingxiu, "Hollington K. Tong"; *Zeng Xubai zizhuan*, vol. 1. Many of Dong's underlings at Wuhan became prominent journalists and diplomats—men like Zeng Xubai, editor of *Zhongyang ribao* for over thirty years, and Ye Gongzhao (George Yeh), who played a key role in international relations of the ROC in the 1950s as ambassador to the United Nations.

18. Hung Chang-tai, *War and Popular Culture*, 151–86; *Hubei xinwen shi huibian*, no.5 (1983): 6. Reportage, or *baogao wenxue*—reporting as personal chronicle—was a new form of journalism that became important at Wuhan and has been a topic of much study in recent years. See Zhang Shaosi, "Kangzhan chuqi de wuhan baogao wenxue."

19. On the boom in publishing at Wuhan, see Wang Jianhui, "Da Wuhan."

20. Gan Hailan, *Lao She nianpu*. His father was a bannerman soldier who died in action during the Boxer Uprising of 1900.

21. For a good general discussion, see many references to Lao She in Spence, *Gate of Heavenly Peace*, and Vohra, *Lao She and the Chinese Revolution*. The standard study of Feng Yuxiang is Sheridan, *Chinese Warlord*. Feng was a product of the alleyways in small north China cities and appreciated Lao She's use of vernacular as well as his focus on the common man.

22. "Sange yuelai de Jinan." See also Lao She, "Diao Jinan," for an essay published in January 1938.

23. Lao She, "Wo weishenmo likai Wuhan." The translation (with permission) is from Liang Kan's unpublished essay, "Rethinking the May Fourth: Vernacular Movement in Wartime Chongqing." For Wu Zuxiang, see Williams, *Village Echoes*. He Rong ended up in Taiwan in the 1950s. On Lao Xiang, see Chang-tai Hung, *War and Popular Culture*, ch. 5, 187–220. As the patron, General Feng made frequent references to these writers in *Feng Yuxiang riji*, vol. 5.

24. Scholars have studied and commented on Gu Jiegang's work in great detail: see Chang-tai Hung, *Going to the People*; Schneider, *Ku Chieh-kang and China's New History*; and Liu Qiyu, *Gu Jiegang xiansheng xueshu*.

25. A good reference work for the 1930s debate on popular literature is the collection of documents edited by Wen Zhenting, *Wenyi dazhonghua wenti taolun ziliao*. For the Anti-Japanese War period, see Lan Hai, *Zhongguo kangzhan wenyi shi*, especially 73–118.

26. In *Lao She wenji*, vol. 15 (1990), see "Wo zemayang xie tongsu wenyi," 218–21; "Zhizuo tongsu wenyi de kutong," 351–58; and "Tan tongsu wenyi," 332–35; the third of these essays appeared originally in *Ziyou Zhongguo* 1, no. 2 (1938). The record of Lao She's addresses at Wenxie meetings survives in *Lao She wenji*, vol. 15, 600–16. Liang Kan, "Rethinking May Fourth."

27. The last of these pamphlets first appeared in *Kang daodi*, no.5 (March 1, 1938): 2–4; the first printing of the fourteen-page pamphlet with woodblock illustrations was on March 27, with regular republication thereafter. For a solid presentation of Lao She and Lao Xiang's old-wine-in-new-bottles work, with many quotes from the originals, see Changtai Hung, *War and Popular Culture*, ch. 5, 187–220. For Lao Xiang's essay in defense of "Anti-Japanese Three-Character Classic," see his "Guanyu kangri sanzijing."

28. Liang Kan, "Rethinking May Fourth."

29. Feng Xuefeng, "Guanyu yishu dazhonghua," 18.

30. Yao Xueyin, "Tongsu wenyi duanlun." Lao Xiang defended himself in "Guanyu kangri sanzijing."

31. In a series of essays, Mao Dun tried to moderate the popularization debate. In *Xinhua ribao*, see "Guanyu dazhong wenyi," (February 13, 1938); in *Jiuwang ribao*, see "Kangzhan wenyi de zhongyao keti," (February 17, 1938), "Duiyu

wenyi tongxun de yijian" (May 23, 1938), and "Wenyi dazhonghua wenti," (March 9 and 10, 1938 [talks given in Hankou]); in *Wenyi zhendi* (all in vol. 1, no.4 [June 1]), see "Liang de tigao yu tongsu," "Liyong jiuxingshi de liang yiyi," as well as "Dazhonghua yu liyong xingshi" 121–22. Three of the above, notably the March 9 and 10 talks, have been reprinted in Wen Zhenting, *Wenyi dazhonghua wenti taolun ziliao,* 377–87.

32. The serialization in *Kang daodi* begins with no. 4 (February 16, 1938) and runs to nos. 13–14, 16–19, and 21–23 (ending on March 29, 1939).

33. For Lao She's 1938 comments about his writing on the play and its popularity, see his essay in *Lao She wenji,* vol. 15, 338–44.

34. Han Suyin, *Destination Chungking,* 65.

35. Zhang Shaosi, *Wuhan kangzhan wenyi shigao.* For commentary by Lao She in *Lao She wenji,* see "Wenjiang xiaxiang, wenjiang ruwu," vol. 15, 467–71 (originally in *Tongsu wenhua yuekan,* no. 9,1 [July 25, 1941]); also see his editorials in *Kang daodi:* "Zhenglunwen: Fa kan si," no. 1 (January 1938), and "Benkan bannianlai di huigu," no.15 (1938), with the latter more accessible in *Lao She wenji,* vol. 15, 348–50; as well as Lao She essays cited in note 26.

36. Roy, *Kuo Mo-jo;* the best overall treatment, touching on highlights such as Guo's relations with Lu Xun and others, is still Spence, *Gate of Heavenly Peace.* Guo's complicated personal and intellectual relationship with Japan is sensitively treated by Lu Yan, *Re-understanding Japan;* see also Gong Jimin and Fang Rennian, *Guo Moruo nianpu,* and *Guo Moruo zhuan.*

37. Lu Yan "Parting with Japan" 170–83; *Lu Xun quanji,* vol. 6, 538–44.

38. Lu Yan, "Parting with Japan," especially 180–87. See also the slightly different version in Sang Fengkang, *Guo Moruo he tade sanwei furen,* 204–22.

39. Interview with Yu Feng on June 18, 2001, in Beijing; also Sang Fengkang, *Haoguang* and *Guo Moruo he tade sanwei furen,* especially 204–22; a more sanitized version of the story appears in Lai Zhenghe, *Guo Moruo de hunlian yu jiaoyou;* as well as in English by Lu Yan (*Re-understanding Japan,* 187–90). I have known Yu Feng since the 1970s but interviewed her on this subject on June 18, 2001.

40. Interview with Yu Feng, June 18, 2001, in Beijing. Yu Feng became an artist with a national reputation, joined the Communist Party, and after 1949 headed the National Art Museum in Beijing. She married the calligrapher Huang Miaozi in Wuhan. She died in 2007.

41. The most detailed memoir is by Yang Hansheng: "Disanting—guotongqu kangri minzutong—zhanxian de yige zhantou baozhong."

42. Typical Guo Moruo speeches and statements are available in *Xinhua ribao,* April 8, 1938, 4; May 12, 1938, 2, 4; and in *Dagong bao,* May 2, 1938, 2.

43. Gunn, "Literature and Art," 261. See also Guo's statement on the popularization issue in "Kangzhan yu wenhua wenti."

44. For a selection of the most successful plays at the time, see Ma Yanxiang, *Zuijia kangzhan juxuan;* Tian Han, *Zhongguo huaju yundong wushinian shiliao ji,* vol. 1, covers the war years.

45. This poetic memoir, first published in 1939, was revised and reprinted a number of times before Guo's death in 1980. The accessible version is the 1997 edition of *Guo Moruo sizhuan* published in Anhui. For a thorough and useful

examination of the original text and subsequent revisions with an eye to errors, see Yi Mingshan, "Kangzhan shiqi Guo Moruo zai Wuhan huodong jilue."

46. See the exchange of letters that has surfaced recently in *Bainian zhao:* Li Ling, "Wen Yiduo de hunyin he aqing." The best portrait of Wen Yiduo in English is still the one by Jonathan Spence in *Gate of Heavenly Peace.* On Xinan Lianda—the wartime university where Wen taught in Kunming—see Israel, *Lianda.*

47. Certainly one can make the case that the wartime devastation of Chinese high culture had terrible long-term consequences; see Li Zehou, *Zhongguo xiandai sixiang shilun,* and Feng Chongyi, *Guogui zai guonanzhong,* on this point. Modris Eksteins has made a similar argument by eloquently describing the vulgarization of European high culture as a result of World War I in *Rites of Spring.* Eksteins and others connect the cultural impact of the Great War to the subsequent rise of fascism in Europe, especially in Germany. See also Winter, "Catastrophe and Culture."

6. MOBILIZING YOUTH

1. Epstein, *People's War,* 151–53.
2. *Geming wenxian,* vol. 58, 60–61 (official statistics on education since 1937); for the travails of one middle school, see *Hubei wenshi ziliao,* no. 19 (1987): 164–68; and for the graphic story of one foreign-supported secondary school as it moved inland to Yichang, see Gulick, *Teaching in Wartime China.*
3. On family background and statistics, see Israel and Klein, *Rebels and Bureaucrats,* 13; and Olga Lang's extensive sampling of college and secondary-school students in *Chinese Family and Society,* appendix, 365 (table 15). *China Year Book, 1935–36,* 505, 512.
4. Wasserstrom, *Student Protests.*
5. See Wasserstrom and Perry, *Popular Protest and Political Culture.*
6. Mei Yin, "Hubei xueyun de guoqu, xianzai, yu jianglai." On Chiang Kai-shek's crackdown on the universities in the late 1920s, see Yeh, *Alienated Academy.*
7. *Kangdi qingnian juntuan.*
8. *Zhengzhi tongxun.*
9. Coble, *Facing Japan;* and Israel and Klein, *Rebels and Bureaucrats.* See Wasserstrom, *Student Protests,* as well.
10. Both Communist and Guomindang histories written later have claimed organizational credit without presenting convincing evidence.
11. *Wuhan kangzhan shiyao,* 175, 181; as well as *Zhanshi jiaoyu,* no. 9 (December 5, 1937); and documents in *Wuhan kangzhan shiliao xuanbian.*
12. The final documents, found in *Wuhan kangzhan shiliao xuanbian,* 147–49, are taken from *Zhanshi jiaoyu,* no. 9 (December 5, 1937).
13. *Qingnian qianxian,* no. 4 (February 15, 1938): 18–21.
14. Epstein, *People's War,* 152.
15. *Qingnian qianxian,* no. 4 (February 15, 1938): 22–23.
16. In praise of this approach, see *Saodang bao,* April 12, 1938, 3.
17. Interview with Chen Lifu on June 23, 1992, in Taibei.

18. Eastman, *The Abortive Revolution*; Wakeman, "A Revisionist View" and *Policing Shanghai*; and Zheng Yuanzhong, "Xin Shenghuo yundong de zhengzhi yiyi."

19. Hu Kuo-tai, "Disputes on the Question of Wartime Education"; Chen Lifu, *Zhanshi jiaoyu fangzhen* and *Zhanshi jiaoyu xingzheng hui*; for a general memoir in English, Chang and Myers, *Storm Clouds*; and interview with Chen Lifu on June 23, 1992, in Taibei.

20. *Xuelu*, no. 5 (February 12, 1938): 78; *Jiaoyu tongxun*, no. 1 (March 26, 1938); and *Wuhan ribao*, January 8 and February 13 and 19, 1938.

21. *Zhongshan zhouli*, no. 1 (February 15, 1938), translated in Kuo, "Youth in the War"; *China Year Book*, 1938.

22. *Xinhua ribao*, March 25, 1938; *Wuhan kangzhan shiyao*, 213–15; and *Wuhan kangzhan shiliao xuanbian*, 149–50.

23. Huang Hua is featured in Israel and Klein, *Rebels and Bureaucrats*.

24. See the following 1938 issues of *Saodang bao*: April 20, 2; April 21, 2; April 23, 1–2; April 30, 4; May 31, 4. *Wuhan ribao*, June 24, 1938, 4; *Jiaoyu tongxun*, no. 3 (April 9, 1938): 1–5.

25. Chen Cheng, *Sanmin zhuyi qingniantuan zhi xingzhi ji qi zhanwang*, 35–36.

26. *Geming wenxian*, vol. 70, 117–18, 133–34.

27. Ibid., vol. 62, 16–22, June 16, 1938, message.

28. See *Wuhan kangzhan shiyao*, 366–69, for details on smaller groups that felt coerced.

29. The latter line of analysis dominates in mainland histories of the period, such as Mao Lei, *Wuhan Kangzhan shiyao*. Kang Ze was a Whampoa graduate and a loyal follower of Chiang Kaishek. The leadership chart of the Sanqing in 1938 included very few students.

30. For a definitive work on the plan to make the Sanqing Youth Corps an instrument for defactionalization and rebuilding of the Guomindang, see Huang Jianli, *Politics of Depoliticization*; my analysis closely follows that of chs. 5 and 6 in this work, as well as that of Lincoln Li in chs. 6 and 7 of *Student Nationalism in China*.

31. The German military advisory mission, led by General von Falkenhausen, had completely pulled out by July 1938. Western military aid was nonexistent. See ch. 7 of this book.

32. In retrospect, historians have made much of a perceived divergence between an overly accommodating pro–United Front line of the party in Wuhan and the tougher, less international position taken by Mao and others in Yan'an. On this point, Van Slyke, *Enemies and Friends*, is a standard work. However, more recent scholarship, based in part on new material from the Soviet archives, suggests fewer political differences between Wuhan and Yan'an in 1938. See Yang Guisong, *Zhonggong yu Moscow de guanxi*, and others, including Garver, *Chinese-Soviet Relations*.

33. *Dagong bao*, May 2, 1938, 3. I am grateful to Carl Crook for this point.

34. Israel and Klein, *Rebels and Bureaucrats*, 167–71.

35. *Wuhan kangzhan shiyao*, 215, 266, 366–69; *Jiaoyu tongxun*, no. 10 (May

28, 1938): 2–5; no. 23 (August 27, 1938): 2–3; *Zhongshan zhouli*, no. 15 (May 24, 1938): 1; no. 20 (June 28, 1938): 12–13; *Saodang bao (1938)*, April 8, 3, May 17, 3–4, May 23, 4, May 24, 4, May 27, 3–4.

36. Utley, *China at War*, 82.

37. See note 10 in ch. 5 for detailed citations on the Chen Duxiu–Zhang Guotao "problem."

38. Interviews in Beijing with Ge Baoquan on March 21, 1978; Hu Sheng on June 3, 1992; and Yu Feng on June 3, 2001; see also Li Hui, *Huang Maozi yu Yu Feng*, 83–101. For a detailed study on organizing youth in Henan, see Wou, *Mobilizing the Masses*. For statistics on Communist Party growth in 1938 and later, see Harrison, *Long March to Power*, 271.

39. See Bo Gu's candid comments to Edgar Snow in Snow, *Random Notes*, 23.

40. A young and naïve Han Suyin in her first book, *Destination Chungking*, 59–93, captured the romantic, surreal atmosphere of Wuhan's final days.

41. From "My Friend, you must have smelled the stench," written in 1937 and first published in 1938, reprinted in *Wang Tongchao shixuan*, 129–31, but also available in *Wang Tongchao wenji*, vol. 4, 304–6; the translation here follows Hsu Kaiyu, *Twentieth Century Chinese Poetry*, 250.

7. ROMANTIC HANKOU

1. Auden and Isherwood, *Journey to a War*, 39–40.

2. See, for example, *New York Times* reports for early 1938 and the 1939 book by senior China correspondent Hallett Abend, *Chaos in Asia*.

3. Sun Youli, "Chinese Military Resistance."

4. MacKinnon and Friesen, *China Reporting*; Abend, *Chaos in Asia*; May, "U.S. Press Coverage of Japan."

5. For prewar treaty-port life and the attitudes of many "old China hands," see Bickers, *Britain in China*; Clifford, *Spoilt Children of Empire*; and Wood, *No Dogs and Not Many Chinese*. An exception was J. B. Powell, the editor of *China Weekly Review* (Shanghai), who chose to remain in Shanghai and publish news of Chinese resistance and criticism of the Japanese occupation until he was interned (and tortured) and the *Review* was closed after Pearl Harbor.

6. Whelan, *Robert Capa*, 133–41. Ivens had a well-financed production agreement with the Chinese government to make a major documentary about the war. The film's backers in the United States included the head of the Library of Congress at the time, Archibald MacLeish, and Hollywood studios.

7. MacKinnon and Friesen, *China Reporting*, ch. 3.

8. On Germany's close relationship with Nanjing, see Kirby, *Germany and Republican China*. In *Journey to a War*, Auden and Isherwood tell a story about Madame Chiang Kaishek's cool reaction to the Japanese proposal: "The ambassador [Trautmann] came to tea and delivered his prepared speech [about peace terms]. There was an awkward silence. Somewhat embarrassed, the ambassador added: 'Of course, I give you this message without any comment.' Madame looked at him: 'I should hope so,' she said quietly. Then switching on all her charm: 'Tell me, how are your children?' This was the only answer the Japanese ever received" (59–60).

9. Stephen Craft offers a good summary in English of the British and German policies in English in ch. 5 of *V. K. Wellington Koo*. In Chinese, see Xu Lan, *Yingguo yu zhongri zhanzheng;* Li Shian, *Taipingyang zhanzheng shiqi de zhongying guanxi*. The secondary literature is considerable; see, for example, Huang Fengzhi, "Lun 1937–1939 nian yingguo duihua zhengce"; or Li Zenghui, "1937–41 nian YingMei zhi huanhua zhengce de yanbian yu bijiao."

10. Garver, *Chinese-Soviet Relations*. A major memoir is Chuikov, *Mission to China;* Kalyagin, *Along Alien Roads*. See also Clubb, *China and Russia*, 306–18;Liu, *Military History of Modern China*, 166–70; and Zhang Baijia, "China's Experience." The role of the Soviet advisers was restricted to munitions and gunnery issues (tanks and artillery); they did not advise at the higher, strategic level as the German advisers had done before 1938.

11. Chen Fu'an and Liu Guangming, *Wuhan huizhan yanjiu*, 245–53; *Wuhan kangzhan shiyao*, 276–79.

12. Guillermaz, *Une vie pour la Chine;* Archiv Chateau Vincinnes. The assistant who died of malaria was Lieutenant Colonel Rousselle. Guillermaz remained in China into the late 1960s.

13. Van de Ven, *War and Nationalism;* Tietler and Radtke, *Dutch Spy in China*.

14. Hans J. van de Ven's main argument in *War and Nationalism* is a critique of the analysis and influence of Stilwell and Dorn and their memos of 1938.

15. Harold Ickes diary entries for March 4 and May 1, 1938, Library of Congress, as cited in Sun Youli, "Chinese Military Resistance," 96.

16. Cited in detail in ibid., 81–96.

17. A variety of speeches and photographs from these dinners have survived; see MacKinnon and Friesen, *China Reporting*, ch. 3; and John Paton Davies's memoir, *Dragon by the Tail*.

18. MacKinnon and Friesen, *China Reporting*, 39.

19. Ibid., 25–26, 33, 40, 49, 50, 57, 104–7. Tong, *Dateline: China; Dong Xianguang zizhuan;* and Zeng Xubai, *Zeng Xubai zizhuan*, vol. 1. See also Boorman, *Biographical Dictionary*, vol. 3, 338–40 (quote on 339); and Liu Jingxiu, "Hollington K. Tong."

20. See the files of Guomindang Zhongyang dangbu in No. 2 Archives, Nanjing, nos. 9–69, for February 6 and 18, 1938; June 16, 1938; and January 17, 1939. See the Xuanchuan Bu files in No. 2 Archives, Nanjing, for 1938, nos. 718–5–23, 718-4-4868 and 4547; 718-4-4700; 718-272. See also *Zeng Xubai zizhuan*, 175–77; and the detailed discussion in Akio, "Kangzhan chuqi zhongguo de dui Mei."

21. Xuanchuan Bu files in No. 2 Archives, Nanjing, no. 718-4-4796; the campaign succeeded: Du Pont broke off negotiations, and the deal with the Japanese was never consummated.

22. Snow, "China's Fighting Generalissimo," 625. On Henry Luce and his publications' treatment of China, see Jesperson, *American Images of China*.

23. By September 1939 over thirteen hundred enterprises were in operation, employing over twenty-six thousand people. No good published history of the industrial-cooperative movement is yet available, but Douglas Reynolds has written a fine PhD dissertation on the topic ("Chinese Industrial Cooperative Move-

ment"), as well as an exploratory article in *Republican China*. For a recent, level-headed Chinese appraisal of the overall historical importance of the wartime Indusco movement, see Hou Dezhu, *Jingji yu wenjiao*, 330–59.

24. See also King, *China's American Daughter*, and Snow, *My China Years* (London, Harrap, 1984). Sadly, the Indusco movement became increasingly embroiled in Guomindang-Communist tensions; after the war, it never regained its initial momentum and disappeared after 1949. The movement never achieved its goal of launching thirty thousand enterprises. The movement ended its tenure as a U.N.-supported rural-reconstruction program: see Stepanek, *Town Called Shaoyang: Introducing*; and Stepanek, *Town Called Shaoyang: Witnessing*.

25. MacKinnon, "Refugee Flight."

26. Translation by the author, from *Shimodelai Zhongguo de pengyou*, 40–44, first published in MacKinnon and MacKinnon, *Agnes Smedley*, 209.

27. For coverage in periodicals of the time, see, for example: *Qingnian zhanxian*, no. 7/8 (June 20, 1938), 2; *Quanmin kangzhan*, no. 13; *Zhongshan zhoukan*, no. 15 (May 24, 1938), 1; the most thorough coverage was in the daily press: for 1938, see *Saodangbao*, May 21, 3; May 22, 4; May 23, 4; May 24, 4; May 27, 3, 4. See also *Wuhan ribao*, June 5, 1938, 4.

28. See citations of reports by McHugh, McConnell, Overesch, and Stilwell in Sun Youli, "Chinese Military Resistance," 91.

29. Tobe Ryoichi, "Central Yangzi Campaign."

30. See Zhang Baijia, "China's Experience" and "Kangri zhanzheng qianqi Guoming zhengfu dui Mei zhengce chutan." On Western public opinion, the classic study is Tuchman, *Stilwell and the American Experience*.

CONCLUSION

1. See Ao Wenwei, "Wuhan kangzhan shiqi Jiang Jieshi de zhanlueshu sixiang," for details of the conference and results; also van de Ven, *War and Nationalism*, 230–32. For a narrative account of the battles that followed in the Nanyue region, see MacKinnon, "Defense of Central Yangzi." For Jiang Baili's writing, see ch. 2.

2. *Kangzhanzhong de Wuhan*, 128–61; *Jinian Wuhan kangzhan 60 zhounian*, 783–88; Pi Mingxiu, *Jindai Wuhan chengshi shi*, 499–530; and Chen Fu'an and Liu Guangming, *Wuhan huizhan yanjiu*, 288–95. The Wuhan city archives have a wealth of documents from Zhang Renli's collaborationist government, with good runs of the daily press available at the city library. See also *Wuhan wenshi ziliao* (1985), no. 1: 85–87; and the comprehensive overview of occupied Wuhan in Ao Wenwei, *Hubei kangri zhanzheng shi*, 382–430, 460–67.

3. In English, see Eastman, *Seeds of Destruction* and "Nationalist China"; and Ch'i Hsi-sheng, *Nationalist China at War*.

4. See the lead editorial by Wang Ming, Bo Gu, and Zhou Enlai in *Xinhua ribao*, June 15, 1938.

5. MacKinnon, "Toward a History of the Chinese Press."

6. In English, see the clear accounts by William Kirby, "Continuity and Change in Modern China" and "Chinese War Economy."

7. Li Xuetong, *Weng Wenhao nianpu*, 154–77.

8. Unfortunately, this legacy became a shared global experience. China's 100 million refugees represented the first wave in a series of war-generated forced migrations in the mid-twentieth century. After 1939 war uprooted large populations in Germany, Spain, North Africa, and Eastern Europe. Next came the dislocations of the postcolonial era, notably the 10 million refugees and violence that grew out of the creation of India and Pakistan in 1947–48.

9. Lary and MacKinnon, *Scars of War*, Introduction. Wang, *The Monster That Is History*, is eloquent on this theme in Chinese fiction.

10. See, for example, Ignatieff, *The Warrior's Honour.*

GLOSSARY

TERMS AND PLACES

Anqing 安庆
Baoding junguan xuexiao 保定军官学校
baogao wenxue 报告文学
Baoqing bingzai jishi 宝庆兵灾纪实
Bengbu 蚌埠
Changchun guan 长春观
chijiu zhan 持久战
cishan tang (hui) 慈善堂 (会)
Dabeishan 大别山
Dagong bao 大公报
disanting 第三厅
funu zhidao 妇女指导
Fuyin tang 福音堂
Gaizao 改造
Gongguang diaozhengchu 工矿调整处
guandu shangban 官督商办
Guangji 广济
Guomin canzhenghui 国民参政会
Guomindang linshi quanguo daibiao dahui 国民党临时全国代表会
Guoshedang 国社党
Haida xiyuan 海大戏院
haisen 败战

hanjian 汉奸
Hankou 汉口
Hanyang 汉阳
Hefei 合肥
Hengyang 衡阳
heping qicheng hui 和平期成会
heping qingyuan hui 和平请愿会
hezuo 合作
Huangchuan 潢川
Huangmei 黄梅
Huayuankou 花园口
Huguang 湖广
Hukou 湖口
jingshen liangshi 精神粮食
jiti shenghuo yu ziwo jiaoyu 集体生活与自我教育
Jiujiang 九江
jiuping zhuang xinjiu 旧瓶装新酒
junshi weiyuanhui 軍事委員会
juntong 軍统
Kangzhan jiaoyu yanjiu 抗战教育研究
kangzhan jiaoyu yanjiuhui 抗戰教育研究会
kusheng zhendi 苦声振地
Lian Yungang 连云港

Linyi 临沂
Madang 马当
Matouzhen 碼头鎮
Minzu jiefang xianfengdui 民族解放
　先锋队
nanmin 难民
nanmin ertonghui 难民儿童会
nantong baoyuhui 难童保育会
Nanyue 南岳
Ouzhou wenyi fuxingshi 欧洲文艺
　复兴史
Pengze 彭泽
qi junzi 七君子
qingnian jiuguo tuan 青年救国团
Qu Yuan 屈原
qunzhong 群众
Ruichang 瑞昌
sanmin juyi 三民主义
Saodang bao 扫荡报
Shahe 沙河
Shen bao 申报
Shenghuo jiaoyu she 生活教育社
Shenghuo shudian 生活书店
Shikan Gakko 士官學校
shusan 疏散
Suxian 宿県
Taierzhuang 台儿庄
Taihu 太湖
Teng xian 滕县
Tianjiazhen 田家镇
Tongmenghui 同盟会
tongsu 通俗
tongxianghui 同乡会
tuanlian 團練
Wanjialing 万家岭
Wenxie 文协
wenzhang xiaxiang, wenzhang ruwu
　文章下鄉, 文章入伍
Wuchang 武昌
Wuhan 武汉
xiafang 下放
xian 県
xin xibao 新細胞
Xinhua ribao 新華日报
xinzheng 新政
xuanchuan bu 宣传部
xuesheng jun 学生军

Xuzhou 徐州
Yichang 宜昌
Yishe 蚁社
Yuzhou feng 宇宙风
zhandou xunkanshe 战斗旬刊社
zhanshi 战事
Zhanshi ertong baoyuhui 战時儿童保
　育会
Zhanshi jiaoyu she 战时教育社
Zhenji weiyuanhui 赈济委员会
zhian weiyuanhui 治安委员会
Zhongguo qingnian dang 中国青年党
Zhongguo qingnian xinwen jizhe
　xuehui 中国青年新文记者學会
Zhongguo xuelian daibiao dahui
　中国学联代表大会

PEOPLE

Bai Chongxi 白崇禧
Bo Gu (Qin Bangxian) 博古 (秦邦憲)
Cai E 蔡鄂
Cai Fuqing 蔡辅卿
Cao Juren 曹聚仁
Cao Kun 曹锟
Chen Baichen 陈白尘
Chen Cheng 陈诚
Chen Duxiu 陈独秀
Chen Gongbo 陈公博
Chen Lifu 陈立夫
Chen Mingshu 陈铭枢
Chen Yishen 陈仪深
Cheng Shewo 成舍我
Chi Fengcheng 池峰城
Chiang Chingkuo 蒋经国
Dai Li 戴笠
Ding Wenan 丁文安
Ding Wenjiang 丁文江
Doihara Kenji 土肥原贤二
Dong Biwu 董必武
Dong Xianguang 董显光
Fan Changjiang 范长江
Feng Guozhang 冯国璋
Feng Xuefeng 冯雪峰
Feng Youlan 冯友兰
Feng Yuxiang 冯玉祥
Feng Zikai 豊子愷

Gao Xiaozhen 高孝貞
Gao Zhipeng 高志鵬
Ge Baoquan 戈寶權
Gu Jiegang 顾颉刚
Gu Yuxiu 顧毓琇
Guo Moruo 郭沫若
Han Fuju 韩复渠
Hao Peicun 郝伯村
He Chengjun 何成濬
He Hengfu 贺衡夫
He Yingqin 何应钦
Hong Shen 洪深
Hu Feng 胡风
Hu Qiuyuan 胡秋原
Hu Sheng 胡绳
Hu Zongnan 胡宗南
Huang Hua 黄华
Huang Shaogu 黄少谷
Jiang Baili (Fangzhen) 蒋百里 (方震)
Kang Ze 康泽
Kong Xiangxi 孔祥熙
Lao She 老舍
Lao Xiang (Wang Xiangchen) 老向
　(王向晨)
Li Chang 李昌
Li Chuanye 李传业
Li Dazhao 李大钊
Li Denghui 李登辉
Li Dequan 李德全
Li Gongpu 李公朴
Li Peng 李鹏
Li Siguang 李四光
Li Wenhang 李韫珩
Li Xiannian 李先念
Li Zongren 李宗仁
Liang Qichao (Rengong) 梁启超
　(任公)
Liang Shuming 梁漱溟
Lin Kesheng 林可胜
Liu Liangmo 刘良模
Liu Ruiheng 刘瑞恆
Liu Wendao 刘文岛
Liu Xinsheng 刘歆生
Liu Zunqi 刘尊棋
Lu Xun 鲁迅
Luo Longji 罗隆基
Luo Zhuoying 罗卓英

Mao Dun 茅盾
Mu Mutian 穆木天
Pang Bingxun 庞炳勋
Peng Wenkai 彭文凯
Qian Junrui 钱俊瑞
Qian Zhongshu 錢钟书
Qiao Shi 乔石
Qin Bangxian (Bo Gu) 秦邦宪
　(博古)
Shen Junru 沈钧儒
Shen Zijiu 沈兹九
Shi Liang 史良
Song Meiling 宋美龄
Sun Chuanfang 孙传芳
Sun Lianzhong 孙连仲
Sun Liren 孙立人
Tang Enbo 汤恩伯
Tang Shengzhi 唐生智
Tao Xingzhi 陶行知
Tao Xisheng 陶希圣
Tian Han (Shouchang) 田汉 (寿昌)
Wang Dongyuan 王东原
Wang Jingwei 汪精卫
Wang Ming 王明
Wang Mingzhang 王铭章
Wang Shijie 王世杰
Wang Tongchao 王统照
Wang Zhanyuan 王占元
Wen Yiduo 闻一多
Weng Wenhao 翁文灏
Wu Peifu 吴佩孚
Wu Zuxiang 吳組湘
Xia Yan 夏衍
Xu Beihong 徐悲鸿
Xu Shiying 许世英
Xu Zhimo 徐志摩
Xue Weiying 薛蔚英
Xue Yue 薛岳
Yang Hansheng 阳翰笙
Yang Qingshan 杨庆山
Yang Sen 杨森
Yang Yongtai 杨永泰
Ye Chucang 叶楚伧
Ye Qing 叶青
Ye Ting 叶挺
Yu Dafu 郁达夫
Yu Feng 郁风

Yu Jishi 俞济时
Yu Lichen 于立忱
Yu Lichu 俞理初
Yu Liqun 于立群
Yuan Shikai 袁世凯
Yuan Shuipai 袁水拍
Yun Daiying 恽代英
Zhang Fakui 张发奎
Zhang Guotao 张国焘
Zhang Hanfu 章汉夫
Zhang Jiluan 张季鸾
Zhang Junmai 张君劢

Zhang Renli 张仁蠡
Zhang Shenfu 张申府
Zhang Wentian 张闻天
Zhang Zhidong 张之洞
Zhang Zhizhong 张治中
Zhang Zizhong 张自忠
Zhang Zuolin 张作霖
Zhou Enlai 周恩来
Zhou Fohai 周佛海
Zhou Yang 周扬
Zou Taofen 邹韬奋
Zuo Shunsheng 左舜生

BIBLIOGRAPHY

NEWSPAPERS AND PERIODICALS

The China Quarterly. Chongqing, vol. 4, no. 1 (Winter 1938–39).
Dagong bao (Impartial daily). Hankou, 1937–38.
Gaizao (Reconstruction). Beijing, 1920–22.
Jiaoyu tongxun (Education bulletin). Chongqing, 1938.
Jiu Zhongguo (Save China), edited by Hu Sheng. Hankou, 1938.
Kang daodi (Resist to the end). Hankou, January–November 1938 (monthly).
Kangzhan (Resist), edited by Zou Taofen. Hankou, 1937–38 (weekly).
Kangzhan wenyi (Resistance literature and art). Hankou, May–October 1938 (weekly).
Kangzhan xiangdao (Anti-Japanese war guide). Hankou, April 3–June 30, 1938 (weekly).
Minyi (People's opinion), edited by Tao Xisheng. Chongqing, 1938.
Qingnian qianxian (Youth frontline). Wuchang, January–August 1938.
Qingnian zhanxian (Youth at battlefront). Xi'an, 1938.
Qiyue (July). Hankou, 1938.
Quanmin kangzhan (United resistance). Hankou, Chongqing, 1939–41.
Saodang bao (Exterminate [the enemy] daily). Hankou, 1938.
Shen bao (Shanghai news). Hankou, 1938 (daily).
Shidai ribao (Times daily), published and edited by Hu Qiuyuan. Hankou, April–August 1938.
Wenyi zhendi (Literary battleground), edited by Mao Dun. Hankou, beginning April 1938 (biweekly).
Wuhan ribao (Wuhan daily). Hankou, 1937–38.
Xinhua ribao (New China daily), edited by Bo Gu. Hankou, 1938.
Xinwen jizhe (The reporter). Hankou, beginning April 1938.
Xuelu (Bloody road). Hankou, beginning January 15, 1938 (weekly).

Yuzhou feng (Universal wind). Guangzhou (Canton), 1938.
Zaisheng (Born again), edited by Zuo Shunsheng. Hankou, 1938.
Zhandi (Battleground). Hankou, March–June 1938.
Zhanshi jiaoyu (Wartime education). Shanghai, 1938.
Zhengzhi tongxun (Political communication). Hankou, inaugural issue June 1938.
Zhongshan zhoukan (Sun Yatsen weekly). Hankou, 1938.
Ziyou Zhongguo (Free China). Chongqing, 1938.

BOOKS AND ARTICLES

Abend, Hallett. *Chaos in Asia*. New York: Washburn, 1939.
———. *Treaty Ports*. Garden City, NY: Doubleday, 1944.
Ao Wenwei. "Wuhan kangzhan shiqi Jiang Jieshi de zhanlueshu sixiang" [Chiang Kaishek's battle strategies during the Battle of Wuhan period]. *Jindai shi yanjiu* [Studies in modern history], 1999, no. 6, 128–56.
———. *Hubei kangri zhanzheng shi, 1931–1945* [History of the Anti-Japanese War in Hubei province]. Wuhan: Wuhan daxue chubanshe, 2006.
Archiv Chateau de Vincennes, Paris. *Rapports des attachés militaires, 1938* (Chine), 7N3291 and 7N 3290.
Auden, W. H., and Christopher Isherwood. *Journey to a War*. London: Faber & Faber, 1938.
Baoding lujun junguan xuexiao [Baoding Military Academy]. Shijiazhuang: Hebei renmin chubanshe, 1987.
Bays, Danel. *China Enters the Twentieth Century: Chang Chih-tung and Issues of a New Age, 1895–1909*. Ann Arbor: University of Michigan Press, 1978.
Benton, Gregor. *China's Urban Revolutionaries: Explorations in the History of Chinese Trotskyism*. Atlantic Highlands, New Jersey: Humanities Press International, 1996.
———. *Chen Duxiu's Last Articles and Letters, 1937–1942*. London: Routledge, 1998.
———. *New Fourth Army: Communist Resistance along the Yangtze and the Huai, 1938–1941*. Berkeley: University of California Press, 1999.
Bi Chunfu. "Jinlue rijun wuhan huizhan jijian huaxue zhan shishi jikuang" [Employment of chemical weapons by invading Japanese troops in the Wuhan campaign]. *Minguo dangan*, no. 4 (1991): 134–38.
———. *Kangzhan jianghe juekou mishi* [Secret history of the breaching of river dikes during the Anti-Japanese War]. Taibei: Mingwen shuju, 1995.
Bian Xiuyue. "Kangzhan sunshi wenti yanjiu de quyu yanjiu jichu goujian" [Comments on "Preliminary Research into War Damage in Jiangsu Province"]. *Kangri zhanzheng yanjiu*, 2004, no. 4, 82–89.
Bickers, Robert. *Britain in China: Community, Culture, and Colonialism, 1900–30*. Manchester: Manchester University Press, 1999.
Boorman, Howard L., ed. *Biographical Dictionary of Republican China*. 4 vols. New York: Columbia University Press, 1967–1971.
Brook, Timothy. "Pacification of Jiading." In *Scars of War*, edited by Diana Lary and Stephen R. MacKinnon, 50–75. Vancouver: University of British Columbia Press, 2001.

———. *Collaboration.* Cambridge, MA: Harvard University Press, 2005.

Cai Qi'ao. *Wuhan xinwen shi* [History of Wuhan journalism]. Wuchang: n.p., 1943.

Cao Juren. *Wo yu wode shijie* [Myself and my world]. Beijing: Renmin chubanshe, 1983.

———. *Jiang Baili pingzhuan* [Critical biography of Jiang Baili]. Taibei: Yiqiao, 1998.

Capa, Robert. *Images of War.* New York: Grossman, 1964.

Carlson, Evans. *The Chinese Army.* New York: Institute of Pacific Relations, 1939.

———. *Twin Stars of China.* Westport: Hyperion Press, 1940.

Chang, Iris. *The Rape of Nanjing: The Forgotten Massacre.* New York: Basic Books, 1997.

Chang Jui-te. *Kangzhan shiqi de Guojun renshi* [The personnel system of the National Army during the War of Resistance]. Taibei: Zhongyang yanjiuyuan jindaishi yanjiuso, 1993.

———. "Nationalist Army Officers during the Sino-Japanese War, 1937–1945." *Modern Asian Studies* 30, no. 4 (1996): 1033–56.

———. "Chiang Kaishek's Coordination by Personal Directives." In *China at War: Regions of China, 1937–45,* edited by Stephen R. MacKinnon, Diana Lary, and Ezra Vogel, 65–87. Stanford, CA: Stanford University Press, 2007.

Chang Ke-ming. "A Study of the Import and Export Trade of Hankow." *Chinese Social and Political Science Review* 20, no. 2 (July 1936): 293–94.

Chang, Sidney, and Ramon Myers, eds. *Storm Clouds over China: The Memoir of Ch'en Li-fu, 1900–93.* Stanford, CA: Hoover Institute Press, 1994.

Changjiang (Fan Changjiang). *Cong Lugoqiao dao Zhanghe* [From Marco Polo Bridge to the Zhang River]. Hankou: Shenghuo shudian, 1938.

———. *Huaihe dazhan zhi qianhou* [Before and after the battle of the Huai River]. N.p.: Jiangsheng shushe, 1938.

———. *Lunwang de Ping-Jin* [The fall of Beijing and Tianjin]. Hankou: Shenghuo shudian, 1938.

Chen Cheng. *Sanmin zhuyi qingniantuan zhi xingzhi ji qi zhanwang* [Overview of the establishment of the Three Peoples Principles Youth Corps]. Hankou: n.p., April 1938.

Chen Duxiu zhu zuoxuan [Selected works of Chen Duxiu]. Shanghai: Shanghai renmin chubanshe, 1993.

Chen Feng, ed. *Ming-Qing yilai zhangjiang liuyu shehui fazhan shilun* [Studies of the history of the social development of the central Yangzi River basin since Ming-Qing]. Wuhan: Wuhan daxue chubanshe, 2006.

Chen Fu'an and Liu Guangming, eds. *Wuhan huizhan yanjiu* [Studies on the battle for Wuhan]. Wuhan: Wuhan daxue chubanshe, 1991.

Chen Lifu. *Zhanshi jiaoyu fangzhen* [Educational policies during the war]. N.p.: Zhongyang xunliantuan junshizhengzhibu jiaoguan yanjiuban, 1939.

———. *Four Years of Chinese Education (1937–1941).* Chongqing: China Information Committee, 1944.

———. *Zhanshi jiaoyu xingsheng hui* [Memoir on education during the war years] Taibei: Shangwu yinshuguan, 1973.

Chen Ta. *Population in Modern China.* Chicago: University of Chicago Press, 1946.

Ch'en Yung-fa. *Making Revolution: The Communist Movement in Eastern and Central China, 1937–1945*. Berkeley: University of California Press, 1986.

Cheng Chaoyun. "Kangzhan chuji de nanmin neiqian" [Refugee migration during the early years of the War of Resistance]. *Kangri zhanzheng yanjiu*, 2000, no.2, 79–97.

Cheng Qiheng. *Zhanshi Zhongguo baoye* [China's wartime newspapers]. Guilin: n.p., 1944. Reprint, Taibei: Guomindang dangshi weiyuanhui, 1976.

Ch'i Hsi-sheng. *Nationalist China at War: Military Defeats and Political Collapse, 1937–45*. Ann Arbor: University of Michigan Press, 1982.

———. "The Military Dimension, 1942–45." In *China's Bitter Victory: The War with Japan, 1937–1945*, edited by James Hsiung and Steven Levine, 170–90. Armonk, NY: M. E. Sharpe, 1992.

China Year Book, 1935–36, 1938–39. Edited by H. G. W. Woodhead. Shanghai: North China Daily News, 1936–39.

Chuikov, Vasil I. *Mission to China: Memoirs of a Soviet Military Adviser to Chiang Kaishek* [Missiya v Kitae: Zapiski voenago sovietnika. Moscow: Nawka, 1981]. Translated by David P. Barrett. Norwalk, CT: EastBridge, 2004.

Ci Shanhui. *Ge shantang zhuangli yange ji shiye qingkuang* [The history and activities of (Hankou) benevolent associations]. Hankou: n.p., 1945.

Clifford, Nicholas. *Spoilt Children of Empire: Westerners in Shanghai and the Chinese Revolution of 1925–1927*. Hanover, NH: Universities Press, 1991.

Clubb, O. Edmund. *China and Russia: The Great Game*. New York: Columbia University Press, 1971.

Coble, Parks M. *Facing Japan: Chinese Politics and Japanese Imperialism, 1931–1937*. Cambridge, MA: Council on East Asian Studies, Harvard University, 1991.

———. *Chinese Capitalists in Japan's New Order: The Occupied Lower Yangzi 1937–1945*. Berkeley: University of California Press, 2003.

Coox, Alvin. *Nomonhan: Japan against Russia*. Stanford, CA: Stanford University Press, 1985.

Craft, Stephen. *V. K. Wellington Koo and the Emergence of Modern China*. Lexington: University of Kentucky Press, 2004.

Davies, John Paton. *Dragon by the Tail*. London: Robson Books, 1972.

Documents from the Frontlines, 1987 (see *Kangri zhanzheng zhengmian zhanchang*).

Dong Biwu zhuan [Biography of Dong Biwu]. Beijing: Zhongyang wenxian chubanshe. 2006.

Dong Xianguang. *Dong Xianguang zizhuan* [Autobiography of Dong Xianguang]. Taibei: Taiwan xinsheng bao, 1973.

Dorn, Frank. *The Sino-Japanese War, 1937–1941: From Marco Polo Bridge to Pearl Harbor*. New York: Macmillan, 1974.

Dower, John. "Lessons of Another Occupation." *Nation*, July 7, 2003, 11–14.

Dreyer, Edward. *China at War, 1901–1949*. London: Longman, 1995.

Eastman, Lloyd. *The Abortive Revolution: China under Nationalist Rule*. Cambridge, MA: Harvard University Press, 1974.

———. *Seeds of Destruction: Nationalist China in War and Revolution, 1937–1949*. Stanford, CA: Stanford University Press, 1984.

————. "Nationalist China during the Sino-Japanese War, 1937–1945." In *The Cambridge History of China*, vol.13, *Republican China, 1912–1949*, edited by John Fairbank and Albert Feuerwerker, 547–607. Cambridge: Cambridge University Press, 1986.

Eksteins, Modris. *Rites of Spring: The Great War and the Birth of the Modern Age*. Boston: Houghton Mifflin, 1989.

Epstein, Israel. *The People's War*. London: Gollancz, 1939.

Ershi shiji Hunan renwu [Twentieth-century Hunan personalities], www.library .hn.cn/difangwx /hxrw/xdrw/mgzy/hsg (accessed March 17, 2006).

Esherick, Joseph. *Reform and Revolution in China: The 1911 Revolution in Hunan and Hubei*. Berkeley: University of California Press, 1976.

Fan Changjiang. *See* Changjiang.

Fang Hanqi. *Zhongguo xinwen shiye tongshi* [Comprehensive history of the Chinese press]. 3 vols. Beijing: Renmin daxue chubanshe, 1996.

Fang Zhijin. *Jianghan Aige* [Elegy for Jianghan]. Beijing: Tuanjie chubanshe 1995.

Feng Chongyi. *Guogui zai guonanzhong: kangzhan shiqi de Zhongguo wenhua* [Chinese culture during the Anti-Japanese War]. Guilin: Guangxi shifan daxue chubanshe, 1995.

Feng Xuefeng. "Guanyu yishu dazhonghua." *Kangzhan wenyi* 3, nos. 9–10 (February 1939): 18.

Feng Yi. "Le problème des refugies à Shanghai, 1937–1940." Memoire de DEA. Master's thesis, Université Lumière-Lyon 2, September 1993.

Feng Yuxiang, *Feng Yuxiang riji* [Diary of Feng Yuxiang]. Edited by Zhongguo dier lishi dangan guan. Shanghai: Jiangsu guji chubanshe, 1992.

Fitzgerald, John. *Awakening China: Politics, Culture, and Class in the Nationalist Revolution*. Stanford, CA: Stanford University Press, 1996.

————. "The Origins of the Illiberal Party Newspapers: Print Journalism in China's Nationalist Revolution." *Republican China* 21, no. 2 (November 1996): 1–22.

Fung, Edmund S. K. *In Search of Chinese Democracy: Civil Opposition in Nationalist China, 1929–49*. Cambridge: Cambridge University Press, 2000.

Furth, Charlotte, ed. *The Limits of Change: Essays on Conservative Alternatives in Republican China*. Cambridge, MA: Harvard University Press, 1976.

Gan Hailan. *Lao She nianpu* [Chronological biography of Lao She's life]. Beijing: Shumu wenxian chubanshe, 1989.

Garver, John. *Chinese-Soviet Relations, 1937–1945: The Diplomacy of Nationalism*. Oxford: Oxford University Press, 1988.

Gatrell, Peter. *A Whole Empire Walking: Refugees in Russia During World War I*. Bloomington: Indiana University Press, 1999.

Ge Gongzhen, *Zhongguo baoxue shi* [History of the Chinese press]. Shanghai: Shangwu chubanshe, 1936. Reprint, Taibei: Xuesheng shuju, 1964.

Geming wenxian [Documents on the revolution]. Taibei: Guomindang lishi weiyuanhui, 1953 to present.

Gittings, John. *Real China: From Cannibalism to Karaoke*. London: Simon & Schuster, 1996.

Godley, Michael R. "More Than a Footnote: Jiang Baili and the New Culture Movement." Paper presented at Murdoch University, Perth, Australia, July 1994.

Gong Jimin and Fang Rennian, eds. *Guo Moruo nianpu* [Chronological biography of Guo Moruo]. Tianjin: Renmin chubanshe, 1982.

———. *Guo Moruo zhuan* [Biography]. Beijing: Shiyue wenyi, 1988.

Goodman, Bryna. *Native Place, City, and Nation: Regional Networks and Identities in Shanghai, 1853–1937.* Berkeley: University of California Press, 1995.

Gu Weiming. "Song Meiling quanjiu kangzhan zhong de nantong [Song Meiling's work to save refugee children during the Anti-Japanese War]." *Yanhuang chunqiu,* 2003, no.6, 36–38.

———. "Zhongguo zhanshi ertong baoyuhui shulue" [Overview of the China Wartime Child Welfare Committee]. *Kangri zhanzheng yanjiu,* 2006, no. 4, 1–29.

Guillermaz, Jacques. *Une vie pour la Chine.* Paris: Editions Robert Laffont, 1989.

Gulick, Edward. *Teaching in Wartime China: A Photo-Memoir, 1937–1939.* Amherst: University of Massachusetts Press, 1995.

Gunn, Edward. "Literature and Art." In *China's Bitter Victory: The War with Japan 1937–1945,* edited by James C. Hsiung and Steven I. Levine, 235–73. Armonk, NY: M. E. Sharpe, 1992.

Guo Moruo. *Wairen mudu zhong de Rijun baoxing* [Japanese atrocities as witnessed by foreigners]. Translated by Harold Timperley. Hankou: Guomin chubanshe, 1938.

———. "Kangzhan yu wenhua wenti." *Ziyou Zhongguo,* no. 3 (June 20, 1938).

———. *Zhanshi xuanchuan gongzuo* [Wartime propaganda work]. Printed speech to Zhongyang lujun junguan xuexiao, 1938.

———. *Moruo wenji* [Collected works of Moruo]. 17 vols. Beijing: Renmin wenxue chubanshe; Hong Kong: Sanlian shudian, 1957–1963.

———. *Hongbo qu* [Great wave melody: ode to spirit of Wuhan]. Tianjin: Baihua wenyi chubanshe, 1959.

———. *Guo Moruo sizhuan* [Autobiographical writings]. Hefei: Anhui wenyi chubanshe, 1997.

Guomin Canzhenghui ziliao [Sources for the National People's Consultative Congress]. 2 vols. Chongqing: Sichuan renmin chubanshe, 1985, 1987.

Han Suyin. *Destination Chungking: An Autobiography.* London: Jonathan Cape, 1941.

Hankou Jiujiang shouhui yingzujie ziliao xuanbian [Historical materials on the recovery of the British concessions at Hankou and Jiujiang]. Wuhan: Renmin chubanshe, 1982.

Harrison, James P. *The Long March to Power: A History of the Chinese Communist Party, 1921–72.* New York: Praeger, 1972.

Ho Ping-ti. *Studies of the Population of China, 1368–1953.* Cambridge, MA: Harvard University Press, 1959.

Hou Dezhu. *Jingji yu wenjiao: kangri zhanzheng shiqi* [Economy in relation to culture: War of Resistance period]. Chengdu: Sichuan chubanshe, 2005.

Hsiung, James, and Steven Levine. *China's Bitter Victory: The War with Japan, 1937–1945.* Armonk, NY: M. E. Sharpe, 1992.

Hsu Kai-yu, trans. *Twentieth Century Chinese Poetry: An Anthology.* Garden City, NY: Doubleday, 1963.

Hu Chunhui. *Jinian Kangri zhanzheng shengli wushi zhounian xueshu taolun hui lunwen ji* [Papers from the conference on the fiftieth anniversary of the victory of the war of resistance against Japan]. Hong Kong: Zhuhai daxue, 1996.

Hu Kuo-tai. "Disputes on the Question of Wartime Education and the Formation of an Educational Policy for the Guomindang in the War." *Republican China* 14, no. 1 (1988): 30–56.

———. "The Struggle between Kuomintang and the Chinese Communist Party on Campus during the War of Resistance, 1937–45." *China Quarterly,* no. 118 (June 1989): 300–23.

Hu Qiuyuan, "Wo yu Cheng Shewo xiansheng" [Myself and Mr. Cheng Shewo]. In *Chengshewo xiansheng jinian wencong* [Essays in memory of Cheng Shewo], 48–63. Taibei: Xin shijie daxue chubanshe, 1998.

Huang Fengzhi. "Lun 1937–1939 nian yingguo duihua zhengce" [British policies towards China, 1937–39]. *Xiangtan shifan xueyuan,* no. 2 (1992): 13–19.

Huang Jianli. *The Politics of Depoliticization in Republican China: Guomindang Policy towards Student Political Activism, 1927–1949.* Berne: Peter Lang, 1996.

Hubei wenshi ziliao [Materials on the history and culture of Hubei Province]. Compiled by Hubei Lishi ziliao bianji weiyuanhui. Wuhan: Zhengxie, 1985–1990.

Hubei xinwen shiliao huibian [Compendium of historical materials on the Hubei press]. Wuchang: Hubei shengzhi xinwen chubanshe, 1982–87.

Hung Chang-tai. *Going to the People: Chinese Intellectuals and Folk Literature, 1918–1937.* Cambridge, MA: Council on East Asian Studies, Harvard University, 1985.

———. *War and Popular Culture: Resistance in Modern China, 1937–1945.* Berkeley: University of California Press, 1994.

Ignatieff, Michael. *The Warrior's Honour.* London: Viking, 1997.

"Industries of Hankou." *Chinese Economic Journal and Bulletin* 19, no. 2 (August 1936): 124–43.

Isaacs, Harold. *The Tragedy of the Chinese Revolution.* Stanford, CA: Stanford University Press, 1972. First published 1938.

———. *Re-encounters in China.* Armonk, NY: M. E. Sharpe, 1985.

Israel, John. *Lianda: A Chinese University in War and Revolution.* Stanford, CA: Stanford University Press, 1998.

Israel, John, and Donald Klein. *Rebels and Bureaucrats.* Berkeley: University of California Press, 1976.

Jeans, Roger B. *Roads Not Taken: The Struggle of Opposition Parties in Twentieth Century China.* Boulder, CO: Westview Press, 1992.

Jesperson, T. Christopher. *American Images of China, 1931–46.* Stanford, CA: Stanford University Press, 1996.

Ji Xueren, *Riben luehua zhanzheng de huaxue zhan* [Japanese use of chemical warfare in the invasion of China]. Beijing: Junshi yiwen chubanshe, 1995.

Jiang Baili. "Zizhi wenti yanjiu" [On the question of autonomy]. *Gaizao* 3.4 (March 1921).

———. "Shijie junshi dashi yu Zhongguo guoqing" [General military trends in the world and China's situation]. *Gaizao* 3.9 (August 1921): 55–64.

———. *Ribenren—yige waiguoren de yanjiu* [The Japanese—as studied by a foreigner]. 45-page pamphlet. Hankou: n.p., 1938.

————. *Jiang Baili xiansheng kangzhan lunwenji* [Collection of Jiang Baili's wartime writings (plus essays in memoriam)]. Xi'an: Da gong bao Xi'an fenguan, 1939.

————. *Jiang Baili xiansheng (Jiang Fangzhen) quanji* [Collected works of Jiang Baili]. 6 vols. Edited by Jiang Fucong and Xue Guangqian. Taibei: Zhuanji wenxue chubanshe, 1971.

Jiang Baili and Liang Qichao. *Ouzhou wenyi fuxing shi* [History of Renaissance in Europe]. Shanghai: Shanghai yinshinguan, 1921.

Jiang Baili xiansheng jinianoe [Essays in memory of Jiang Baili]. Zhejiang Haining: Wenshi ziliao, 1993.

Jiang Song Meiling. *Nanmin ertong jiuji yu jiaoyang* [Saving and caring for the children of refugees]. Speech in Hankou, 1938.

Jianghan wenshi ziliao [Materials on the history and culture of Jianghan]. Wuhan: Zhengxie, 1988.

Jin Chongji. *Zhou Enlai zhuan* [Biography of Zhou Enlai]. Beijing: Zhongyang wenxian Chubanshe, 1996.

Jinian Wuhan kangzhan ji zhongshan zhuan yunan 60 zhounian guoji xueshu yantaohui lunwenji [Proceedings of the Chengde conference on the 60th anniversary of the Wuhan resistance war and the Sun Yatsen warship incident]. Wuhan: Hubei renmin chubanshe, 1999.

Johnson, Chalmers. *Peasant Nationalism and the Rise of Communist Power.* Stanford, CA: Stanford University Press, 1962.

————. *Osaki Hotsumi and the Sorge Spy Ring,* 2nd ed. Stanford, CA: Stanford University Press, 1990.

Jordan, Donald. *The Northern Expedition: China's National Revolution of 1926–1928.* Honolulu: University of Hawaii Press, 1976.

Kalyagin, Aleksandr. *Along Alien Roads.* Translated by Steven Levine. New York: Columbia University Press, 1983.

Kangdi qingnian juntuan [Anti-Japanese Youth Military Corps]. Zhonggong Henansheng wei dangshi gongzuo weiyuanhui. Xinyang: Henan renmin chubanshe, 1990.

Kangri zhanshi [History of the Anti-Japanese War]. Compiled by Guofang Bu [Ministry of Defense (Taiwan)]. Taibei: Guofangbu shizhengju, 1962–1966.

Kangri zhanzheng guomindang zhenwang jianglinglu [Chronicle of the heroic sacrifices by Guomindang generals on the front lines of the Anti-Japanese War]. Beijing: Jiefang jun chubanshe, 1987.

Kangri zhanzheng shiqi de Zhongguo xinwenjie [Chinese press during the War of Resistance period]. Edited by the Institute of Journalism, Chinese Academy of Social Sciences. Chongqing: Chongqing chubanshe, 1987.

Kangri zhanzheng zhengmian zhanchang [(Documents from the) frontline battlefields of the War of Resistance]. 2 vols. Edited by Zhongguo di'er lishi dang'an guan. Nanjing: Jiangsu guji chubanshe, 1987. Cited in notes as *Documents from the Frontlines.*

Kangzhan chuqi de Shanghai nanmin gongzuo [Work with refugees during the initial years of the Anti-Japanese War]. Shanghai: Shanghai dangshi ziliao, 1993.

Kangzhan chuqi guogong hezuo Wuhan dashiji [Chronological record of the Communist- Guomindang United Front during the early War of Resistance period]. Wuhan: Balujun Wuhan banshiqu jinianguan, 1985.

Kangzhan de jingyan yu jiaoxun [Lessons and experience (in journalism) from War of Resistance]. Edited by Qian Jiaju, Hu Yuzhi, and Zhang Tiesheng. N.p.: Shenghuo shudian, 1939.

Kangzhan jianguoshi yantaohui lunwenji [Proceedings of the conference on China during the War of Resistance]. Taibei: Modern History Institute, Academia Sinica, 1985.

Kangzhan shiqi neiqian xinan de gongshang zhiye [Evacuation of business and industry to the southwest during the Anti-Japanese War]. Kunming: Yunnan renmin chubanshe, 1989.

Kangzhanzhong de Wuhan [Wuhan in the middle of the War of Resistance]. Wuhan: Zhengxie wenshi weiyuanhui, 1985.

King, Margery. *China's American Daughter: Ida Pruitt, 1888–1985.* Hong Kong: Chinese University of Hong Kong Press, 2004.

Kirby, William. *Germany and Republican China.* Stanford, CA: Stanford University Press, 1984.

———. "Continuity and Change in Modern China: Chinese Economic Planning on the Mainland and on Taiwan, 1943–1958." *Australian Journal of Chinese Affairs* 24 (July 1990): 121–41.

———. "The Chinese War Economy: Mobilization, Control, and Planning in Nationalist China." In *China's Bitter Victory: War with Japan, 1937–45.* Edited by James Hsiung and Steven Levine, 185–212. Armonk, NY: M. E. Sharpe, 1992.

Kubo Toru. "Koa-Institute and Its Research in China." In *China at War: Regions of China, 1937–45,* edited by Stephen R. MacKinnon, Diana Lary, and Ezra Vogel, 44–64. Stanford, CA: Stanford University Press, 2007.

Kuo, P. C. "Youth in the War." *China Quarterly* (Chongqing) 4, no. 1 (Winter 1938–39): 55–66.

Lai Zhenghe, ed. *Guo Moruo de hunlian yu jiaoyou* [Guo Moruo's marriages and friends]. Chengdu: Chengdu chubanshe, 1992.

Lan Hai. *Zhongguo kangzhan wenyi shi* [History of literature and art of the Chinese War of Resistance]. Ji'nan: Shandong wenyi chubanshe, 1984.

Lang, Olga, *Chinese Family and Society.* New Haven, CT: Yale University Press, 1946.

Lao She. "Sange yuelai de Jinan" [Jinan over the last three months]. *Dagong bao,* December 4–6, 1937.

———. *Tongsu wenyi wujiang* [Five lectures on the popular literature]. Chongqing: Zhonghua wenyijie kangdi xiehui, 1939

———. *Lao She wenji* [Collected works of Lao She]. 16 vols. Beijing: Renmin wenxue chubanshe, 1985–1990.

———. "Diao Jinan" [Mourning Jinan]. In *Lao She wenji* [Collected works of Lao She], vol. 14, 96–100. Beijing: Renmin wenxue chubanshe, 1989.

Lao Xiang (Wang Xiangchen). *Kangri sanzi jing* [Anti-Japanese Three Character Classic]. Introduction by Lao She. Hankou: Sanhu dushu she, 1938.

———. "Guanyu kangri sanzijing." *Kangzhan wenyi* 1.7 (June 5, 1938): 19.
Lary, Diana. *Region and Nation: The Kwangsi Clique in Republican Politics.* Cambridge: Cambridge University Press, 1975.
———. "Defending China: The Battles of the Xuzhou Campaign." In *Warfare in Chinese History,* edited by Hans van de Ven, 398–427. Leiden: Brill, 2000.
———. "Drowned Earth: The Strategic Breaching of the Yellow River Dyke, 1938." *War in History* 8, no. 2 (2001): 191–207.
———. "A Ravaged Place: The Devastation of the Xuzhou Region, 1938." In *Scars of War: The Impact of Warfare on Modern China,* edited by Diana Lary and Stephen R. MacKinnon, 98–117. Vancouver: University of British Columbia Press, 2001.
———. "Treachery, Disgrace, and Death: Han Fuju and China's Resistance to Japan." *War in History* 13, no. 1 (2006): 65–90.
———. "Guangxi's Experience of War." In *China at War: Regions of China, 1937–45,* edited by Stephen R. MacKinnon, Diana Lary, and Ezra Vogel, 314–34. Stanford, CA: Stanford University Press, 2007.
Lary, Diana, and Stephen R. MacKinnon, eds. *Scars of War: The Impact of Warfare on Modern China.* Vancouver: University of British Columbia Press, 2001.
Leys, Simon (Pierre Rickmans). *Chinese Shadows.* New York: Viking, 1977.
———. *Burning Forest.* New York: Henry Holt, 1985.
Li Enhan. *Ribenjun zhanzheng baoxing zhiyanjiu* [A study of Japan's war atrocities]. Taibei: Taiwan shangwu chubanshe, 1994.
Li Hui. *Jianyu yinying de rensheng* [A life under the shadow of prison]. Changsha: Hunan wenyi chubanshe, 1989.
———. *Huang Maozi yu Yu Feng* [Huang Miaozi and Yu Feng]. Wuchang: Hubei renmin chubanshe, 2005.
Li Juanli. *Junxue qicai—Jiang Baili* (Lanzhou: Lanzhou dakue chubanshe, 1998).
Li, Lincoln. *Student Nationalism in China (1924–1949).* Albany, NY: State University of New York Press, 1994.
Li Ling. "Wen Yiduo de hunyin he aiqing" [Love and marriage of Wen Yiduo]. *Bainianchao* 15, no. 3 (1999): 65–73.
Li Shian. *Taipingyang zhanzheng shiqi de zhongying guanxi* [Chinese-British relations during the Pacific War]. Beijing: Zhongguo shehui kexue chubanshe, 1994.
Li Tsung-jen (Li Zongren) and Tong Te-kong. *The Memoirs of Li Tsung-jen.* Boulder, CO: Westview Press, 1979.
Li Wenzhi. *Zhongguo jindai nongye shi ziliao* [Materials on China's modern agriculture], vol.1 (1840–1911). Beijing: Sanlian, 1957.
Li Xuetong. "Zhanshi ertong baoyuhui de lishi yu zuoyong" [History and function of the Wartime Child Welfare Committee]. In *Qingnian xueshu luntan* [Studies by young scholars], *Year 2000,* edited by the Chinese Academy of Social Sciences Modern History Institute, 245–62. Beijing: Shehui kexue wenxian chubanshe, 2001.
———. *Weng Wenhao nianpu* [Chronological biography of Weng Wenhao]. Jinan: Shandong jiaoyu chubanshe, 2005.
Li Yongming. *1938: Wuhan dahuizhan* [Battle of Wuhan]. Wuhan: Hubei chubanshe, 2005.

Li Zehou. *Zhongguo xiandai sixiang shilun* [Essays on modern Chinese thought]. Vol. 2. Beijing: Renmin chubanshe, 1987. Revised in *Zhongguo sixiang shilun*. Heifei: Anhui wenyi chubanshe, 1999.

Li Zenghui. "1937–41 nian YingMei zhi huanhua zhengce de yanbian yu bijiao" [Comparative analysis of British and U.S. control of aid to China policies from 1937–41]. *Dangan shiliao yu yanjiu*, no. 2/3 (2000): 94–106.

Li Zhiying. *Bo Gu zhuan* [Biography of Bo Gu]. Beijing: Dangdai Zhongguo chubanshe, 1994.

Liang Hsi-huey. *The Sino-German Connection: Alexander von Falkenhausen between China and Germany, 1900–1941*. Assen, Netherlands: Van Gorcum, 1978.

———. "General Alexander von Falkenhausen." In *Die deutsche Beraterschaft in China, 1927–1938*, edited by Bernard Martin, 175–86. Dusseldorf: Droste, 1980.

Liang Jialu. *Zhongguo xinwen yeshi* [Business history of the Chinese press]. Nanning: Guangxi renmin chubanshe, 1984.

Liang Kan. "Chinese Intellectuals in the War: Chongqing, 1937–1945." PhD diss., Yale University, 1995.

———. "Rethinking May Fourth: Vernacular Movement in Wartime Chongqing." Unpublished paper, n.d.

Lin Dezheng, *Baoding junguan xuexiao zhi yanjiu* [A study of Baoding Military Academy]. Master's thesis, Taibei, Institute of Modern History, 1980.

Liu Bing. "Kangri zhanzheng yu zhongguo renkou wenti xueshu luntan zongshu" [Summary of discussions at a research conference on population questions during the Anti-Japanese War]. *Kangri zhanzheng yanjiu*, 2000, no.2, 249–53.

Liu, F. F. *A Military History of Modern China, 1926–1956*. Princeton, NJ: Princeton University Press, 1956.

Liu Fenghan. "Wuhan huizhan yanjiu" [Examination of the Battle for Wuhan]. In *Kangzhan jianguo shiyan taolunhui wenji*, vol. 1, 99–162. Taibei: Zhongyang yanjiuyuan jindai so, 1985.

Liu Jingxiu. "Hollington K. Tong and the Nationalist Government's Wartime Image Creation Efforts, 1937–1945." Master's thesis, Arizona State University, 1996.

Liu Liangmo, *Shimodelai Zhongguo renmin zhi you* [Agnes Smedley: friend of the Chinese people]. Beijing: Renmin chubanshe, 1950.

Liu Lu. "A Whole Nation Walking: The Great Retreat in the War of Resistance, 1937–1945." PhD diss., University of California, San Diego, 2002.

Liu Qi. *Xuzhou huizhan* [Battle for Xuzhou]. Beijing: Zhongguo wenshi chubanshe, 1985.

Liu Qiyu. *Gu Jiegang xiansheng xueshe* [Description of Gu Jiegang's scholarship]. Beijing: Zhonghua shuju, 1986.

Liu Wangling. *Heixue jingu: xinghai qianhou Hubei baokan shishi zhangbian* [Dark blood, golden drum: extensive history of the Hubei press before and after 1911]. Wuhan: Huazhong. 1991.

Liu Zunqi. "Zhandi jizhe de yixie yinxing" [Impressions of a war correspondent]. In *Kangzhan de jingyan yu jiaoxun*, edited by Qian Jiaju, Hu Yuzhi, and Zhang Tiesheng. N.p.: Shenghuo shudian, 1939.

————. *Tongxun zazhixuan* [Miscellaneous essays and writings]. Beijing: Xinhua, 1989.

Lo Fu (Zhang Wentian). *Xi shinian lai de CCP* [Last ten years of the Communist Party], pamphlet, 1938.

Lu Fangshang. "Lingyizhong weizuzhi: Kangzhan shiqi de jiating yu hunyin wenti" [Marriage and family during the Resistance War]. *Jindai Zhongguo funushi yanjiu* (Taibei), no. 3 (August 1995): 97–121.

————. "Kangzhan shiqi de qiandu yundong" [Moving the capital during the War of Resistance]. In *Jinian kangri zhanzheng shengli wushi zhounian*, edited by Hu Chunhui, 21–43. Zhuhai: Xianggang Zhuhai shuyuan yazhou yanjiu zhongxin, 1996

Lu Xun. *Lu Xun quanji* [Complete works of Lu Xun]. Beijing: Renmin wenxue chubanshe, 1981.

Lu Yan. *Re-understanding Japan: Chinese Perspectives, 1895–1945.* Honolulu: University of Hawaii Press, 2004.

Ma Yanxiang, ed. *Zuijia kangzhan juxuan* [The best War of Resistance plays]. Hankou: Shanghai zazhi gongsi, 1938.

MacKinnon, Stephen R. "The Tragedy of Wuhan, 1938." *Modern Asian Studies* 30, no. 4 (1996): 931–43.

————. "Toward a History of the Chinese Press in the Republican Period." *Modern China* 23, no. 1 (January 1997): 3–32.

————. "Wuhan's Search for Identity in the Republican Period." In *Remaking the Chinese City: Modernity and National Identity, 1900–1950,* edited by Joseph Esherick, 161–71. Honolulu: University of Hawaii Press, 2000.

————. "Refugee Flight at the Outset of the Anti-Japanese War." In *Scars of War: The Impact of Warfare on Modern China,* edited by Diana Lary and Stephen R. MacKinnon, 118–34. Vancouver: University of British Columbia Press, 2001.

————. "Defense of the Central Yangzi Valley, 1938–1940." Unpublished research paper, Hawaii, 2004.

MacKinnon, Stephen R., and Oris Friesen. *China Reporting: An Oral History of American Journalism in the 1930s and 1940s.* Berkeley: University of California Press, 1987.

MacKinnon, Stephen R., Diana Lary, and Ezra Vogel, eds. *China at War: Regions of China, 1937–45.* Stanford, CA: Stanford University Press, 2007.

MacKinnon, Stephen R., and Janice R. MacKinnon. *Agnes Smedley: The Life and Times of an American Radical.* Berkeley: University of California Press, 1988.

Malraux, André. *Man's Fate (La Condition Humaine).* Paris: Gallimard, 1933.

Mao Zedong. "On Protracted War." In *Selected Works of Mao Zedong,* 113–94. Beijing: Foreign Languages Press, 1967.

Martin, Bernard, ed. *Die deutsche Beraterschaft in China, 1927–1938.* Dusseldorf: Droste, 1980.

Masako, Kohama. "The Problem of Refugees in Shanghai during the Sino-Japanese War and the Transformation of the 'Public' Arena." Presented at the Research Conference on Society and Culture in China during the Sino-Japanese War, Hakone, Japan, November 24–28, 2006.

May, Ernst. "U.S. Press Coverage of Japan, 1931–41." In *Pearl Harbor as History*, edited by D. Borg and Shumpei Okamoto, 511–32. New York: Columbia University Press, 1973.

McCord, Edward. "Burn, Kill, Rape, and Rob: Military Atrocities, Warlordism, and Anti-Warlordism in Republican China." In *Scars of War: The Impact of Warfare on Modern China*, edited by Diana Lary and Stephen R. MacKinnon, 18–47. Vancouver: University of British Columbia Press, 2001.

Mei Yin. "Hubei xueyun de guoqu, xianzai, yu jianglai" [Past, present, and future of the Hubei student movement]. *Qingnian qianxian*, no. 5 (May 4, 1938).

Merker, Peter. "The Guomindang Regions of Jiangxi." In *China at War: Regions of China, 1937–45*, edited by Stephen R. MacKinnon, Diana Lary, and Ezra Vogel, 288–313. Stanford, CA: Stanford University Press, 2007.

Miao Fenglin. *Taierzhuang dazhan he Zhongguo Kangzhan* [Battle of Taierzhuang and China's Anti-Japanese War]. Jinan: Shandong daxue chubanshe, 1997.

Peattie, Mark. "Attacking a Continent: The Navy's Air War in China, 1937–41." Ch. 5 in *Sunburst: Rise of Japanese Naval Air Power, 1909–1941*. Annapolis, MD: Naval Institute, 2002.

Pi Mingxiu. *Wuhan jinbainianshi* [One hundred year history of Wuhan, 1840–1949]. Wuhan: Hubei renmin chubanshe, 1985.

———. *Jindai Wuhan chengshi shi* [A history of modern Wuhan]. Wuhan: Zhongguo shehui kexue chubanshe, 1993.

Pi Mingxiu and Yang Fulin, eds. *Wuhan chengshi fazhanjiuyi* [Collected essays on the developmental path of the city of Wuhan]. Tianjin: Nankai daxue chubanshe, 1990.

Plum, M. Colette. "Unlikely Heirs: War Orphans during the Second Sino-Japanese War, 1937–45." PhD diss., Stanford University, 2006.

Qian Zhongshu. *Fortress Besieged*. Translation of *Weicheng* (1947), by Nathan Mao and Jeanne Kelly. New York: New Directions, 2004.

Qin Feng, *Kangzhan Yishunjian* [The War of Resistance through the wink of an eye (photos)]. Guilin: Guangxi shifan daxue chubanshe, 2005.

Rankin, Mary. *Elite Activism and Political Transformation in China: Zhejiang, 1865–1911*. Stanford, CA: Stanford University Press, 1986.

Rapports des attachés militaires, 1938 (Chine). 7N3291 and 7N 3290. Archiv Chateau de Vincennes, Paris.

Ray Huang. "Chiang Kaishek and His Diary." *Chinese Studies in History* 29, nos. 1 and 2 (Fall-Winter 1995–96), and 30, nos. 1 and 2 (Fall-Winter 1996–97).

Reynolds, Douglas. "Chinese Industrial Cooperative Movement and Political Polarization of Wartime China, 1938–1945," University Microfilms 76–13, 192. PhD diss., Columbia University, 1976.

———. "The Indusco Files at Columbia University: Primary Source for the Wartime Gung Ho Movement." *Republican China* 12.2 (April 1987): 44–64.

Rowe, William T. *Hankow: Commerce and Society in a Chinese City, 1796–1889*. Stanford, CA: Stanford University Press, 1984.

———. *Hankow: Conflict and Community in a Chinese City, 1796–1895*. Stanford, CA: Stanford University Press, 1989.

————. "Wuhan and Its Region, 1736–1938." In *Les metropoles chinoises au Xxe siècle*, edited by Christian Henriot. Paris: Editions Arguments, 1995.

————. *Crimson Pain: Seven Centuries of Violence in a Chinese County*. Stanford, CA: Stanford University Press, 2007.

Roy, David Tod. *Kuo Mo-jo: The Early Years*. Cambridge, MA: Harvard University Press, 1971.

Sang Fengkang. *Haoguang: Guo Moruo yu Anna de hunlian* [Brilliant: Guo Moruo and love match with Anna]. Taiyuan: Beiyao wenyi chubanshe, 1992.

————. *Guo Moruo he tade sanwei furen* [Guo Moruo and his three wives]. N.p.: Hainan chubanshe, 1994.

Sawyer, Ralph, trans. *Sun-tzu: Art of War*. Boulder, CO: Westview Press, 1994.

Schencking, Charles. Edited by Ger Teitler and Kurt Radtke. "A Dutch Spy in China: Reports on the First Phase of the Sino-Japanese War (1937–1939)." *Journal of the Royal Asiatic Society* 11, no. 1 (2001): 51–132.

Schneider, Lawrence. *Ku Chieh-kang and China's New History*. Berkeley: University of California Press, 1971.

Schwarcz, Vera. *The Chinese Enlightenment: Intellectuals and the Legacy of the May Fourth Movement of 1919*. Berkeley: University of California Press, 1986.

————. *Time for Telling Truth is Running Out: Conversations with Zhang Shenfu*. New Haven, CT: Yale University Press, 1992.

Shen Benwen. *Xiandai shehui wenti* [Contemporary social problems]. Chongqing: Shangwu, 1942. Revised as *Xiandai Zhongguo wenti*. Shanghai: Shangwu, 1946.

Sheng Renxue, ed. *Zhang Guotao wenti yanjiu ziliao* [Source materials for the study of the Zhang Guotao question]. Chengdu: Sichuan renmin, 1982.

Sheridan, James. *Chinese Warlord: The Career of Feng Yu-hsiang*. Stanford, CA: Stanford University Press, 1966.

Shi Liang. "Wode shenghuo daolu" [The path of my life]. *Renwu*, no. 5 (1983): 22–33, and no. 6 (1983): 76–90.

Shi Sheling. "Baoding junguan xuexiao cangsangji" [The vicissitudes of the Baoding Military Academy].*Yiwen zhi*, nos.34, 35, and 36 (July, August, and September 1957): 16–21, 9–14, and 35–38.

Shina shobetsu zenshi [Comprehensive gazetteer of Chinese provinces]. 18 vols. Tokyo: Toa Dobunkai, 1917–20.

Sih, Paul. *Nationalist China during the Sino-Japanese War*. Hicksville, NY: Exposition Press, 1977

Smedley, Agnes. *Battle Hymn of China*. New York: Knopf, 1943.

Snow, Edgar. "China's Fighting Generalissimo (Chiang Kaishek)." *Foreign Affairs*, no. 16 (July 1938): 612–25.

————. *Random Notes on Red China, 1936–1945*. Cambridge, MA: Harvard East Asian Research Center, Harvard University, 1957.

————. *Red Star over China*. New York: Random House, 1938. Rev. ed., New York: Grove Press, 1969.

Snow, Helen F. *My China Years*. London: Harrap, 1984.

Solinger, Dorothy J. *Contesting Citizenship in Urban China: Peasants, Migrants, State, and the Local Market*. Berkeley: University of California Press, 1999.

Spence, Jonathan. *Gate of Heavenly Peace: The Chinese and Their Revolution, 1895–1980*. New York: Viking, 1981.

———. *God's Chinese Son: The Taiping Heavenly Kingdom of Hong Xiuquan*. New York: Norton, 1996.

Stepanek, Antoinette. F. *A Town Called Shaoyang: Witnessing Dynastic Changes in China*. Boulder, CO: Gold Hill Press, 1992.

Stepanek, Joseph E. *A Town Called Shaoyang: Introducing Industry Appropriate to China*. Boulder, CO: Gold Hill Press, 1992.

Stranahan, Patricia. "Radicalization of Refugees: Communist Party Activity in Wartime Shanghai's Displaced Persons Camps." *Modern China* 25, no. 3 (1999): 166–93.

Su Yun-feng. *Zhongguo xiandaihua quyu yanjiu: Hubei sheng* [Regional studies in China's modernization: Hubei Province, 1860–1916]. Taibei: Zhongyang yanjiu yuan, 1981.

Sun Dongxuan, "Han Fuju beike qianhou" [Circumstances of Han Fuju's execution]. *Wenshi ziliao xuanji*, no. 54 (1962): 99–109.

Sun Yankui. *Gunande renliu: Kangzhan shiqi de nanmin* [Refugees during the War of Resistance]. Guilin: Guangxi shifan daxue chubanshe, 1994.

———. "Kangzhan chuqi Wuhan nanmin jiuji zouyi [Refugee relief work in wartime Wuhan]. *Wuhan luntan*, no. 6 (1996): 43–48.

Sun Youli. "Chinese Military Resistance and Changing American Perceptions, 1937–38." In *On Cultural Ground*, edited by Robert David Johnson, 81–96. Chicago: Imprint Press, 1994.

Tang Baolin. *Zhongguo tuopai shi* [History of the Chinese Trotsykism]. Taibei: Dongda dushu, 1994.

Tang Xuefeng. *Zhongguo kongjun kangzhan shi* [History of Chinese Air Force during War of Resistance]. Chengdu: Sichuan daxue chubanshe, 2000.

Tao Juyin. *Jiang Baili xiansheng zhuan* [Biography of Mr. Jiang Baili]. Shanghai: Zhonghua shuju, 1948; Beijing: Zhonghua shuju, 1985.

Teitler, Ger, and Kurt Radtke. *A Dutch Spy in China: Reports on the First Phase of the Sino-Japanese War, 1937–1939*. Leiden: Brill, 1999.

Tian Han. *Zhongguo huaju yundong wushinian shiliao ji* [Historical materials on the Chinese drama movement of the last fifty years]. 3 vols. Beijing: Xiju chubanshe, 1985.

Timperley, Harold. *Japanese Terror in China*. New York: Modern Age Books, 1938.

Tobe Ryoichi. "Central Yangzi Campaign, 1938–41." Paper presented at the Research Conference on Military History of the Anti-Japanese War, Hawaii, January 2004. Published in Japanese in *Nicchu senso no gunji teki tenkai* [Military developments in the Sino-Japanese War], edited by Tobe Ryoichi and Hatano Sumio, 157–88. Tokyo: Keio University Press, 2006.

Tong, Hollington K. *China and the World Press*. N.p., 1948.

———. *Dateline: China—The beginning of China's Press Relations with the World* New York: Rockport Press, 1950.

Tsuchida Akio. "Kangzhan chuqi zhongguo de dui mei 'guomin waijiao gongzuo'" [China's public diplomacy towards U.S. at beginning of War of Resistance]. Presented at the Research Conference on 1930s China, Chengdu, August 2005.

Tuchman, Barbara. *Stilwell and the American Experience in China*. New York: Bantam Books, 1971.

U.S. Military Intelligence Reports: China 1911–1941. Frederick, MD: University Publications of America, 1983.

Utley, Freda. *China at War*. New York: John Day, 1939.

van de Ven, Hans J. *War and Nationalism in China, 1925–1945*. London: Routledge Curzon, 2003.

Van Slyke, Lyman. *Enemies and Friends: The United Front in Chinese Communist History*. Stanford, CA: Stanford University Press, 1967.

———. "The Chinese Communist Movement during the Sino-Japanese War, 1937–1945." In *The Cambridge History of China*, edited by John K. Fairbank and Albert Feuerwerker. Vol. 13, *Republican China, 1912–49, part 2*. Cambridge: Cambridge University Press, 1986.

———. "The Battle of the Hundred Regiments: Problems of Coordination and Control during the Sino-Japanese War." *Modern Asian Studies* 30, no. 4 (1996): 979–1005.

Vohra, Ranbir. *Lao She and the Chinese Revolution*. Cambridge, MA: East Asian Research Center, Harvard University, 1974.

Wakeman, Frederic, Jr. *Policing Shanghai: 1927–1937*. Berkeley: University of California Press, 1995.

———. *The Shanghai Badlands*. Cambridge: Cambridge University Press, 1996.

———. "A Revisionist View of the Nanjing Decade: Confucian Fascism." *China Quarterly* 150 (1997): 395–432.

Waldron, Arthur. *From War to Nationalism: China's Turning Point, 1924–1925*. Cambridge: Cambridge University Press, 1995.

———. "China's New Remembering of World War II: The Case of Zhang Zizhong." *Modern Asian Studies* 30, no. 4 (October 1996): 945–78.

Wang, David Der-Wer. *The Monster That Is History: History, Violence, and Fictional Writing in Twentieth-Century China*. Berkeley: University of California Press, 2004.

Wang Jianhui. "Da Wuhan: 1937–38 nian de quanguo zhuban zhongxin" [Wuhan as the nation's publishing center in 1937–38]. *Jianghan luntan*, no. 12 (December 2000): 85–90.

Wang Ming. *Weiduli ziyou xingfude Zhongguo douzheng* [Struggles within independent free China]. Pamphlet. 1938.

Wang Shaoguang. *Failure of Charisma: Cultural Revolution in Wuhan*. Oxford: Oxford University Press, 1995.

Wang, Sophia. "The Independent Press and Authoritarian Regimes: Case of the *Dagong Bao* in Republican China." *Pacific Affairs* 67, no. 2 (Summer 1994): 216–41.

Wang Tongchao shixuan [Selected poetry of Wang Tongchao]. Beijing: Renmin chubanshe. 1958.

Wang Tongchao wenji [Collected works of Wang Tongchao]. Jinan: Shandong renmin chubanshe, 1982.

Wang Yimin. "Guanyu Han Fuju tongzhi Shandong he bei busha di jianwen" [Concerning Han Fuju in Shandong and witnessing his execution]. *Wenshi ziliao xuanji*, no. 12 (1961): 57–78.

Wang Zhen. *Dongdangzhong de tongmeng: kangzhan shiqi de zhongsu guanxi* [Uneasy alliance: Chinese Soviet relations during the War of Resistance]. Guilin: Guangxi shifan daxue chubanshe, 1993.

Wasserstrom, Jeffrey. *Student Protests in Twentieth-Century China: The View from Shanghai*. Stanford, CA: Stanford University Press, 1991.

Wasserstrom, Jeffrey, and Elizabeth Perry, eds. *Popular Protest and Political Culture in Modern China*. Boulder, CO: Westview Press, 1994.

Wei Hongyun. *Kangri zhanzheng yu Zhongguo shehui* [The Anti-Japanese War and Chinese society]. Shenyang: Liaoning renmin chubanshe, 1997.

Wen Zhenting, ed. *Wenyi dazhonghua wenti taolun ziliao* [Sources materials on the discussion of how to popularize literature and art]. Shanghai: Shanghai wenyi chubanshe, 1987.

Weston, Timothy B. "Theory and Practice of Newspaper Journalism in 1920s China." *Twentieth-Century China* 31, no. 2 (April 2006): 1–32.

Weyl, Walter, "The Chicago of China." *Harper's*, October 1918, 716–24.

Whelan, Richard. *Robert Capa: A Biography*. New York: Knopf, 1985.

White, Theodore, and Annalee Jacoby, *Thunder out of China*. New York: William Sloane, 1946.

Wilbur, C. Martin. *The Nationalist Revolution in China, 1923–1928*. Cambridge: Cambridge University Press, 1983.

Wilson, Dick. *When Tigers Fight: The Story of the Sino-Japanese War, 1937–1945*. New York: Hutchinson, 1982.

Winter, J. M. "Catastrophe and Culture: Recent Trends in the Historiography of the First World War." *Journal of Modern History* 64, no. 3 (September 1992): 525–32.

Wood, Frances. *No Dogs and Not Many Chinese*. London: John Murray, 1998.

Woodcuts of Wartime China, 1937–45 [Kangzhan banian muke xuanji]. Shanghai: Kaiming Book Co., 1946. Text in English and Chinese.

Wou, Odoric. *Mobilizing the Masses: Building Revolution in Henan*. Stanford, CA: Stanford University Press, 1994.

Wu Renshu. "Kangzhan yu jiyi: Kangzhan zhanqi de yiqi yu yizhong (1940–45)" [Anti- Japanese War and malaria]. *Zhonghua junshi xuehui huikan* [Proceedings of Chinese Military History Association], vol. 3, no. 1:323–64. Taibei: Guofangbu chubanshe, 1997.

Wu Xiangxiang. "Total Strategy Used by China and Some Major Engagements in the Sino-Japanese War of 1937–45." In *Nationalist China during the Sino-Japanese War, 1937–45*, edited by Paul Sih, 37–80. Hicksville, NY: Exposition Press, 1977. Later published in Chinese in *Zhuanji wenxue*, no. 302 (July 1987): 61–70.

"Wuhan Commerce after the Flood." *Chinese Economic Journal* 11, no. 2 (August 1932): 201–2.

Wuhan daxuexiao shi [History of Wuhan University]. Wuhan: Wuhan daxue chubanshe, 1993.

Wuhan guomin zhengfu shi [History of the Wuhan Republican Government]. Compiled by Liu Jizeng, Mao Lei, and Yuan Jicheng. Wuhan: Hubei renmin chubanshe, 1986

Wuhan huizhan [Recollections of the battle for Wuhan]. Edited by Wenshi ziliao weiyuanhui. Beijing: Zhongguo wenshi chubanshe, 1989.

"Wuhan Industries after the Flood." *Chinese Economic Journal* 11(2)(August 1932): 83–100.

Wuhan kangzhan shi [History of Wuhan during the Anti-Japanese War]. Wuhan: Hubei renmin chubanshe, 1995.

Wuhan kangzhan shiliao xuanbian [Source materials on Wuhan during the Anti-Japanese War]. Wuhan: Hubei renmin chubanshe, 1985.

Wuhan kangzhan shiyao [Important historical points in the history of Wuhan during the Anti-Japanese War]. Compiled by Mao Lei. Wuhan: Hubei renmin chubanshe, 1985.

Wuhan renwu xuanlu [Selected biographies of Wuhan personalities]. Wuhan: Wuhan wenshi ziliao weiyuanhui, 1988.

"Wuhan sanzhen zhi xianzai ji qi jianglai" [The three Wuhan cities and their future]. *Dongfang zazhi* 21, no. 5 (March 10, 1924): 62–86.

Wuhan wenshi ziliao [Materials on the history and culture of Wuhan]. Wuhan: Wuhan wenshi ziliao weiyuanhui, 1981–95.

Wuhan xinwen shiliao [Historical materials on the Wuhan press]. Wuhan: Zhangjiang ribao, xinwen yanjiuso chubanshe, 1983.

Xia Mingfang. "Kangzhan shiqi zhongguo de huozangyu renkou qianyi" [Famine and migration during the War of Resistance]. *Kangri zhanzheng yanjiu*, 2000, no.2, 59–78.

Xie Bingying. *Nubing zizhuan* [Autobiography of a woman soldier]. Chengdu: Sichuan Wenyi chubanshe, 1985. Also available in English translation: *A Woman Soldier's Own Story: The Autobiography of Xie Bingying*. Translated by Lily Chia Brissman and Barry Brissman. New York: Columbia University Press, 2001.

Xin Ping. *1937: Shenchong de cainan yu lishi de zhuanzhe* [1937: the great catastrophe and turning point in history]. Shanghai: Shanghai renmin chubanshe, 1999.

Xinwenxue shiliao [Historical materials on the history of journalism]. Beijing: Wenxue chubanshe, 1978–.

Xu Lan. *Yingguo yu zhongri zhanzheng: 1931–41* [Britain and Sino-Japanese War]. Beijing: Shifan xueyuan, 1991.

Xu Yiyun. *Jiang Baili nianpu, 1882–1938* [Chronological biography of Jiang Baili]. Beijing: Tuanjie chubanshe, 1992.

Xu Yong. *Zhengfu zhi Meng: Riben luehua zhanlue* [Pacification dreams: Japanese war strategies in China]. Guilin: Guangxi shifan daxue, 1993.

Xue Guangqin. *Jiang Baili de wannian yu junshi sixiang* [Jiang Baili's military thought during his later years]. Taibei: Zhuanji wenxue chubanshe, 1969.

Xuzhou huizhan [Recollections of the battle for Xuzhou]. Edited by Wenshi ziliao weiyuanhui. Beijing: Zhongguo wenshi chubanshe, 1985.

Yang Bingde. *Zhongguo jindai chengshi yu jianzhu, 1840–1949* [Cities and architecture of modern China, 1840–1949]. Beijing: Zhongguo jianzhu gongye chubanshe, 1993.

Yang Guisong. *Zhonggong yu Moscow de guanxi (1920–1960)* [Relations between Chinese Communists and Moscow]. Taibei: Dongda dushu, 1997.

Yang Hansheng. "Disanting—guotongqu kangri minzutong: zhanxian de yige zhantou baolei" [Number Three section—frontline defense in the United Front Guomindang controlled areas]. *Xinwenxue shiliao*, 1980, no. 4, 16–27; 1981, no. 1, 11–22; and 1981, no. 2, 27–39.

Yang Tianshi, ed. *Renwu shuwang: Bainianchao jingpin xilie* [Notes on people: selections from *Bainianchao*]. 2 vols. Shanghai: Shanghai zizhu chubanshe, 2005.

Yao Xueyin. "Tongsu wenyi duanlun" [Debating tongsu wenyi], *Kangzhan wenyi*, vol. 1, no. 5 (May 20, 1938), 42.

Ye Qing. "Guanyu zhengzhi dangpai" [Concerning political party divisions]. *Xuelu*, no. 2 (January 1938): 27–34.

———. *Zhongguo dixian jietuan jiqi jianglai*. Wuhan: n.p. 1938.

Yeh, Wen-hsin. *Alienated Academy: Culture and Politics in Republican China, 1919–1937*. Cambridge, MA: East Asian Research Center, Harvard University, 1990.

———. "Progressive Journalism and Shanghai's Petty Urbanites: Zou Taofen and the *Shenghuo Weekly*, 1926–1945." In *Shanghai Sojourners*, edited by Frederic Wakeman and Yeh Wen-hsin, 186–238.Berkeley: East Asian Institute, 1992.

Yi Mingshan. "Kangzhan shiqi Guo Moruo zai Wuhan huodong jilue" [Analysis of Guo Moruo activities in Wuhan during the War of Resistance]. *Wuhan shifanxueyuan xuebao*, no. 4 (1980): 17–28.

Yip, Ka-che. *Health and National Reconstruction in Nationalist China: The Development of Modern Health Services, 1928–1937*. Ann Arbor, MI: Association of Asian Studies, 1996.

———. "Disease and the Fighting Men: Nationalist Anti-Epidemic Efforts in Wartime China, 1937–1945." In *China in the Anti-Japanese War, 1937–1945: Politics, Culture, Society*, edited by David P. Barrett and Larry N. Shyu, 171–88. New York: Peter Lang, 2001.

Yu Lipang. *Zhang Zhizhong* [Biography of Zhang Zhizhong]. Jilin: Jilin wenshi chubanshe, 1992.

Yu You. *Liu Zunqi* [Biography of Liu Zunqi]. Beijing: Renmin ribao chubanshe, 1995.

Yuan Jicheng. "Kangzhan chuqi Wuhan de baozhi kanwu" [Wuhan's press during the Anti Japanese War]." *Hubei xinwen shiliao huibian*, no. 11 (1987): 25–112.

Yuan Shuipai. *Mafantuo de shange* [Hill songs of Ma Fantuo]. Shanghai: Shenghuo chubanshe, 1946.

———. *Yuan Shuipai shige xuan* [Selection of Yuan Shuipai's poetry and lyrics]. Beijing: Renmin wenxue chubanshe, 1985.

Zeng Xubai zizhuan [Autobiography of Zeng Xubai]. Taibei: Lianjing chuban shiye gongsi, 1988.

Zhang Baijia. "China's Experience in Seeking Foreign Military Aid and Cooperation for Resisting Japanese Aggression." Presented at the Research Conference on Military History of the Anti-Japanese War, Hawaii, January 2004.

Zhang Shaosi. *Wuhan kangzhan wenyi shigao* [Draft history of literature and the arts at Wuhan during the War of Resistance]. Wuhan: Zhangjiang wenyi chubanshe, 1988.

————. "Kangzhan chuqi de wuhan baogao wenxue" [Reportage at Wuhan in the early Anti-Japanese War period]. *Zhongnan minzu xueyuan xuebao,* 1995, no. 1, 72–76.

Zhang Xianwen. *Kangri zhanzheng de zhengmian zhanchang* [Battles on the front-lines of the War of Resistance]. Zhengzhou: Henan renmin chubanshe, 1987.

————. *Zhongguo kangri zhanzheng shi* [History of China's War of Resistance]. Nanjing: Nanjing daxue chubanshe, 2001.

Zhang Zhizhong. *Zhang Zhizhong huiyi lu* [Memoir of Zhang Zhizhong]. Beijing: Wenshi chubanshe, 1985.

Zhao Puchu. "Kangzhan chuqi de Shanghai nanmin gongzuo" [Work with refugees in Shanghai during the first part of the Resistance War]. *Lishi ziliao yanjiu,* 1986, no. 4, 31–50.

Zheng Yuanzhong. "Xin Shenghuo yundong de zhengzhi yiyi" [The political meaning of the New Life Movement]. In *Kangzhan qian shinian guojia jianshe shi yantaohui lunwenji* [Proceedings of the Conference on Nation Building in the Ten Years before the War of Resistance]. Taibei: Academia Sinica, Jindaishi chubanshe, 1984.

Zhongguo funu yundong lishi ziliao (1937–45) [Collection of historical documents on the Chinese women's movement, 1937–45]. Edited by the Women's Movement History Research Group, All China Women's Association. Beijing: Zhongguo funu chubanshe (44–135 for documents on Wuhan in 1938).

Zhongguo Qingnian dang [Chinese Youth Party (documents)]. Beijing: Zhongguo shekexue chubanshe, 1982.

Zhou Enlai zhenglunxuan [Selected political works of Zhou Enlai]. Beijing: Zhongyang wenxian chubanshe, 1993.

Zhou Tiandu. *Qi junzi zhuan* [Biographies of the Seven Gentlemen]. Beijing: Wenshi chubanshe, 1999.

Zou Taofen nianpu [Chronological biography of Zou Taofen]. Shanghai: Fudan daxue chubanshe, 1982.

INDEX

Illustrations follow page 80 and are indicated in italics by the abbreviation "illus."

DESIGNER
J. G. Braun

TEXT
10/13 Sabon

DISPLAY
Interstate

INDEXER
Kevin Millham

CARTOGRAPHER
Bill Nelson

COMPOSITOR
Integrated Composition Systems

PRINTER AND BINDER
Thomson-Shore, Inc.